THE COMPLETE
garden
MAKEOVER BOOK

Better Homes and Gardens

THE COMPLETE
garden
MAKEOVER BOOK

MEREHURST

Contents

Planning

The best way to start planning your garden makeover is to assess what you have. Consider your plot, as if for the first time, and examine its qualities and defects. In which directions does the land slope? Do trees give you privacy, but block out winter sun? Which parts of your garden are exposed to cold winds or the extremes of summer sun?

These considerations, as well as your lifestyle, will affect the way you shape your ideal garden. You may be planning a number of features: entertaining areas, a variety of different garden areas, paths, a shaded patio, a courtyard and pergola or a pool. As you consider ways to integrate your house with these features, issues such as sun, shade, privacy, and the qualities of the plot and its aspect will be important.

In most cases, you can use the characteristics of your garden to great effect to meet your needs. Sometimes, however, you may have to consider major works such as excavating, building retaining walls, adding drainage and removing trees.

As you sketch your plans, keep in mind all your possible needs. Have you incorporated special areas for all members of your family, including children? Have you considered the positioning of trees and shrubs to allow for their growth?

Finally, create a realistic timetable and spread the workload over an extended period, perhaps years rather than months if it is an ambitious project. In this way, you are more likely to enjoy living in your garden as you complete the process.

The aim of many garden designers is to bring the tranquillity of the garden into the home. Here an outdoor living area leads effortlessly into the garden. The pergola and umbrella create a shaded and protected spot for outdoor dining. Screens and lavender borders separate different sections of the garden, yet all elements combine well.

Look at what you have

Can you move comfortably from the house to the garden? It's not as common as it used to be to find the only door to the back garden is from the kitchen. Do you have a door from the living room; would it be desirable to have one from the utility room, or even a main bedroom if you live in a bungalow? Replacing a window with a door isn't a major job for a builder, and it might allow you to step out on to a terrace or deck, maybe into the sunshine, perhaps with a pergola overhead for shade. If there is already a patio, is it adequate for your purposes, or should you think of making it more generous? If the ground is flat, you may be able to walk out at the same level as the house. In many cases, there will be a slope, however slight (you can see it most clearly along the walls of the house) this will need to be taken into account, and if the house is old and sits a little above the ground, steps will be needed. Should they be at the door, or do you want to create a terrace leading to it?

Paths and pavements are another matter. If they fit your purposes, fine, but if they don't – and some builders seem to have a genius for putting them in strange places – the cost of replacing them will be money well spent.

Sloping ground

A sloping site may call for the movement of soil to create level areas for outdoor living, with banks and possibly retaining walls and steps to link it all together. Here you have another design theme, one that can be so effective that people have been known to create level changes where they weren't really needed, just for interest. But remember that earthworks will mean either spending money on a contractor or backbreaking work – a level site is easier to develop.

ABOVE: This large, sun-filled backyard is obviously enjoyed by the owners. They could gain greater use of their outdoor living space by creating a paved patio area, perhaps covered by a pergola and linked to a garden screen or arched bower.

RIGHT: It's rare for a house to stand alone without neighbours. In the average street, you're likely to have no less than five properties adjoining your own. Their houses, sheds and trees impinge on your landscape and need to be taken into account in your plans.

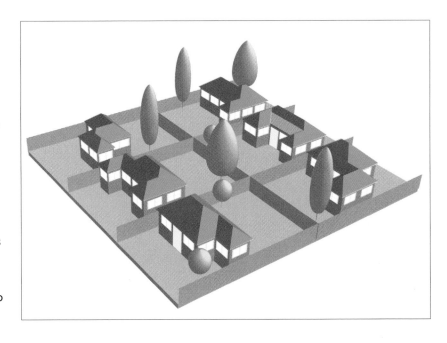

On the other hand, a steeply sloping hillside site may offer fine views, and you will want to ensure that your plants frame them while, at the same time, masking visual distractions – which usually take the form of neighbouring houses and telephone poles. Don't forget to make your garden look good from the upper floor, or floors, of your house, too.

Existing trees

Are there trees growing in the garden? There is nothing like trees to give the garden a head start, and you should think very carefully indeed before deciding to remove any. Even if a tree looks a little scruffy now, a few years' care may turn it into a beauty. Judicious pruning may be needed to reveal handsome trunks and branches. However, if you have doubts about pruning or the safety of any tree, consult a tree surgeon.

Soil and drainage

What sort of soil do you have to work with? If it's not the ideal deep, crumbly loam, don't worry, as beautiful gardens have been made with all soil types. It's almost always better to work with what you have than to import topsoil (unless the house builder has carried all your natural topsoil away or buried it irretrievably under subsoil and rubble). Any soil can be improved by cultivation and the addition of as much organic matter – compost and the like – as you can manage.

Check the drainage. Simply dig a couple of holes about half a metre deep and fill them with water; if it has drained away after 24 hours, you have no worries. If it hasn't, you might think of laying land drains or creating a number of raised beds. Alternatively, you could accept the soil as it is and choose plants that like 'wet feet' – there is a wide range to choose from in addition to willows.

It's essential to know whether your soil is alkaline or acid, as this will determine many of the types of plant that you can grow. For example, many heathers and rhododendrons require an acid soil to flourish. If you can wait until summer, look at the colour of hydrangeas growing in your area; if they are blue, the soil is acid, if pink, it is alkaline. Although this will give you a rough idea of local soil type, to check your garden accurately, you can use an inexpensive soil testing kit available from garden centres.

ABOVE: Even the 'flattest' ground will have some fall. The slope of the ground can be difficult to assess; however, if you can see it against the walls of the house, you can measure it against the brick courses.

LEFT: A steep site – and rocky – with the only soil being thin and sandy. With planning and an understanding of the site's features, an attractive bushland garden can be created.

What you hope to achieve

Now that you have assessed the physical features and aspect of your garden, the next task is to define what you hope to achieve. What are the features you want to introduce? Prepare a wish list and arrange it in order of priority.

Once you have collected together the key features that represent how you want to transform your garden, consider what needs to be done to make these changes possible. Will they require earthworks and building structures – such as retaining walls, decks and fences? If so, these will have to be completed first. Also they will have a definite impact on your garden and how you then develop the rest of your plans for it. For instance, if you are planning a courtyard and pergola, have you considered a pathway and garden beds?

Your ideal garden

In listing the features of your planned garden, you will need to consider your interests and lifestyle. Do you want to entertain outdoors, retreat to a private garden nook or grow herbs and vegetables? Where can you position that private, sun-drenched deck you have always longed for? Now is the time for you to summarise the key elements of your ideal garden design.

You might start by listing particular aspects that matter most to you, even if you cannot plan the specifics. This could include general goals, such as being able to sit and eat outdoors in a sheltered spot; to have a deck connecting your house to the garden; or to design a number of separate garden areas.

Later on, once your list develops, you can progress from 'what you want' to 'how to do it'. In many cases, it is the latter that presents the biggest challenges of all. This may involve the issues of limited

space and designing to make the most of garden features (trees, driveways and slopes).

Entertaining areas

Your plans will also be influenced by how you want to use your garden in the future. If you have a young family, no doubt your needs and those of your children will overlap for most purposes. Perhaps building a swimming pool for the children is your initial focus, but you would also like to have a separate entertaining area. One option

ABOVE: This sloping garden has been terraced into two levels, with broad, curved steps linking the sections.

BELOW: An outdoor living area, paved for year-round use, can extend your home and provide a connection with the garden.

might be to extend the pool surrounds to create a paved area that includes enough space for a table setting and barbecue.

In some instances, the garden may also contain a carport or a garage, separate from your house and existing with a 'personality' all of its own. You might consider adapting the generous, sheltered area beneath a carport as an entertaining area. It could be linked to an adjoining courtyard or patio, with a

uniform paving style beneath and an attractive pergola that connects the structures.

Many houses only have internal living areas, limiting the ways in which you can entertain. Adding a deck or courtyard can connect the house to the garden and make it possible to enjoy the garden when the climate suits. You might need to plan for screens to provide wind protection and privacy, or a pergola for shade in the summer months.

ABOVE: Happiness is being able to enjoy the delights of the garden from many vantage points, such as this meandering red path.

ABOVE: A narrow garden with high-rise neighbours at the rear presents difficulties. With careful positioning of screens and shrubs, privacy can be secured while still retaining an accessible sunny spot.

Special considerations

Although every family has its own special needs to consider when designing features for the garden, there are some aspects that are commonly encountered, which can pose problems. These aspects need to be given a bit of thought.

Limited space

Space may not be a problem if you have a quarter-acre plot, but for inner-city dwellers, making the most of limited space can present quite a challenge.

Plant trees

When the garden is long and narrow, and overlooked by tall buildings to boot, the problem of space becomes acute. High walls would create a cooped-up feeling, and there just isn't room for tall shrubs to spread themselves. Trees, quite substantial ones, provide the answer. They take up little usable ground space, as you can walk under them, while even the bare winter branches of deciduous trees give a sense of protection.

Keep it simple

The plan is straightforward – virtually wall-to-wall brick paving, wide enough so that it doesn't look like a path to nowhere, with the trees and lower plantings hard against the fences on each side. There's subtlety, too, in the way that the corridor-like perspective is broken, first

RIGHT: To divide space you can use:

1 Shrubs – for total separation.
2 Trees – which allow you to see under the branches.
3 Low planting – for a gentle division, maybe with a pergola or roof overhead.
4 A screen fence, or a wall, softened with creepers.
5 & 6 A change of level – with steps as a link, and perhaps some planting associated with them.

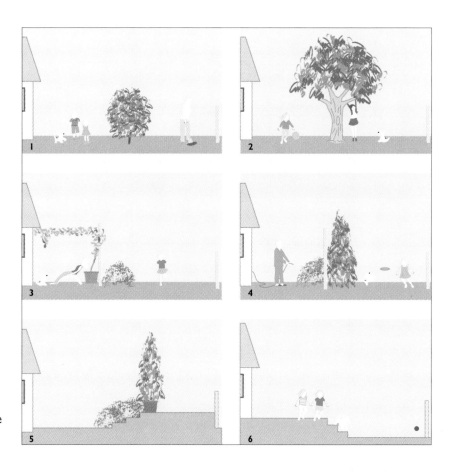

by changing the pattern of the bricks at each end, and then by the placing of two semi-circular beds that jut into the space at the far end so that you have to walk around them to the side gate.

The car and the garden

It is always desirable to be able to park your car off the street, but what do you do when you don't have a garage and the car is parked in your garden? The photo below shows a brilliant compromise. The car is let in through a roller-door, painted to match the walls, and is relegated to the street at weekends and when there are visitors. Its standing space then becomes a patio for people. A raised bed, squaring off the awkward angle of the plot, allows for some shrubs and flowers, but most of the greenery is provided by cladding the high walls all around with Virginia creeper (*Parthenocissus*), which needs no trellis to climb and takes up next to no ground area. It could be augmented with flowering climbers like jasmine (*Jasminum*) or morning glory (*Ipomoea*), or even climbing roses if you wished. The dense foliage not only looks good, but it also cuts down the reflected heat from the masonry that used to turn the garden into an oven every summer. The eye is drawn down into the garden by the panel of lawn, in the centre of which a tiny pond contains a single water lily. With pot plants moved into strategic positions, you'd hardly know the car had ever been there.

Privacy

In a country garden, the question of privacy may hardly arise, while in a large suburban plot, there's room for banks of shrubs, even if the fences are only 1.5 metres high. But in a very small space, the problem of ensuring that you won't feel you're conducting your life under the public gaze can determine much of your garden planning.

Usually, it isn't so much the presence of the neighbours themselves in their gardens (unless you happen to dislike them), but their windows – most of us find the idea of being watched by unseen eyes distinctly invasive and unnerving.

Watering systems

As you plan your garden, give some thought to the watering needs of different areas. For instance, lawns will obviously need more water than potted plants or shaded garden areas. Installing a watering system might be the answer.

These systems attach to the tap and consist of a small-diameter hose, upright extension rods for elevating the sprays and a range of different nozzles. The thin tubing is flexible, easy to handle and can be buried just below the surface. Watering systems are easily assembled to deliver varying quantities of water to different parts of your gar-

den. Trickle nozzles deliver water slowly to the roots of your plants; mini-sprinklers water an area of a couple of square metres. The sprays are designed to distribute water in specific spray patterns and coverage 'shapes' – from thin strips (ideal for narrow garden beds) to quarter- and half-circles. The sprays are rated by their water output (in litres per hour), allowing you to determine the amount of soaking different plants receive.

An automatic timer can be a useful addition to a watering system. Battery-operated timers are available that allow you to program the duration of your garden watering for specific times during the week.

During long, hot summers, water authorities may issue hosepipe bans to prevent the indiscriminate use of the mains supply for garden watering. Bear this in mind and consider installing rainwater butts or diverting water from a washing machine into the garden.

BELOW: The garden is set for visitors, with the car banished to the street. Here, limited space is cleverly overcome by having the space usually occupied by the car double as an entertaining and leisure area.

Design for the climate

A comfortable garden needs a balance between sun and shade, through the day and through the year, and once you know which way your property faces, you can plan for it quite easily.

We all know, of course, that the sun rises in the east, sets in the west and is at its highest at noon, when it's never quite overhead, but somewhere to the south. This is why the south side of the house gets the sun and the north side is in its own shade for most of the year. But not in summer, because the summer sunrise and sunset are quite a bit to the north of an east-west line. This means that at midsummer, the hot afternoon sun will hit your 'shady' north side patio at about mid-after-noon and stay there for the rest of the day, upsetting any shade-loving plants growing there. Unshaded paving will absorb a lot of the heat and radiate it into the house long after sunset.

Conversely, the winter sun moves to the south and doesn't rise so high; shadows are longer, and that spot you chose in July for the veg-etable garden because it was so sunny may turn out to receive no winter sun at all, and precious little in autumn and spring.

BELOW: Methods of controlling the wind, and the effects of a windbreak.

BOTTOM: Sun and shade move as the trajectory of the sun changes with the seasons.

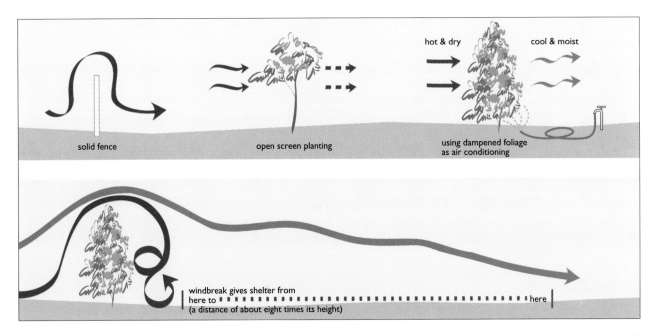

hot & dry   cool & moist

solid fence   open screen planting   using dampened foliage as air conditioning

windbreak gives shelter from here to ▪ here
(a distance of about eight times its height)

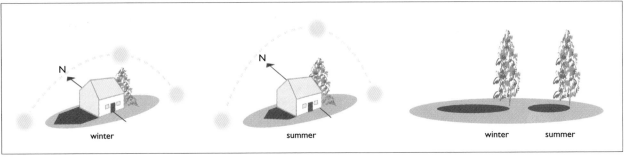

winter   summer   winter   summer

The ideal aspect

The ideal aspect for outdoor living is the south or south-east side of the house, where the winter sun is assured. An area of paving here can reflect its warmth into the house, but you'll need to provide shade for the summer. You could rig up awnings or sun umbrellas, but the natural shade of trees is cooler (the constant transpiration of water from their leaves acts as an effective natural air conditioner). Deciduous trees let the winter sun through their bare branches; plant them on the east for the early winter sun. Evergreens can go to the north, and maybe the west, too, as during a very hot summer the thick foliage can offer welcome protection from the afternoon sun.

Shading the house

Tall trees shading the roof of a bungalow or ground-floor extension can make quite a difference to your comfort inside, while large areas of glass cry out for shade. Remember that once the sun gets into your rooms, so does the heat. If shade trees will dominate the garden too much, don't forget the climate-control device of the vine-covered pergola. A pergola needn't always be attached to the house, but can be positioned in the garden, too.

> ### Tip
> It's probably better to err on the side of too much shade than too little; most trees will put up with a bit of judicious pruning and thinning if they get too dense.

BELOW: The low afternoon sun just shines straight in underneath this veranda. An awning of vines (trained on one or two wires) provides an attractive solution. Cooler than canvas, the vines let in breeze, do not trap hot air, and create cool air through their transpiration.

Developing your plan

A stroll around your local area to look at neighbouring gardens will give a good idea of the best plants for your own garden. Local nurseries will also recommend suitable plants.

BELOW: The first stage in making a design is to assemble a plan of the property as it exists. Architects' and builders' plans can serve as a basis (the local council may have copies if you haven't), but you'll still need to measure fences, trees, sewer lines and such. Show everything that might affect your design. Graph paper helps to keep everything in scale (1:100 is usual).

By-laws and regulations

It is worth talking to your local council to check if they have any regulations or policies that might affect you. You may need planning permission for a tall fence or wall, a large outbuilding or a swimming pool (your water authority will also need to know about the last). In some areas, the pruning and removal of trees cannot be done without council approval.

Initial sketches

Making sketches on a small scale with a pencil, felt-tip pens or crayons is the heart of the design process. If it doesn't look good in a small sketch, then it is likely that it won't when it's built. There's nothing to be gained by being in a hurry; sooner or later, you'll come up with an idea that seems to incorporate all the things you want and that looks promising.

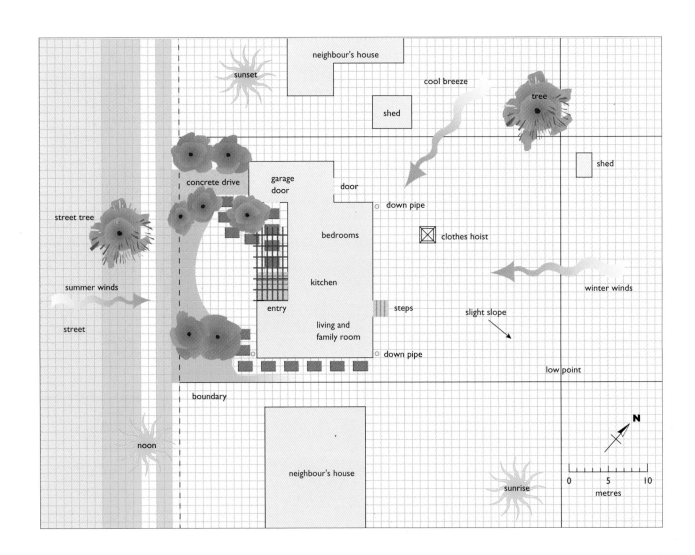

neighbour's house

sunset

cool breeze

tree

shed

shed

concrete drive   garage door   door

down pipe

street tree

bedrooms

clothes hoist

kitchen

winter winds

summer winds

entry   steps

slight slope

street   living and family room   down pipe

low point

boundary

noon

N

neighbour's house

sunrise

0   5   10
metres

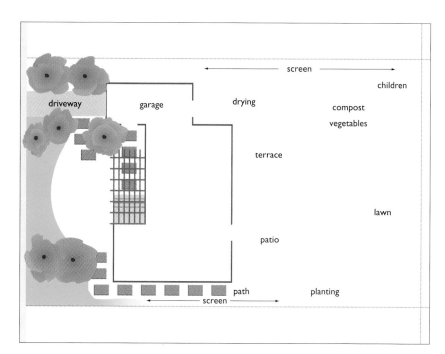

screen

children

driveway | garage | drying | compost

vegetables

terrace

lawn

patio

path | planting

screen

LEFT: Lay a piece of tracing paper over your site plan (see opposite) and you can begin designing by assigning locations to the various activities the garden is to accommodate. Initially this only needs to be a rough guide to ensure you can fit them all in.

BELOW LEFT: It always helps to have a theme for a garden design. Here we are doodling with a combination of circles and straight lines based on our plan opposite.

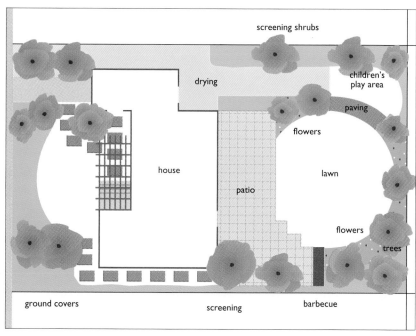

screening shrubs

drying

children's play area

paving

flowers

house

lawn

patio

flowers

trees

ground covers

screening

barbecue

BELOW: This informal path creates a ragged look alongside the fence, cleverly avoiding any straight lines and establishing a large curved garden in the centre.

Then you can lay a piece of tracing paper over your original site plan and transfer the sketched idea to it. Now is the time for accuracy, to make sure the paths are wide enough, that the patio is adequate, that there is room for that row of shrubs. The result might begin to be taking shape – an exciting stage. You still have a lot of pleasant choices to make – the kind of trees, the patio in bricks or slabs – but

now you have a design to provide a framework for your thinking.

How much detail you include in your plan from here on is up to you; a professional landscape designer might want to show everything down to the most intricate details of the planting.

If you are undertaking the project yourself and doing it in stages, you may decide to leave the details until later on.

Design and planning checklist

You need to consider:

- summer shade, winter sun
- windbreaks
- blocking undesirable views, privacy
- drying the washing, compost heaps, storage for garden equipment and furniture
- level changes, steps and/or retaining walls, paved areas and lawn levels
- lighting
- drainage
- overhead telephone and power lines, drains
- the width of paths, gates and steps, the size of paved areas and patios, the shape of lawns and the ease of mowing
- security, especially for swimming pools
- space for children's games, herbs, vegetables or other special garden projects
- access for the car
- access to the garden during construction and afterwards
- comfortable access to the house
- Can you/do you need to build the garden in stages?
- Have you allowed enough space for planting so that plants won't outgrow themselves and need constant cutting back?
- Do you need official approval for fences, structures and pools and for cutting trees?

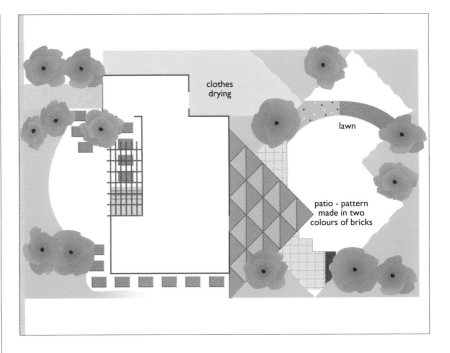

clothes drying

lawn

patio - pattern made in two colours of bricks

ABOVE: Another option is being explored here. The plan is now interpreted with a triangular theme.

RIGHT: Advanced trees are perfect for screening in a hurry. These 'mop top' robinias fill a gap above the fenceline where an apartment building overlooked the garden.

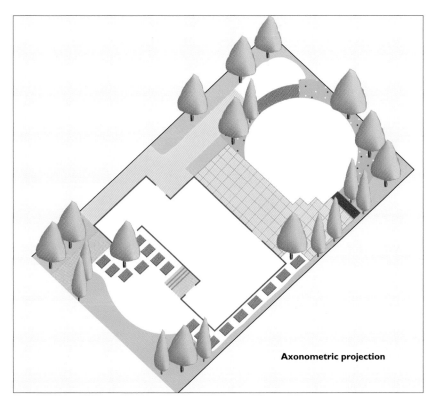

Axonometric projection

LEFT: A bird's-eye (axonometric) view of the circles-and-straight-lines design which helps you to see the third dimension. You can make it by simply tipping the plan over at an angle and extending your heights to scale.

BELOW: The finished design, based on the circles design on page 17 and traced onto graph paper.

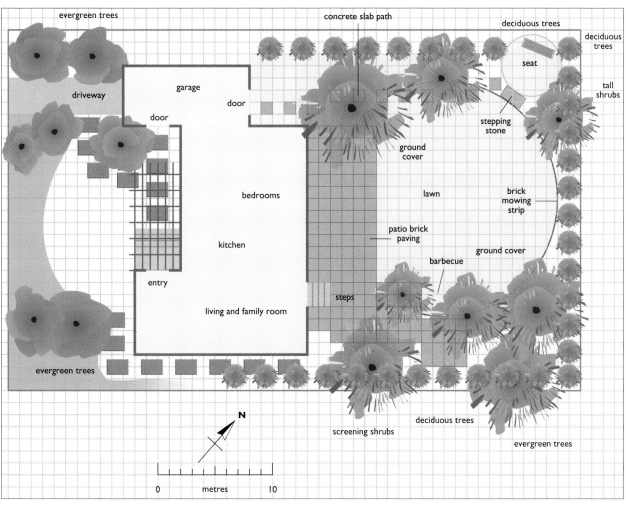

evergreen trees

concrete slab path

deciduous trees

deciduous trees

seat

garage

driveway

tall shrubs

door

door

stepping stone

ground cover

bedrooms

lawn

brick mowing strip

patio brick paving

kitchen

ground cover

barbecue

entry

steps

living and family room

evergreen trees

screening shrubs

deciduous trees

evergreen trees

N

0   metres   10

From plan to reality

Having made your plans, how do you set about turning them into a garden? The deluxe method is to hire a contractor to do it all, from the initial earthworks to the final planting, and there are advantages in this, especially if heavy work is involved.

It saves you time and a lot of hard work, of course; a contractor probably knows more people in the business than you do, and he may well be able to find plants and materials more easily than you can. You should expect a high standard of workmanship, and once the contract has been signed, you should have a clear picture of what it will all cost (but budget for another ten per cent of the total cost or so for any unforeseen extras).

Naturally, this is the most expensive way, and you can save money by having the contractor take on only part of the project and finishing it off yourself. There is a lot to be said for having him carry out the heavy work (earthworks, grading, drainage, possibly structures like pergolas and at least the major portion of the paving), reserving the less arduous task of planting for yourself. If one of your contractor's workers is injured whilst carrying out the heavy work, it's the contractor's problem. However, if you are laid up for days or weeks, let alone a friend who's offered to lend you a hand, it could be disastrous.

Working with a contractor

Let us say you decide to call in a contractor, either for the whole job or part of it. How do you find one? If you've used a landscape designer to plan the garden, he or she will be able to make a recommendation; if, at the same time, you're altering the house, your builder may be able to take on the garden as part of his job (he'll probably sub-contract at least the planting part). Otherwise, ask your neighbours for recommen-

dations (this is often the most reliable method), ask at local nurseries and garden centres, or consult the Yellow Pages. Whatever you do, it is well worth obtaining at least three quotes. Prices for landscape work can vary enormously, and you may find that the highest quote is more than double the lowest.

It's courteous to tell each prospective contractor that you're seeking other tenders, but you're not obliged to say from whom. You're entitled to ask to see some examples of the contractor's work (and to ask the clients about his performance), and for assurance of his solvency – a contractor going bankrupt in the middle of a job is a real nightmare.

Getting quotes

Make sure you obtain the quotes in writing, and that you understand what each includes. If you're contracting for the complete job, you may find included a 'maintenance' or 'establishment' period. This doesn't mean you'll be getting a full-time gardener for the period specified, which could be three or six months, but you can expect the contractor to visit the finished job from time to time to give the new plantings and grass the basic aftercare they need to become properly established. It's rather like the after-sales service you get when you buy a new car. If you are confident of your ability to look after the new plantings, you can save money by not accepting aftercare in the contract.

Once you've accepted a price, you have an agreement and work can begin. Confirm it in writing and

ABOVE: The initial earthworks are well under way. Here, a wooden retaining wall has been built following excavation of the garden, while the areas for formwork and paving have been marked out.

make sure you know whether you will be expected to pay on completion of the work or in progress payments, and, if so, when they are due. You may also need to pay a deposit before work begins. Don't forget to confirm the start date.

Keeping to the plan

Ask any contractor and he'll tell you that his pet hate are customers who can't make up their mind what they want. If you gave him drawings (no matter how sketchy) to work from, you will have got off to a good start, but as the design takes shape on the ground, it is easy to fall prey to second thoughts. If the contractor asks you questions, give him definite answers. He'll often have suggestions about how best to do things; don't be afraid to ask if they will involve extra cost. And always talk to the contractor himself; he won't be doing everything, and it can cause much confusion if you leave your instructions with his sub-contractor. Remember, he is as keen as you are that his work will do credit to you both.

On the following pages, we show the building of the garden of a terraced house from beginning to successful conclusion.

Working out a timetable

If you decide to do the lion's share of the work yourself, the first question is whether to do it all at once or spread it out over two or three years. Spreading the work has the double advantage of making it easier to pay for and allowing you some weekends for something other than garden construction. The scope of the job is also a factor. A tiny city courtyard, calling only for paving that can be laid in a couple of weekends and a few plants to follow, might be best tackled in a single campaign; a larger suburban garden, with paving, perhaps a pergola, and more extensive plantings, may well be better staged over three or four years.

ABOVE: Retaining walls are being completed in this large scale project. Now the owners can look forward to establishing the garden.

The contractor, for whom time is money, usually organises his job something like this:

1 *Earthworks* Any major ground shaping that needs machinery (he might take down a section of the fence for access), followed at once by any drains that have to be laid on the site.

2 *Rough carpentry* Formwork for concrete, timber retaining walls and similar structures.

3 *Masonry and Paving* Constructing retaining walls and a driveway.

4 *Large trees* Mature trees that need to be moved by trucks.

5 *Fine carpentry* Fences (if they're not there already), pergolas and garden benches.

6 *Topsoil and fine grading of planting beds and lawns* Watering systems usually go in at this stage, garden lighting, too (hoses and cables that run beneath paths will have been laid at paving time).

7 *Planting and grassing* A timetable that allows you to leave planting and grassing until the very end of the project is ideal. However, if you are doing it in stages, you should try to avoid the upset of having to pull out plantings to bring in a load of bricks or adjust some ground levels.

An in-ground swimming pool is a big construction, and is best done as early as possible. As it's also a major expense, it may have to be put off until after Year 3. In the meantime, its site could be grassed or spread with gravel, and you should take care not to put any permanent features across the future contractor's access to the site. It will be frustrating watching the destruction of a garden you have taken 3 years to achieve.

Many people rush in with grass first of all, then find themselves doing a lot of digging and cursing as they try to get rid of bits of it, or find themselves having to repair the damage caused by loads of pavers trundled over it. Sowing the rough-graded area with clover may not be orthodox, but it works; it gives you a cover against dust and is dug in at lawn-preparation time to the benefit of the grass or other plantings.

The timetable outlined on page 23 may need adjusting to suit your priorities. However, when you've worked out your timetable, try to keep to it.

1 Looking from an upstairs window down the length of the garden. The ground has a sizeable slope. This can be transformed into terraces, making a series of levels connected by single steps.

2 The garden looks like a disaster area, but things are happening. Soil is being levelled, bricks are being put in place. The fate of the odd lot of plants 'inherited' from the previous owners is still to be decided.

3 Just below the house, the main change of level has been established and steps built.

4 Right at the bottom of the garden – dirt and junk. If it were a bigger place, this area could be left for a second stage, after the side next to the house was finished.

1

2

3

4

RIGHT: Some time later, the area beside the house has been covered with a pergola for shade and comfort. The long bench and coffee table make for a marvellous outdoor living area. In time, vines will cover the walls and soften the severe lines.

Your garden plan over three years

Year 1

Major earthworks (by a contractor?)

Fences

Main paths and driveways (so that you can get into the house without muddy boots)

Set out the patio, either planting it with grass or laying gravel as a temporary surface that will serve as the base for paving later

Trees, not to be overlooked

Grass, which could be left to Year 2 and a green manure crop (such as clover or potatoes) planted this year to improve the soil

Green manure or holding crop (Nasturtiums etc) on future planting areas

Year 2

Retaining walls, steps, lawn, prepare planting beds

Patio (a first stage perhaps)

Pergola framework, with the vines planted at its base (the joists can come now or next year)

Set out planting areas, plant major shrubs

Year 3

Finish patio and pergola

Finish plantings, groundcovers

Ornaments (sculpture etc)

RIGHT: From the house, the garden looks much bigger than it is. Beyond the pergola-roofed living and outdoor dining space is a soothing view of lushness and green.

Constructing Your Site

One of the first tasks in putting your plan to work is to prepare your site. Often this may involve nothing more than plotting the area for a patio, flower bed or pathway. However, in other cases, dead or unsuitable trees may need to be removed; sloping sites may require retaining walls; a site for a deck or courtyard may have to be cleared and excavated.

Sloping sites offer a number of options. One is to create retaining walls and effectively terrace the slope. By using walls, you prevent topsoil from being washed away, control water run-off and gain the benefit of new beds. Another option is to keep the slope and construct a natural-looking rock garden. You can support the slope and create a varied garden by carefully positioning large and small rocks.

All walls need to be built with water drainage in mind. Tree roots and water erosion are common destroyers of walls, so plan carefully at the outset. By using gravel, land drains and weep holes, water can be diverted so that it does little damage.

A number of wall types are featured on the following pages: dry stone, timber, concrete and masonry. Some important skills (such as using a water level and mixing concrete and mortar) are described in the Reference Section at the back of the book.

Many gardens can be improved by the introduction of raised flower beds. These create different levels in the garden, retaining moisture and holding back topsoil, and add areas of interest, with multiple layers of plants on view.

A dry stone retaining wall supports a newly created patio, while a broad gravel path leads down into the garden. Hardwood timber, used in the path retaining wall, is cleverly extended to create garden edgings and steps. In time this, together with the newly laid sandstone steps, will blend into soft grey tones and complement the gravel.

From slope to rock garden

If you're fighting an uphill battle in your garden, stop thinking of the slope as a problem. Instead, think of it as the ideal site for a rock garden. In fact, many gardeners with level plots create a slope so they can have a rock garden and enjoy a visually pleasing change of levels. It's also an attractive way to show off some of the delicate flowers that are often completely lost in a horizontal bed. A patch of uneven ground can be transformed simply by setting a few rocks and adding some good, loamy soil before putting the plants in.

Choosing the rocks

Careful planning is the essential first step in establishing a good rock garden. Before you cut into your bank or slope, you must decide the type and size of rock you'll be using. Plot where rocks will go and where you want interesting undulations in the slope. The best rockeries look as though nature did the groundwork. If you are lucky enough to live in a naturally rocky area, you'll be able to study local outcrops and boulders. You'll see that large rocks usually have their broadest side partly embedded, that the grain or strata lines all lie in the same direction, and that some rocks have matching faces and look as if they were once part of a larger outcrop.

Where possible, choose rocks that would occur naturally in your area. That way, the rockery will not look out of place. Lightweight porous rocks, such as sandstone, are ideal. They absorb moisture and act as a buffer during dry spells. Non-porous rocks, such as granite, can cause rapid drying-out of surrounding soil because they don't absorb moisture. Avoid using rocks that call too much attention to themselves and overshadow the plants.

Laying the rocks

Many garden centres will sell and deliver rocks. If your garden slope is ready, the more unwieldy ones can be dropped into their positions when delivered. For a natural effect, embed the bottom third of most rocks, including large boulders. If the rocks have a grain, lay them so that it runs in the same direction as it would in their natural state. Position smaller rocks, bedding in every third or fourth one and setting others between them, and pack in soil as you go.

1 The first step is to remove rubble and weeds, then excavate some 'shelves' to take a few large rocks. Keep smaller rocks to position among the large ones later.

2 Have large rocks dropped as close as possible to their permanent locations. Then manoeuvre them into place with a long crowbar or thick-walled pipe.

3 Fill the voids between large rocks with soil, then position smaller rocks and stones and partially bury them. Pack soil well into crevices. Now you can plant.

1

2

3

Alpine plants are the most suitable for a rockery, but to flourish they need good drainage, so a sandy type of soil is ideal for packing into the pockets between the rocks. Start with a base of loam and mix it with one part peat or garden compost and one part gravel. If the loam is of particularly good quality, simply mix it with the gravel.

Finish by half-burying smaller rocks and stones in the soil mixture. It's important that the soil you use should be weed-free, as persistent weeds are impossible to get rid of if they sprout deep under stones. Slant flat rocks back into the soil to divert water to plant roots. Pack soil well down around the rocks so that there are no voids, then walk over and around your structure to make sure

the whole construction is firm and of pleasing shape. Now it is ready for planting.

Choosing your plants

There is a wide variety of alpine plants to choose from for a rock garden, but they fall into four basic categories, which determine where on the rockery they should be planted: upright, prostrate, rosette-forming and bushy. Upright forms, such as conifers and shrubs, are best planted at the base of rocks to provide the display with height. Prostrate types should be planted behind rocks so that they can spill over them, while rosette formers will fill vertical crevices between rocks, preventing rainwater from

ABOVE: The completed rock garden in summer flower. Annuals and foliage plants provide mounds of colour. Petunias cascade from beneath geraniums; begonias and marigolds are enhanced by the colourful foliage of *Senecio cineraria* and assorted *Sedums*.

Tips

- Use a pointed stick to make room for delicate plant roots.
- To improve drainage in your rock garden, remove some topsoil, put down a layer of broken brick and stone, then tamp gravel and soil back down.
- To improve close-textured soil, mix in about one third organic material.

ABOVE: Pansies, heart's ease and forget-me-nots will grow well in soil pockets of rocky beds and rock walls.

BELOW: It's simple to create a pretty rock garden. Make sure your rocks have a few indentations which you can fill with rich, moist soil. Simply plant them with low-growing alpine plants such as pink primula, white *Saxifraga* and yellow *Draba* or *Sedum* as shown here.

collecting in their rosettes and rotting them. Bushy plants, or groups of individual plants, should be used to fill the areas of soil between the horizontal layers of rock.

See our list on this page to help you choose suitable plants.

Planting your garden

Most alpine plants are bought in very small pots. Before removing them, water well and allow to drain. Then place your fingers around the plant and on the soil, tip upside-down and tap the pot sharply on its base. The plant should drop into your hand with the soil intact. Use a pointed stick or an old table fork to make room for the roots of delicate plants that like to be right in among the rocks. Then carefully insert their roots in the holes you've made and tamp the soil back with a blunt stick.

Cover the soil around plants and rocks with a layer of gravel. This will keep down weeds and help to prevent the soil from drying out. It will give a more natural look, too.

Maintaining your rock garden

Remove weeds as they appear, being careful not to disturb delicate plants. Watch that more vigorous plants don't spread over and crowd out the less-vigorous varieties. Clip back and prune ruthlessly, but try to maintain a natural look. Your rock garden should be controlled, but not look too regimented.

Water well and regularly in dry weather, but only occasionally in winter when plants are dormant.

Miniature rock garden

Very little space is needed for these fascinating rock gardens. You need a few shapely pieces of weathered rock, some dainty alpine plants and a cool position. If necessary, level the rocks with a few dabs of mortar, which can be hidden by surrounding plants or stones.

Suitable plants for rock gardens

- Moss phlox (*Phlox subulata*). Mat-forming perennial. Cold climate. 12 cm spring flowers; red, pink, white, mauve. Likes sun.
- Edelweiss (*Leontopodium alpinum*). Cushion-forming perennial. White woolly leaves surrounding yellow discs in summer. Likes sun.
- Bugle (*Ajuga reptans*). Perennial, spreading. 25 cm. Leaf varieties, dark blue flower spikes, spring. Likes shade.
- Cinquefoil (*Potentilla* spp). Perennials and shrubs to 1 m. Strawberry-type leaves. Yellow summer flowers. Likes sun.
- Heuchera (*Heuchera*). Perennial, spreading. Stems of bell-like flowers in various colours. Early summer. Likes sun.
- Dwarf juniper (*Juniperus communis*). Low-growing columnar conifer. Blue-green foliage. Likes sun.
- Senecio cineraria (*Senecio cineraria*). Grey-leaved perennial. 75 cm. Yellow daisy flowers. Summer. Likes sun.
- Flame nettle (*Coleus blumei* hybrid). Bushy annual. 45 cm. Red and green leaves. Summer. Warm. In sun or partial shade.
- Geranium (*Pelargonium* spp). Shrubby perennial. Many flower and foliage varieties. Spring and summer. Dry position. Likes sun.
- Convulvulus (*Convulvulus sabatius*). Tender trailing perennial. Blue 25 mm flowers. Summer. Likes sun.
- Ice plant (*Sedum spectabile*). Succulent sub-shrubs. Spreading. 45 cm. Red, orange, white, pink flowers. Spring. Likes sun.
- Knotweed (*Persicaria affinis*). Trailing shrubby perennial. Green leaves turning red. Pink pompom flowers. Spring. Likes sun.

Retaining walls

There are certain common denominators in the construction of any retaining wall. These walls hold back a lot of weight in terms of soil and water, so they have to be built well. Any wall up to about a metre high falls within the scope of the practical person. Walls higher than this will require something more substantial in terms of experience as well as footings. Water must be allowed to escape through weep holes in the wall and land drainage pipes behind it. Walls will generally be 'battered', that is constructed so that they slope back into the ground they are supporting.

The construction of retaining walls that are more than about a metre high is best left to professionals, but you can often avoid calling them in by terracing a steep slope with two or more low retaining walls.

Providing drainage

Water is the worst enemy of a retaining wall. Without proper drainage, water will soon cause any structure you put up to buckle. In colder areas, alternating freeze/thaw cycles can also wreak havoc on a retaining wall.

There are many different drainage methods you can use, the easiest being to leave open perpendicular joints every five or six joints in a masonry wall so that water can drain out, or to make weep holes by drilling through timber or inserting short lengths of pipe through a wall near its base. You can also provide drainage by burying a PVC land drainage pipe behind the wall. This is perforated so that water drains into it. Ensure it extends well beyond the end of the wall. Slope the pipe in one direction at least 3 mm per 300 mm and arrange for it to discharge into a rubble-filled soakaway. With proper drainage, your wall should be secure.

Types of wall

The easiest retaining walls to build are those made from materials pre-fabricated for the purpose. These include pressure-treated timber logs and interlocking concrete blocks. If you prefer a more traditional look, you can use local stone, brick or concrete blocks on a strong concrete footing. Alternatively, old railway sleepers are ideal.

If you have plenty of stone, a dry stone wall – that is one that is not mortared together – makes an interesting alternative. It should be built with a slight backward incline for maximum strength. Alternatively, you can build a freestanding dry stone wall with both sides sloping inwards towards the top. Build up the soil on one side.

Constructing a wall

Excavate the area behind the wall site so that it can be refilled with coarse drainage material (gravel, for example). Next, lay the foundations for the wall. These must be strong – we recommend a concrete strip 300 mm deep and 150 mm wider than the thickness of the wall. If using hollow concrete blocks, insert steel reinforcing rods into the wet concrete, ensuring that their spacing will match the hollows in the blocks when mortared together. When the concrete has set and you begin to build the wall, keep checking that the courses are level horizontally and true vertically. Leave enough unmortared vertical joints in the

---

Tips

- Include a brick or concrete mowing strip at the base of your wall if lawn is to be laid up to it.
- To prevent collapse, water must be able to escape from behind the wall.

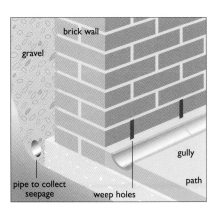

ABOVE: Retaining wall drainage. Note the provisions made to disperse water.

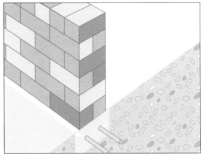

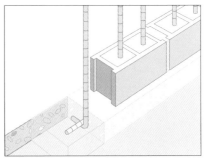

ABOVE: Crib walls simply slot together and have a built-in backwards lean for stability. Units come in several sizes, and there are both concrete and timber versions. Though not particularly attractive, the earth-filled gaps allow such walls to be completely covered with plants.

TOP: Don't skimp on foundations. They must be strong and secure. Use reinforcing rods if necessary.

ABOVE: Use steel reinforcing rods to strengthen concrete block walls.

lowest courses to allow water to escape from behind the wall. This is most important.

Levelling a slope

A sloping site can be levelled using the 'cut and fill' technique. This involves the construction of at least two walls, with the soil on the lower side of the upper wall being excavated and used to fill the upper side of the lower wall. Don't tip the excavated topsoil into the site to be filled first. Instead, put it to one side, placing the poorer quality subsoil behind the lower wall, topping it off with the more fertile topsoil. If any soil has to be disposed of, let it be the subsoil.

Crib walling

Crib walls are based on a module so that they simply slot together.

They often have gaps for plants to cover an otherwise monotonous face. Interlocking concrete blocks are commonly used for crib walls. However, pressure-treated timber beams are good options, while old railway sleepers are ideal.

Set up a string line and dig down to firm subsoil. If your wall is less than a metre high, you can use sleepers as a footing. When you have built the footing, lay a length of 100 mm land drainage pipe behind the wall's position and cover it with a layer of coarse gravel.

Leave spaces for planting between the beams or sleepers and stagger them as you are laying them. Don't forget to batter the wall into the embankment. Cut sleepers in half and insert them through the wall like reinforcing rods. Build these in when you're about half-way up the wall. For

BELOW: A single brick wall requires plenty of drainage material behind to shed ground water. Note that the land drain is positioned at the base to collect the seepage.

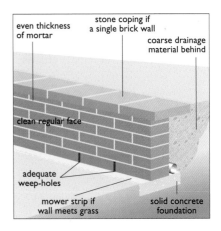

even thickness of mortar

stone coping if a single brick wall

coarse drainage material behind

clean regular face

adequate weep-holes

mower strip if wall meets grass

solid concrete foundation

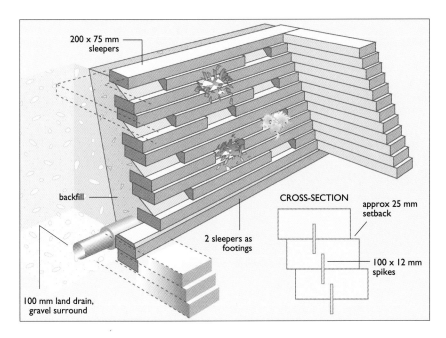

200 x 75 mm sleepers

backfill

2 sleepers as footings

100 mm land drain, gravel surround

CROSS-SECTION

approx 25 mm setback

100 x 12 mm spikes

LEFT: A timber crib wall of railway sleepers can be constructed to suit your slope. Each layer is slightly set back and secured by steel rods or spikes.

BELOW LEFT: Sloping sites can be levelled, using the 'cut and fill' technique.

BELOW: A stone wall (beyond the large tree fern) has been constructed to terrace the slope. Sleepers of treated timber have been used for the steps and the garden edging.

strength, every sleeper must be well fastened to another so that the wall becomes a single unit.

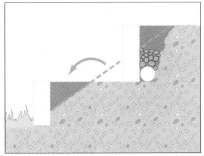

Equipment for crib walling and stone walling

- tape measure
- square, pencil
- claw hammer
- pick and spade
- spirit level
- string line
- sledgehammer
- crowbar
- thick gloves
- circular saw or chainsaw for sleepers; lump hammer and bolster for stones

Tips

- Be sure to wear gloves when you're building your wall. They will protect your hands from abrasions and splinters.
- Check your wall with a spirit level at frequent intervals.
- You can use a hammer and bolster to alter the shape of any stone too awkward to deal with.

Concrete retaining wall

1 Dig a trench across the slope for the wall, making it approximately 150–220 mm deep. Make the trench wide enough to accommodate the wall and provide enough extra space for you to work in. You will need to build the formwork in it.

2 Cut 19 mm plywood into panels 90 mm taller than the height your wall will extend above the ground (earth provides the form for the footing). Coat plywood with motor oil for easier removal. Nail studs of 100 x 50 mm timber to the plywood, 600 mm apart.

3 Assemble the form with end pieces of plywood and interior spreaders of 100 x 50 mm wood.

Set the form in place, make sure it is level and plumb, then brace it with outriggers and stakes. Push the form into place with one foot while you drive in the stakes.

4 To strengthen the wall, drive lengths of reinforcing rod into the ground every 450 mm. Tie reinforcing rods to the spreaders with wire. Tie horizontal reinforcing rods to the vertical ones every 450 mm. If you plan to cap the wall with concrete, let the vertical reinforcing rods protrude 25 mm or so above the spreaders' bottom edges.

5 Pour the concrete. This can be a big job, and you will need to be well prepared. Think out the

process carefully and have a helper. We built a wheelbarrow ramp to the top of the form. As you pour, have a helper tamp the concrete to squeeze out air bubbles. After the concrete has set slightly, smooth its surface with a float and leave it to cure.

6 After the concrete cures, remove the forms. Install perforated drainpipe by laying it in a bed of gravel as shown in the diagram on page 31 then backfill. Cap the wall with brick, wood or precast concrete coping, if desired. Use the terrace created by the wall as a garden or cover with lawn or paving for recreational use.

Masonry retaining wall

This wall (left and below) was built from stones trimmed to a regular, rectangular shape and laid without mortar. They fit together neatly, but leave enough space between them to allow drainage. Precast concrete blocks could also be used in this way.

Other, less regular stone shapes work equally well, but as they fit together less neatly, they may not be quite as stable. Solve this problem by tipping the wall further back into the slope; a sloping wall is just as attractive. The gaps between stones can be filled with small stones wedged into the crevices, or you can plant flowers or foliage plants in them giving the wall a softer, less stark appearance. Even in a wall made from regular-shaped stones, small gaps can be left for planting to soften its appearance.

If you use mortar when building a masonry wall, remember to leave weep holes for drainage.

1   Lay out the wall with stakes and string, and then dig a shallow trench, cutting its back side at a slight angle to the slope. For drainage, lay about 25 mm of gravel in the trench. Our wall will turn a corner, but the same techniques apply to straight walls.

2   Lay your longest stones on the bottom; the fewer the joints in the first course, the stronger the wall will be. As you lay stones, level them as best you can by tapping with the handle of a club hammer. (Remember, to avoid back injury as you lift, you should bend at the knees.)

3   Lay succeeding courses so that each stone bridges a joint below. If you must cut a stone, use a club hammer and bolster. If a stone wobbles, pack more soil underneath.

4   Dig a hole into the slope every 1.5 m and lay a long stone at right-angles to the wall. Pressure from the soil above these stones will stabilise the wall.

1

2

3

4

ABOVE: A timber retaining wall will quickly become part of the garden as it is weathered, especially if it is covered with cascading plants.

Timber retaining wall

For our timber retaining wall, we used 200 x 200 mm lengths of pressure-treated pine. Other heavy timbers, such as oak, are also good options, although they may be expensive. Old railway sleepers are sometimes available from garden centres and would work well, provided you could obtain enough of them. Even heavy fence posts could be used for a low wall. Reinforcing rods hold the structure together securely.

1 Cut a bevelled trench into the slope, wet the trench and tamp well. Set the first timber in place and level it. This course will be completely buried in the ground. We planned our-wall to turn a corner; however, the same techniques apply to a straight wall.

2 Set a second timber on top of the first and bore a hole through the two. (Use a heavy-duty drill with an extension bit; small drills burn out on long holes such as these.) Drive 19 mm reinforcing rods through the holes and into the ground. These rods will hold the timbers firmly together.

3 Continue to place the timbers, staggering joints from one course to the next. Drill holes and use reinforcing rods to pin each timber to the one below on each side of every joint. Cut timbers with a sharp chainsaw. Wear protective leggings, gloves and a face shield.

4 Backfill as necessary. For drainage, drill weep holes every 1.2 m along the wall's length. One row of holes about 300 mm above ground level is fine. An alternative to drilling holes is to provide 25 mm drainage gaps between the timbers. Plant trailing flowers above and in the crevices, if you like.

Dry stone wall

Dry stone walls are built without the use of mortar or any other bonding agent. Their strength depends solely on the selection of stones and their careful placement, along with a combination of gravity and friction. When properly built, these walls are beautiful, very strong and extremely durable.

A dry stone wall can be built to almost any height, a rough guide being that the width of the wall under the copestone should be half that of the base. If in doubt, make the wall wider rather than narrower. Use large, flat-bottomed stones for a stable structure – the stones become smaller as the wall rises.

Raising the wall

1 Use string stretched taut to mark out the line of both sides of the wall. On softer ground, dig a trench 10–20 cm deep so that loose soil and grass can be removed. On stony or compacted ground, this may not be necessary as long as the site is level and free of all obstructions, such as large tree roots.

2 Build logically, placing the largest stones first, with the flattest side down. Pack around and under them with smaller stones. If there is a cavity inside the wall, fill it with one large stone rather than a lot of small ones. Never use soil to fill the cavities

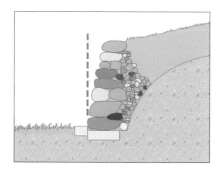

TOP: Fill the area behind the wall with coarse drainage material and include weep holes at the base. Note the slope of the wall and the use of a drainage pipe to collect water at the base.

ABOVE: Inward-sloping dry stone walls can be built freestanding then backfilled.

RIGHT: Dry stone walls look very attractive and provide strong and durable walling. They are especially suitable for country gardens, where the stones may also be locally available.

Mind your back

Remember these simple rules when lifting large stones:
- Work with someone else.
- Use a wheelbarrow wherever you can.
- Roll a stone rather than lift it.
- Keep the work area clear.
- Always lift by bending your knees while keeping your back as straight as possible.

RIGHT: A tall, dry stone wall such as this needs a base of large, flat foundation stones. Note that it will need to be secured by through-stones halfway up. The capping can be an attractive finishing touch.

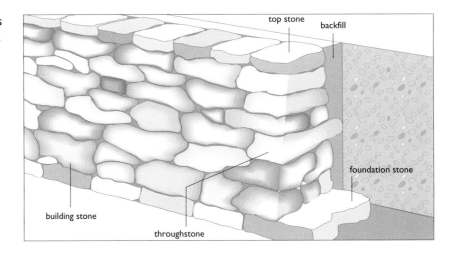

BELOW: The 'dos and don'ts' of wall building are straightforward: the weight of the rock has to be used to make the wall stable and avoid the possibility of movement of the stones over time.

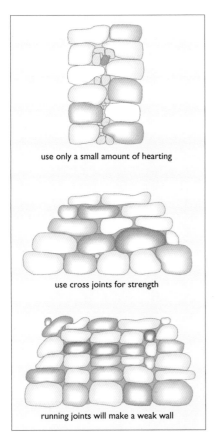

use only a small amount of hearting

use cross joints for strength

running joints will make a weak wall

within the wall, as it will tend to weaken the structure.

3 Lay the stones so that they lie with the longer side running into the wall, not along the face. This makes a much stronger wall, as less hearting material is required.

4 Use the bigger stones towards the bottom of the wall. As the wall rises, it becomes thinner and there may not be enough width for the big stones at the top.

5 Make sure each stone is firmly in place before moving on.

6 Always cover the joints between the stones below, otherwise lines of weakness (running joints) will develop in the wall.

7 Build up both sides of the wall at the same time, and keep each side roughly the same height.

8 Fill the wall as the work proceeds, that is course by course. Do not leave this step until the end of the job.

Throughstones

Throughstones are stones laid through the wall from one side to the other. In some areas, large enough stones are not found and so cannot be used, but they do help make the wall stronger. Place them at one-metre intervals along the wall, about half-way up the wall. Place the flatter side down and make sure they cover a joint on both sides of the wall.

Copestones

Copestones are placed along the top of the wall, not only to make it more attractive, but also to help bind the wall together.

Place each copestone beside the last one, although it should not be supported by it, otherwise you will create a domino effect. Each stone should be self-supporting. Once the copestones are all in place, they are pinned by taking V-shaped slices of stone and driving them into the spaces between the copestones. If this is done properly, you will be able to walk along the top of the wall without creating any movement of stones.

BELOW: The ideal stone wall should be twice as wide at the base as it is at the top. Throughstones should be inserted where possible for strength. The largest stones should be used at the base.

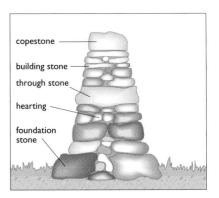

Raised garden beds

Large wooden slabs, such as old railway sleepers, can be used to construct a self-contained structure that supports itself and its contents in all directions. Use 100 mm deep slabs (either recycled or new) and join them at the corners with half-lap joints (see the diagram, right). As you proceed, drill and insert spikes from each layer through to the one below. Add 150-mm-wide capping timber to the top slabs of timber to serve as a ledge seat.

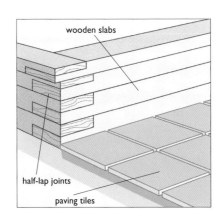

By constructing retaining walls in a U-shape, you can create a large raised bed enclosing a small sunken area. This is an ideal way to make a paved spot surrounded by planting. For a 2.5-m-square paved area surrounded by 2.5-m-wide raised beds, you will need an area 7.5 x 5 m. If you don't have that much space to devote to the project, make the beds slightly narrower, but don't reduce the size of the area you have planned to pave too much, otherwise it will be too small to use comfortably.

The walls of your garden beds can also be constructed of stone. Choose flattish stones and embed the lowest course in the ground, in a shallow foundation trench. Use the larger stones in the lower courses for stability. If your wall is to be more than three or four courses high, see the section on retaining walls on pages 29–34.

ABOVE: A wall of timber beams is easily constructed and can make an attractive raised garden bed.

BELOW: Raised garden beds in staggered boxes against a wall can be a real feature. Hardy plants such as *Impatiens* and geraniums are often the best choice as they can withstand difficult conditions. Any green shrub with dark or light foliage will enliven a dull area.

ABOVE: Pressure-treated log walls are durable and easy to assemble. The supporting posts must be set firmly into the ground and this is the hardest part of the job. Though the finished, 'Fort Apache' look may not suit everyone, these walls can be quickly disguised with shrubs or trailing plants.

ABOVE: This raised garden bed retains the drainage where it is needed – in the garden. The timber walls will soon weather and be covered by greenery.

FAR LEFT: A background of greenery is the perfect foil for white flowering plants cascading over a sandstone wall.

LEFT: Long-lasting sleepers make very attractive low walls, especially in bush or informal gardens. They can also be used to make matching steps and paths.

OPPOSITE: In a formal garden, neatly trimmed stones can be used for a pleasing wall and steps. Here they lead down to a shallow sunken area.

Paths and Steps

Paths and steps have an important role to play in establishing the look and feel of your garden, so it's worth taking time to consider their design and route. Paths should be practical and follow a convenient route, although not necessarily the shortest one. The straight and narrow is fine for service paths, say between the back door and clothes line, but paths designed for strolling should curve gently. Naturally, if the garden itself is laid out in a strict geometric fashion, the paths should match.

Of course, the cost of paths and steps will depend on the materials used, but they should reflect the style of the garden and house and any other paving or walling (existing or planned). As a rule, try to standardise materials. For example, if you have an area paved with concrete slabs and retaining walls of railway sleepers, it makes sense to build paths from the same slabs and use sleepers for steps. Forming the paths from bricks or pavers similar in appearance to those used for the house helps unify the house and garden.

The time and effort put into preparing the foundations for paths and steps will determine their life and appearance. A path laid on a poorly prepared base will soon develop an uneven or cracked surface and detract from the appearance and value of the garden. Further information on essential groundwork is given in our construction diagrams.

Also we look at path edgings (in timber, concrete and brick), planting next to paths, building steps and constructing a ramp. Well-designed steps can transform your deck, complement your pathway and be a feature of your garden. The ideas shown on these pages will give you plenty of inspiration.

A path can be a feature in a well-designed garden. Here stone boulders are used to contain raised garden beds while the path moves in gentle curves down from the rear gate. The pavers are a muted tone, matching the fence, and accentuate the variety of colours and textures of the garden.

BELOW: This well-established garden on two levels is linked by six steps built from concrete slabs on a concrete base. Solid and totally in character with the whole feeling of the area, the steps join courtyards of similar slabs and are flanked by lush and colourful growth of geraniums, petunias, roses, felicia, irises and leafy climbers.

Paths – the possibilities

Thoughtfully planned walkways invite you to stroll and admire the sights, sounds and scents of a pretty garden. This selection of paths, steps and walkways offers lots of possibilities. They're all very different – some are formal, others informal – but what they all have in common is that each helps make the garden a thing of real beauty.

ABOVE: This sloping path of non-slip pavers is laid on a foundation of hardcore gravel, 20 mm of sand and 50 mm of 1:3 cement and sand mortar. This is essential to provide the base necessary on a sloping site. The corrugated pavers are a good choice in this damp position. Curve the profile slightly and lay a shallow gutter on either side.

ABOVE RIGHT: A cement pathway might seem a little utilitarian, but when it is surrounded by a garden such as this, any harshness soon goes. Building the path on a curve helps to soften the line, as does the red oxide colouring which can be added to the concrete when laying. The path leads to a plum tree in the corner of a garden filled with primroses, lobelia, begonias, busy lizzies, irises, columbine and fuchsias.

RIGHT: Oblong blocks of sandstone create a walkway alongside a garden of juniper bushes and candytuft. Sandstone facing blocks such as these are sometimes available from demolition sites; alternatively, a landscape supplier will have them. Laying them is simple: just place in a shallow trench on a bed of sand, and sow grass right to the edges.

RIGHT: A broad brick path provides a boulevard feel in this open garden setting. The mellow tonings of brick always harmonise well. Clever use of a gentle camber in the construction of the path ensures effective water run-off.

BELOW: The many varieties and colours of slate, from almost as many countries, are ideal for landscaping projects. In this instance, slabs of slate have been laid a few centimetres apart on a cement base for stability. Tiny pebbles are used to border each slab and blend the area with the pebbled section in the background.

RIGHT: River boulders make an eye-catching pathway in this garden of sweet williams, pinks and carnations. When using boulders as stepping stones, ensure that they are laid in such a way that they look like they've been there forever. Make sure that you bury at least half the boulders' mass beneath ground level to prevent them rocking when stepped on.

BELOW: Here, red house bricks are combined with wooden railway sleepers to create a casual garden setting. The railway sleepers also act as edging to the path, as well as set the height for the integral step.

ABOVE: The jungle look of this tropical-style garden area has been achieved by dense planting of shrubs and groundcovers. The pathway edges are marked by boulder 'walls' which have gradually become overgrown. The path itself has a thick covering of pine flake and other dried plant material with a footway of log rounds.

ABOVE LEFT: Tulips and daffodils make the ideal accompaniment to an imaginative system of garden steps. The hardwood railway sleepers, held in place by heavy spikes at each end, are virtually indestructible. They have been used as the risers for what is really a terrace system of hard-packed clay soil.

LEFT: To build steps such as these, use bricks or small concrete slabs for the risers after you have dug out the shape to be followed. Lay the crazy paving steps in a 1:3 cement–sand mortar. Keep the risers less than 180 mm high and support the bottom riser on a concrete slab of about 100 mm thickness to provide a sound footing.

Concrete paths

Often considered too plain, concrete is nevertheless a practical and durable material for paths, and with a little thought and extra effort it can be given quite a pleasing appearance. For example, concrete can be colour-dyed and contained within a border of bricks, or it can be broken up with a transverse row of bricks.In the garden below, interest has been added to the plainest of paths by varying its width, defining the edges with raised borders and giving it a sinuous course through the garden.

Constructing a concrete garden path

1 Excavate the route of the path to a depth of about 150 mm.

2 Build forms of 100 x 25 mm timber held in place by 50 x 25 mm stakes. Use several hardboard strips for curves, or retain concrete with permanent edging of brick, stone or treated timber.

3 Compact the soil, then lay a 25–50 mm bed of sand and level it with a straightedge.

4 Lay steel mesh reinforcement on wooden stakes at half the depth of the path.

5 Wet removable forms and shovel in mixed concrete. Level it with straight-edged timber. Smooth with a wooden trowel. Allow excess water to rise to the surface and evaporate, use a steel trowel for a smooth finish. If an exposed aggregate finish is desired, add pebbles at this stage.

6 Add expansion-joint grooves at regular intervals along the path to prevent it from cracking.

7 If you have added aggregate, use a wide, stiff broom or wire brush and a fine spray from a hose to clean off the pebbles when the concrete is partially dry. If you have to walk over the concrete, use a plank.

8 Cover the newly-laid path with moist sacking and leave this in place for seven days. Remove the temporary forms once the concrete has dried – at least 24 hours should be allowed.

BELOW: Formwork and construction materials for a concrete path.

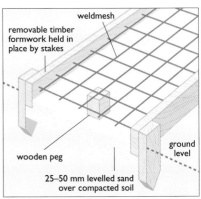

weldmesh

removable timber formwork held in place by stakes

wooden peg

ground level

25–50 mm levelled sand over compacted soil

Paths made of pavers

Paths made of bricks, concrete pavers or stone setts are the hardest to lay, but often give the most satisfying results. They allow you to create pleasing effects by varying the paving colours and patterns. Because pavers offer such a great variety of textures, colours and finishes, more than is available in other path materials, you have the opportunity of laying a path that is unique to you. In the path below, rectangular concrete pavers give way to bricks laid on edge, herringbone fashion.

ABOVE: The rich textures and colours of brick pavers give a rustic feel to this informal pathway – with highlights provided by sections of stone paving.

Hints for laying paths

1 Take the time and trouble to prepare and consolidate the base for your path. Your efforts will be repaid with a smooth surface free from subsidence for many years to come.

2 Service paths may be narrow, but make major paths at least 1.8 m wide; that is wide enough for two people to stroll abreast.

3 Before laying permanently, check that your proposed pattern will fit by setting out a sample on the prepared base.

4 Lay the paving stones on top of 5 cm of compacted, damp, level sand contained between a permanent formwork of preservative-treated planks. Hold the formwork in position with stakes driven into the ground on the outside of the planks and with removable crossbeams placed at regular intervals.

5 Settle pavers into position by tapping with a mallet.

6 Cut the pavers using a brick bolster and club hammer. Score all around the paver, then strike sharply with the bolster, tilted slightly towards the waste piece.

7 Ensure the pathway drains by incorporating a slight slope.

8 Brush dry sand into the joints of unmortared paths on completion.

BELOW: Laying bricks and block pavers on sand.

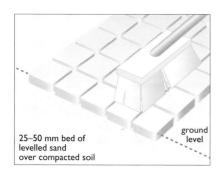

25–50 mm bed of levelled sand over compacted soil

ground level

RIGHT: Block pavers provide rich colour in this path. Here, plants conceal the edges and spill on to the path, creating the curving appearance. Low timber steps are in perfect harmony.

BELOW: THE brick paving on this elegant, curved path is complemented by sandstone block edgings which have been used creatively to establish a raised patio and garden bed.

Timber paths

Sawn logs, wooden slabs and sleepers make beautiful and innovative paths that will be long lived if treated with preservative and built on a suitable foundation. The path shown below right is made of transverse planks that lead to a wooden bridge, while an interesting effect (bottom left) has been created by laying the slabs lengthways and allowing them to weather to a soft grey. Wood is good for 'natural-style' gardens, but not for perpetually shaded areas.

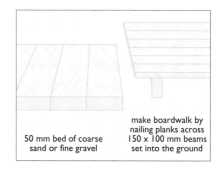

50 mm bed of coarse sand or fine gravel

make boardwalk by nailing planks across 150 x 100 mm beams set into the ground

ABOVE: Methods of constructing timber paths and boardwalks. Pressure-treated timber or naturally rot-resistant hardwood slabs can be set into the ground on a bed of coarse sand or fine gravel. Alternatively, a boardwalk can be built by nailing planks across 150 x 100 mm beams of hardwood set into the ground.

BELOW AND BELOW LEFT: Creative ways of using timber for walkways.

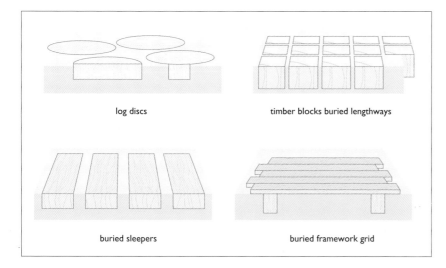

log discs

timber blocks buried lengthways

buried sleepers

buried framework grid

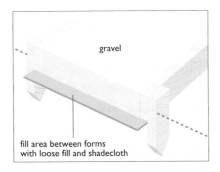

gravel

fill area between forms
with loose fill and shadecloth

ABOVE: Construction details for laying stepping stones.

Stepping stones

Stepping stones can be used to make a very attractive and practical path – and it isn't too difficult to do. Just plan the route of the path to complement the shape of your garden and lay out the stones on the surface to make sure you have enough.

1 Excavate the route of the path to the depth of the stepping stones plus 25 mm.
2 Build forms of 100 x 25 mm timber inside the edges of the excavated path, and retain them in place with timber stakes nailed to the outside. Alternatively, use brick, stone, treated logs or sleepers to edge the area.
3 Compact the base of the path and cover it with crushed stone to a depth of at least 25 mm. Tamp the stone to compact it.
4 Set stones in 25 mm of sand (or mortar if you use thin stone –

RIGHT: Use concrete squares as stepping stones to create a quick and easy path. Here they are laid in a diamond pattern for added effect and their impact softened by flowing ground cover. A string line can be used for correct alignment.

mix one part of cement with two parts soft sand and three parts sharp sand). Tap into place with a rubber mallet. Fill around the stones with pea gravel, bark chippings or mortar until level with the surface of the paving.

You can also set stepping stones directly into loose material such as gravel or bark chips for a quick and easy path. You can use flat stones, sections of log, bricks, concrete slabs or homemade concrete rounds. Whatever you use, they should be set flush with the surrounding surface so that they are not a trip hazard, be flat, firm and non-slip, and be spaced for comfortable walking. The last aspect is the hardest to achieve, for everyone's step is different, but a path with closely-spaced stones will be a pleasant, easy walk for anyone.

TOP: Using stepping stones to cross a lawn can be much less intrusive than a pathway.

ABOVE LEFT: To create interest in an informal garden, stones of many different sizes can be laid in a random pattern.

Gravel paths

The easiest of all paths to construct is one of pea gravel or similar crushed stone. A quick method of construction is to stretch a layer of shadecloth between the outer edging pieces and fill with the gravel. The edging prevents the infill from escaping sideways, while the shadecloth stops it from being trodden into the soil. Around 3–5 cm of pea gravel is enough, if the infill is any deeper it will only make the surface too soft and difficult to walk on. Rake the surface regularly to preserve its appearance.

If your path will be well trodden, it may be advisable to lay it with a hardcore foundation, as this makes it a more durable structure.

1 Mark out the path and remove soil to a depth of 75–100 mm.
2 Edge the path with formwork of 100 x 25 mm timber bedded to the level required. Hold it in place with strong timber stakes driven into the soil and nailed to the outside of the formwork.

Alternatively, use brick, stone, treated logs or other materials to obtain a permanent edging.

3 Add a layer of hardcore or crushed stone to a depth of about 50–75 mm. Consolidate this layer with a roller or rammer. The base must be firm.
4 When the base material ceases to sink into the soil, fill the path with your loose material and grade the surface.

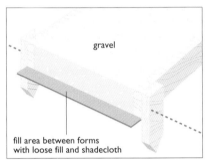

gravel

fill area between forms
with loose fill and shadecloth

TOP: Loose materials such as gravel can be cheap as well as attractive. In this case, a contrasting edging provides an attractive highlight to the red gravel.

ABOVE: Construction of a gravel path using shadecloth.

LEFT: Natural gravel provides a soft contrast to this colourful garden. Raised edging makes it easy to prevent the gravel entering the garden beds.

Chipped-bark paths

If you have a woodland area in your garden, a formal, hard-surfaced path would look out of place and too harsh for its surroundings. A shredded- or chipped-bark path, however, would be perfect.

As with most loose paving material, edge restraints will be essential to prevent the bark chips from spreading. To complement the natural appearance of the bark, choose rustic logs; their irregular shapes and sizes will fit right in. To ensure their long life, soak them in clear preservative. Rustic logs are rarely straight, so you should be able to find curved examples to follow a sinuous path. Nail them to sharpened rustic-log stakes driven into the ground. Wooden boards or sleepers are also suitable as edging.

The route for the chipped-bark path should be dug out to remove the topsoil, then the subsoil compacted by treading it down or rolling it. Soft areas should be filled with a little rubble to stabilise them. Once this has been done and the edging put in place, the chipped bark can be added. Spread a thick (about 75 mm) layer of chips along the path, raking them out to provide an even surface that is a uniform distance below the top of the edging.

From time to time, rake over the bark chips to maintain an even surface, and pull out any weeds as they appear.

LEFT: A consolidated chipped-bark path, when well tamped and cambered, will shed excess water and require little maintenance. It creates the perfect look for a casual flower or cottage garden.

Path edgings

Edgings can be used to dress up a plain path, provide crisp lines between paving and landscaping materials, or hold paving slabs or bricks in place. In most cases, all you need to do is decide on the material you'd like to use, excavate shallow trenches on each side of the path, and stake or set the edging in place. However, integral concrete edging needs to be made at the same time as the path.

Edging options

Edging materials can vary just as much as the paving they border. Choose from concrete, brick, stone, tile or timber. Edging styles, however, fall into just two broad categories: a mowing strip that is laid flush with the path so that you can run one wheel of a lawnmower along it; or a raised edging that puts a lip at each side of a path.

Mowing strips

Mowing strips should be 150–300 mm wide. Concrete, brick, tile and other smooth-surface masonry materials are best for mowing strips. You can use lengths of timber, but be warned that they are easily nicked by the mower blade and will rot away in time.

Raised edgings

A raised edging keeps aggressive groundcover plants from growing over a path, channels water run-off and makes a clean break between different surfaces. If you are planning a path of gravel, or similar loose material, a raised edging is the only way to go.

Keep a raised edging low, say 10 mm or so above the surface, or make it at least 75 mm high – anything in between can easily be tripped over. Below and opposite we give instructions for installing several types of raised edging.

Brick edging

Bricks are probably the most popular path edging, whether set on edge, on end or at an angle for a sawtooth effect. They make excellent borders for concrete, loose materials and, of course, brick paving. Use engineering bricks to withstand the damp.

Brick edging should be set in sand or mortared to a concrete base. See the section on stepping stones (pages 52–53). Make sure

BELOW: Timber edging

1 Dig a trench alongside the path. Make it about 90 mm deep, deep enough to accommodate 10 mm of gravel and all but 10 mm of 75 x 38 mm timber. The gravel bed should be about 250 mm wide to ensure adequate drainage. This will prevent premature rotting of the timber.

2 Lay the gravel bed, and then stake 75 x 38 mm boards in place. Mitre-cut end-to-end joints to make them less conspicuous. Drive in nails for the stakes so that their tops will be about 25 mm below the top edges of the boards. Projecting stakes can be dangerous.

3 Backfill with enough topsoil to cover the stakes. Compact the soil, and then cover it with turf, if you want your lawn to continue right up to the path, or mulch. Or you may prefer to create a bed beside the path, planting it with good edging plants to soften the edges.

Timber edging

1

2

3

Integral concrete edging

1

2

3

ABOVE: Here, timber edging butts up against small concrete pavers to create a raised flower bed. Both materials mix well as their colours are closely matched.

the edging is firmly set in place, otherwise the bricks will soon work themselves loose.

Victorian-style edging

In Victorian times, paths were commonly edged with terracotta edging tiles. These were produced in a variety of patterns, one of the most common being 'rope' edging, the top edge of which was shaped in a spiral like a length of rope.

Today, it is possible to buy reproduction Victorian edging tiles, but you can often find the real thing at architectural salvage yards. These edging tiles have a shaped lower portion, allowing them to be easily set in the ground.

ABOVE: Integral concrete edging

1 Construct plywood forms at the edge of your planned path. For a 90 mm thick path, leave a 90 mm gap between the gravel bed and inside board. Temporarily nail short pieces of timber between the inside and outside boards. Stake forms every 900 mm or so.

2 Lay reinforcing mesh, bending it so that its tips stick up into the curb forms. These tie the path and edging into an integral unit. When pouring the concrete, pull the mesh into the middle of the slab and curb it with a claw hammer or rake.

3 Pour concrete into the edging forms first, then into the path area, pulling out timber spacers as you pour. Strike off and trowel the surface but do not make it too smooth or it may become slippery. Let the concrete cure for a week, and then remove stakes and forms.

LEFT: Neat and tidy brick edgings can provide the perfect border for most types of paths.

Pathway plantings

An attractive array of plants softens the outlines of harsh edges and always adds a welcome splash of colour.

ABOVE: Red brick garden beds and box hedges create a delightful border for these flower gardens and meandering pathways.

Plants for formal paths

Even with a formal garden and pathway, it is more attractive to plant the edges with clumps of low plants so that the edges 'disappear' into the garden. Suitable plants for this are *Ophiopogon planiscapus nigrescens*, with purple-black grass-like leaves, and lilyturf (*Liriope*), which has a blue or a white flower. The blue-flowering lilyturf has variegated leaves; the white-flowering one has dark green leaves.

Other low hedging plants include Japanese box (*Buxus microphylla*), with its lightish green leaves, and common box (*B. sempervirens*), which has dark green leaves. Both are slow growing and are usually clipped into shape. Boxleaf honeysuckle (*Lonicera nitida*), is another choice that looks wonderful when clipped low along a formal path. Or try *Teucrium*, which needs constant clipping and has a little blue flower.

Plants for informal paths

For edgings in informal gardens, shrubs should spill over paths, softening their edges. Different varieties of lavender and daisies, clumps of salvia, day lilies, iris, stokes' aster (*Stokesia*), rosemary, lamb's ears (*Stachys bizantina*) and *Santolina* all look wonderful together. *Erigeron*, snow-in-summer (*Cerastium tomentosum*), *Convolvulus*, *Campanula*, *Saxifraga*, foxgloves and violets should also be considered. Lavender, rosemary, daisies, day lilies and iris all need sun, but violets, *Campanula*, *Saxifraga*, foxgloves and most lilies don't need a lot of sun and are happy in partial shade.

Plants behind the shrubs edging a pathway could include Chinese lantern (*Physalis alkekengei franchetii*), *Plumbago*, *Buddleja*, *Philadelphus*, gardenia and camellia.

Informal pathways call for pockets of flowers poking their heads up between paving slabs. Heartsease, miniature baby's breath (*Gypsophila repens*), violets, forget-me-nots and alyssum are particularly suitable. Wherever possible, simply sprinkle seeds between the slabs.

BELOW LEFT: Unmortared crazy paving flows like a river through this colourful sunny garden. This style of path is particularly suited to today's informal gardens, is relatively easy to lay and needs no special edging. Unfilled joints as shown could prove hard to walk on and we'd recommend either filling the joints with pea gravel or mortaring the stones together. Wayside plants are a colourful mixture of annuals and perennials, cottage-garden style.

BELOW: There's so much colour and interest in the garden you hardly notice the neat brick path shown here. This pattern is quick and easy to lay but more stylish results can be had using a fancier laying pattern. Lilac *Ageratums* and orange nasturtiums provide the bulk of the colour.

FAR LEFT: Lush ferns soften a sandstone path.

LEFT: Plant-filled urns on each side of sandstone steps give added interest and warmth to a paved area. Any paving, whether it be on patio or pool surround, pathway or driveway, will be made more charming with plants.

LEFT : This elegant pathway effect is a result of careful design, control of the colour range and the use of tiered formal hedges.

Garden steps

A flight of steps makes an attractive link between levels, and will add interest and character to the landscape.

Once, levelling the plot was the first thing a gardener did, and that was a pity. As well as being a back-breaking task, it was such a waste of a marvellous asset – a natural change in level. Highlight a slope with a flight of steps, and you will change the entire character of the landscape, adding fresh interest and opening up new vistas.

As with paths, steps should be compatible with their surroundings. For a formal garden, you could use bricks, pavers, tiles, cut stone or split rock embedded in mortar or, if the soil is heavy, in a sandy base. Informal steps can be made with railway sleepers, logs, rock or compressed soil with timber risers. Make your steps as wide as possible so you can allow plants to grow over the edges slightly to soften them. Ensure that they have a good deep tread and that the risers aren't too high for comfort. On a long, steep slope, build in one or two resting platforms if you can; a handrail is essential. A drainage ditch on one side will help to channel rainwater away from the steps. Line it with rocks to stop erosion, and plant it with water-tolerant species. Plants flanking your steps must never be prickly or spiky. Consider perfumed varieties that will release their scent when brushed against.

Constructing steps

Properly constructed garden steps not only connect different levels in the garden, but they also serve as a retaining wall. They must be carefully planned and securely anchored into the slope.

Tips
- The ground at the bottom of the steps will be wetter than elsewhere. Install a drainage system if you can, and choose water-loving plants.
- Strategically-placed rocks, large planters and embedded stumps can be used as alternatives to a handrail on steeply sloping sites.
- Choose sleepers and natural rocks carefully. Edges should be sharp, not rounded or splintered, and surfaces must be as even as possible.

BELOW: A combination of brick paving and large hardwood sleepers creates an impressive effect in these steps as they lead down from a patio.

Suitable materials

Select materials to match or contrast with the paths above and below. Steps can be built from brick, concrete, timber or any combination of these materials. For a natural look, you can terrace the slope with timber risers and surface the treads with gravel, bark chips or similar loose-fill.

Laying out

Whatever materials you choose, first you must decide how many steps you will need, how deep each horizontal tread will be, and how high to make each vertical riser. Here's a useful tip: the tread dimension plus the riser dimension should equal about 430 mm. Try to make your riser dimension no more than 180 mm and no less than 100 mm. No matter how you juggle the figures, make sure that all the treads will be exactly the same depth and all the risers exactly the

same height; any change may break a person's stride and could cause a stumble. Also, when planning a concrete foundation, be sure that you take into account the overall depth of the tread-surfacing materials and mortar.

Use stakes and a stringline or board to determine the total rise your steps will ascend and the total run they will traverse (see section on page 133). To determine how many steps you will need, divide these measurements by various combinations of tread and riser sizes until you have obtained steps of equal-size.

A handrail will be necessary if the flight exceeds five risers.

Paved steps

The method described (right) can be used for any paving materials — pavers, bricks, stone slabs or small concrete slabs. For the project illustrated opposite, we used bricks.

BELOW: Building paved steps

1 Cut into the slope, digging deeper under the bottom tread for an integral footing. Mark and dig the space for each tread 50 mm or so longer than the tread will be so that the forms can overlap as shown in step 2.

2 Construct forms so that the front edge of each tread will be double thickness. Pour gravel into the forms, and then add reinforcing mesh. Suspend horizontal reinforcing rod at the points where treads and risers will meet; tie the bottom tread to its footing with vertical reinforcing rod.

3 Shovel and pour wet concrete into the forms. Poke the mix from time to time with a piece of reinforcing rod to remove air pockets. Lift the mesh midway

into the concrete's thickness. Strike off and trowel. Let the concrete cure for about a week, and then remove the forms. The steps are now ready for the pavers.

4 Spread a 100 mm thick bed of mortar over the riser and tread of one step. Screed the bed, and then press the pavers into place, first on the riser and then on the tread below. A stringline keeps them level.

5 If a brick is too high, tap it down with the handle of a hammer or trowel. If it's too low, lift it out and trowel on more mortar to the bottom of the brick. Use 10 mm spacers to maintain even gaps between bricks.

6 Pack mortar between the bricks; shape the joints with a trowel or piece of pipe. When the mortar is almost dry, clean the bricks with water and a brush. Leave to cure for at least a week.

ABOVE: The gradual slope of this garden has been accentuated by the winding brick path. The low steps consist of frameworks of timber with brick infill to match the path. The timber frameworks are fixed securely to the path edging, which is also of large timbers, so there is no possibility of movement.

RIGHT: Making timber steps

1 Cut carefully into the slope, making room for the desired tread and riser dimensions. Each of our steps consisted of two 200 x 200 mm timbers with an overlap of 100 mm (that is, a tread width of 300 mm). Lay the timbers, knock them into place with a sledge and check for level.

2 Using a long wood-boring bit, drill holes at the front edge of each timber into the one below it, and then drive in reinforcing rods to tie them together. Also bore horizontal holes to secure each timber to the one behind it. These rods will hold the steps together firmly and prevent any movement.

Timber steps

Timber steps can take many forms, from a staircase such as that described on pages 133–6 to the simple steps shown below. Use only heavy-duty timber sections, making sure that they have been pressure-treated with preservative. Old railway sleepers are ideal and readily available from garden centres. Inspect timber steps regularly for signs of rot, as rotten steps can cause accidents.

Timber is relatively simple to work with, and timber steps can be constructed extremely quickly. They also blend well into informal settings, and are ideal if you wish to create a natural looking garden.

1

2

ABOVE: In this garden, solid timber sleepers have the size to balance the surrounding bush rocks and provide a rugged theme.

ABOVE RIGHT: Since plants are important to this design, the broad, platform-style steps are spaced randomly to form pockets which the gazanias fill with colour. These steps replace a dreary concrete path. Their frame is 100 x 50 mm hardwood set on edge, and the steps are 150 x 25 mm hardwood. Timber steps are best in a sunny position like this; they tend to become slippery in shade.

Sandstone steps

You can see below the problem faced by these home owners — inadequate, unattractive and broken steps, obstructed by overgrown foliage. Their solution was to build a new flight of steps flanked with beds of more suitable plants. The paving materials they used were lengths of shaped sandstone that framed crazy-paved treads.

Start by calculating the number of steps you'll need. Do this by attaching a stringline to the proposed top of the flight. Tie the other end to a stake and adjust the stringline until it is both taut and level. Measure the distance from this point to the ground, then

RIGHT: Broken, dangerous and narrow concrete steps did nothing but detract from this property. To make matters worse, access was obstructed by inappropriate siting of a large shrub.

1

2

3

divide that by the planned height of each step; 150 mm is a good, comfortable height. Allow at least 350 mm for the depth of the treads. The width of the flight is up to you and the site, but do remember that, gen-erally, the wider the steps, the better they will look. Using a sharp spade, dig out the shape of the steps, trying not to loosen too much of the soil that remains, then build your steps from the bottom up.

ABOVE: Building sandstone steps

1 Use a spirit level to check that the steps slope slightly to shed water. Lay 50 mm of sand as a bed for the stones.

2 Measure the step width to determine the length of the wall stone. Finished steps should be at least a metre wide.

3 Add a 3:1 dry mixture of sand and cement to the top of the laid stones. Sweep into spaces, brush off excess then, using a very fine mist, moisten the mixture thoroughly.

LEFT: The finished project looks stylish, and makes a much more practical and inviting entrance to the garden. Surrounding plantings will never grow big enough to obstruct traffic but will eventually hide garbage bins from sight.

Combination steps

These steps are constructed of three different building materials that make decorative shapes and forms. The framework consists of 150 x 75 mm wooden beams, with concrete paving slabs (we used 400 x 200 x 200 mm examples). The infill of the steps is of crushed stone, the chips being about 10 mm in size.

1 Mark out the dimensions of each step with string and carefully cut out the steps.

2 Drill and nail together the framework for each step so that the timber on the edge of the tread runs its full length. The frames should be about twice as wide as the desired tread width.

3 Place the frames on the cut-out steps and skew-nail them to each other, as shown in the diagram.

4 Fill the frames with gravel and bed the pavers within the gravel, making sure they are central within the wooden frame.

ABOVE: The timber frames of these combination steps are ideal for use on uneven ground as the timbers can be lengthened where necessary to extend into the slope. As the materials weather, the steps will blend into the garden.

LEFT: These combination steps employ three different materials: timber surrounds, concrete paving slabs and gravel. The timber framework is skew-nailed together, then the cavities are filled with gravel and surfaced with slabs. The size of the pavers can be adjusted to cover just a part or all of the step.

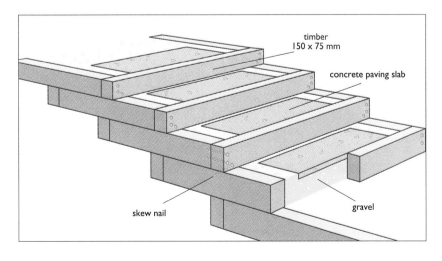

timber
150 x 75 mm

concrete paving slab

skew nail

gravel

Planting near steps

LEFT: Small plants and sprawling groundcover mingle well with these steps. The plants soften the rock edges by spilling over into the bark chips and leaf litter.

BELOW: Slabs of flat stone pave these steps to create a formal look. Their appearance is softened by tiny succulents in the crevices.

BOTTOM: Tamped earth steps with railway-sleeper risers are suitable for slopes with good drainage. Groundcovers help to prevent erosion. Curved steps look best on long slopes like this.

LEFT: Where the slope is not great, a ramp is a practical alternative to steps, allowing easier access for people with limited mobility.

BELOW: A wooden walkway can be an innovative solution over rough ground. In this case a formal stairway cut into the ground would have spoiled the natural woodland feel of the garden. The answer was to build a wooden ramp. Durable hardwood has been used and left unstained to weather gradually to a grey tone.

When a ramp is needed

Ramps make a gentle transition from one level to another, smoothing the path for everything from wheelbarrows to, most especially, wheelchairs. If you have a family member or friend who relies on a wheelchair, you will need a ramp to approach at least one of your home's entrances and possibly to reach the garden.

You can use a variety of materials for a ramp, including concrete, wood or even earth topped with fine gravel. Do, however, make sure that the surface is non-skid. Textured rubber toppings, such as skid-resistant polymer, and textured concrete work well.

Design considerations

Safety and ease of use are the prime considerations for any ramp. Appearance, though, also plays a part in its design.

Slope a wheelchair ramp at no more than 1 in 12. This can result in a very long ramp (a total rise of one metre, for example, requires a length of at least 12 metres), but a gentle incline is essential for those who will need it the most. Even if

your ramp will not be used by anyone in a wheelchair, give it no more than a 1-in-8 slope.

For wheelchair use, include handrails on both sides of the ramp and make the ramp wide enough so that the distance between the handrails is at least 900 mm. Landings should be placed at the top and bottom. Any incline longer than about 7 m needs an extra landing where a wheelchair user can rest and manoeuvre the chair. Whether your project calls for an L-shaped, U-shaped or simple straight ramp, all landings must be as long as the path is wide, but not less than 900 mm long. Where doors open outwards, the landing must be at least 1.5 x 2.0 m in order to allow the wheelchair user to move back safely and comfortably.

RIGHT: Building a concrete ramp

1 Use stringlines to lay out your ramp, planning it according to the directions given opposite. A concrete ramp must be tied into the slope with footings on each side of each landing. Make the ramp at least 100 mm thick.

2 We extended our ramp down from an existing slab, which we fitted with a piece of expansion strip. Cut and fill the earth as necessary. Construct forms with 100 x 50 mm timber. Double-check that the forms do not slope more than desired. Add gravel and reinforcing mesh.

3 Tie in footings with reinforcing rod. Pour concrete. Use a rather stiffer mix than you would for a level slab so that the concrete will hold the incline. Strike off. Float with a darby float. Define edges with an edging trowel, and then tool control joints every 1 m or so.

4 To make your ramp skidproof, pull a damp broom across the surface of the just-trowelled concrete. For a fine texture, use a soft-bristled broom; for a coarser one, use a stiffer bristle. Let the concrete cure for at least a week before removing the forms.

RIGHT: Metal handrails are a practical option, especially for a concrete ramp where they can be fixed to the curb or surface.

Building a concrete ramp

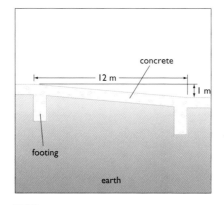

Installing handrails

It you are building a ramp that will be used by people in wheelchairs, fit handrails to both sides so that they can pull themselves up. The handrails should be about 865 mm high and have a grip width of about 38 mm. On flights of steps, install a handrail on at least one side. It should be at least 865 mm high.

To attach wooden railings to a wooden ramp, follow the instructions for fitting railings to a raised deck (pages 132–3) and be sure to fix the balusters securely to the ramp's structure, not its surface. Similarly, for wooden steps, it is important to attach the railing to the structure, not the treads.

To fix a metal railing to a concrete ramp, first drill holes into the ramp's surface (or into a concrete curb along its edge, as shown here). Install the brackets with expanding bolts. Slip the vertical balusters into their brackets, and tighten the set screws. Install the rails and assemble the intermediate balusters.

If you are installing handrails on concrete steps, attach the rail brackets to the treads.

Patios and Courtyards

Garden paving can form an extremely attractive feature that never needs mowing, feeding or watering. But more importantly, it provides a practical, level, hardwearing surface for outdoor eating, entertaining, relaxing and playing. As more people begin to appreciate the value of the land that surrounds their homes, interest in paving patterns, styles and colours steadily grows.

A patio or a courtyard provides a valuable extended living area, which can be a design feature of your garden as well as adding flexibility to your lifestyle. The patio often flows from the house and acts as an important link between house and garden. However, it may also be situated away from the house, perhaps in a spot that catches the evening sun or is protected from the winds. In this way, if a patio is well designed, it can extend your use of the garden considerably.

A pergola, adding shade and privacy, offers a visual connection between the patio and the house. Special plantings (of climbers, potted plants and small trees) add interest and allow your garden to flow beyond the formal flower beds and on to the patio.

On the following pages, we feature ideas for patio planting as well as detailed advice on how to lay paving, including a range of paving styles and materials, from terracotta to brick, slate, tessellated tiles and concrete pavers.

French doors lead on to a rustic, brick-paved patio, complete with an outdoor setting and tables. The effects of shade and sunlight, accentuated by the combination of potted plants and colourful shrubs, present a wonderful outlook from the house and create a delightful area in which to sit and enjoy it all.

The planning stage

Paving isn't at all difficult to lay, but it is important to prepare the ground carefully so that in the years to come undulations will not develop as the material settles. On the following pages, we give full, easy-to-follow instructions on getting the groundwork right. But first, consider carefully where the paving should go. In a small garden, you may not have a choice, but there may be several possibilities in a larger plot of land.

A patio needs to be more spacious than an indoor living room; it isn't just that we like the idea of 'the great outdoors', we do need more room outside. We walk with longer strides, our gestures are larger and we tend to sprawl in deckchairs. Six people can dine in reasonable comfort in a room measuring 3 x 3.5 m, but a patio of that size would seem crowded with only four people sitting around a table.

As a rule of thumb, whatever shape your patio may be – you're not confined to rectangles – its smallest dimension should not be less than 3 m, allowing for encroachment on the space by foliage.

Finding the best spot

Ideally, the patio should be sheltered from the wind, shaded from the hot summer sun, yet positioned so it can catch the autumn and spring sunshine, and big enough to be useful, not merely a path-like strip of paving beneath the living-room windows.

The south side of the house isn't the only spot; you can make a comfortable patio on the east, west and north sides, too. It's more important that it relates comfortably to your living rooms, maybe to the kitchen as well. You will be taking guests there, and it would be nice not to have to lead them out through the utility room or garage.

If the design of the house allows, it is always pleasant to be able to step straight out on to the patio through wide doors, so that it becomes physically an extension of the living room (or the family room,

BELOW RIGHT: Almost detached from the house and shaded by blossoming crab-apple trees, this patio forms the focus for entertaining in a large garden. The expanse of brick paving is broken up by groundcover.

BELOW: It is interesting to note that although both patios use the same area of paving, B feels more spacious. This may be because patio B uses two levels and extends further out into the garden.

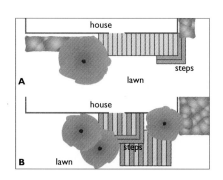

or the dining room). In this way, you break down the distinction between indoors and out. You may prefer to set your patio further out into the garden, perhaps to catch the sun or to take advantage of a fine view – or maybe just so that you can get away from the house and among the trees and greenery. The shape of the land may suggest a spot, too.

Carry out a 'trial run'

As you make your plans for a patio, take a chair outside and sit for a while in various spots to try out your ideas. You'll soon know if you've chosen a good location, and what you'll have to add in the way of planting, shade or whatever to make it perfect. There are no 'rules' – the right spot is where you feel most comfortable.

LEFT: This patio opens on to the driveway at the side of the house via a substantial gate. As well as being a place for sitting out, it also serves as an entry garden for the owners, who use their 'back' door much more than their front one.

BELOW: This sun-filled patio has undoubtedly expanded the possibilities for outdoor living for the owners of this home. The brick pavers are arranged in random blocks of colour, creating a distinctive effect.

Brick paving

Brick pavers, laid correctly, provide an attractive, durable and virtually maintenance-free surface. Nowadays, there are myriad colours and textures from which you can choose. Different shades are achieved by using different clays, mixing in additives (such as oxides), and by varying both the burning temperature and the amount of kiln time.

The darker colours are characteristically harder, stronger and more chemical- and salt-resistant. They are ideal for driveways and swimming-pool surrounds (for pools, choose a texture that isn't slippery).

Altering the surface finish of the mould in which the bricks are pressed and adding sand, gravel, etc to the clay provides different and interesting textures. Laying bricks in patterns adds further variation.

ABOVE: The brick terrace is large enough for dining. Small deciduous trees on the north side give summer shade, which doesn't reach to the formal herb and flower garden at a higher level.

RIGHT: A range of popular styles for brick paving.

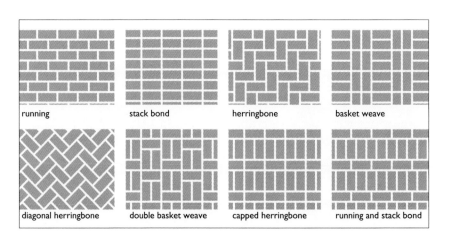

running stack bond herringbone basket weave

diagonal herringbone double basket weave capped herringbone running and stack bond

Brick patterns

Bricks can be laid in many patterns, from simple to complex. As standard bricks are 215 x 102.5 x 65 mm, they are difficult to lay in regular patterns – specially made paving bricks are easier to use.

Some popular patterns (or bonds) for brick paving are stretcher (the same as many brick walls), herringbone (either diagonal or square pattern; recommended for driveways), stack, basketweave and running bond.

With some ingenuity, you could come up with something original, but don't get too carried away; remember that fancy curved patterns, while stunning, may require many cut bricks. Although some cut easily with a bolster and club hammer, others are best cut with a diamond saw, which you will have to hire. Check with your supplier or, better still, obtain just a few bricks to test how easy they are to cut.

If you are paving near the house, the finished surface of the pavers should not come any closer than 150 mm to the walls' damp-proof course (a waterproof layer of bitumen, felt or lead built into a horizontal brick joint near ground

BELOW: This contemporary-style house is complemented by a concrete-paved patio. It provides a pleasant, level area for entertaining, family meals or just sitting.

level). This is because of the danger of moisture entering the wall through water splashing or surface build-up.

Calculating brick quantities

Estimating quantities of bricks involves some basic area calculations (in square metres).

1 For a square or rectangle, multiply the length in metres by the width: e.g., a rectangle 4.67 by 6.29 = 29. 37 square metres. (Order an additional five to ten per cent for wastage because of cutting, chipped bricks, etc.) If the area is L-, T- or U-shaped, divide it into separate rectangles, calculate the area of each, then add them together.

2 If the area is circular (or rectangular with a circular pool in the centre), calculate the area by multiplying pi (3.143) by the radius squared (the radius is the distance from the outside of the circle to the centre). For example, where the radius is 5 m, the area is 3.143 x 25 = 78.57 square metres (plus allowance for wastage).

For difficult shapes, you may be able to ask your brick supplier to calculate the quantity required. However, you must give him an accurate plan.

Calculating sand and cement quantities

To calculate the amount required for a sand-only bed, take the number of square metres of paving and multiply it by the thickness required. For example, 45 square metres of sand, 50 mm thick = 45 x 0.05 (50 mm is 0.05 of a metre) = 2.2 cubic metres of sand.

For cement in mortar mixes, quantities depend on the mix you require. If you want a 1:5 mix (common for laying paving), a close approximation is that you'll need one-fifth the volume of sand. Using the previous example, 2.2 divided

by 5 = 0.44 cubic metre of cement. Allowing that a bag of cement holds 0.035 cubic metre, you'll need 12–13 bags of cement (0.44 divided by 0.035).

Preparing for paving

As with any job, the finished product will only be as good as the preparation, and correct subsurface, drainage, bedding and edging are essential for a good result.

Subsurface

The subsurface must be stable, otherwise the pavers will settle unevenly. Remove all topsoil and grass plus any loose-fill. As you are working, use a straightedge and level and try to achieve a fall in the subsurface of 10–20 mm per metre (otherwise you'll have to create the fall with the bedding). If the soil appears to be unusually soft or unstable, compact it with a flat-bed vibrator (you can hire one). If it's still unsuitable, you will have to add a well-compacted 75–100 mm layer of hardcore or crushed stone.

Drainage

Slope the subsurface towards an area where the water will drain away easily, or create a collecting gutter that discharges into a stormwater drain. If this is impossible, you may have to use a mortar bed under the paver, which won't wash out. For badly drained areas, you may have to put in an underground drainage system.

Edging

The paving should be secured around the edge so that lateral movement is impossible and the bedding cannot be eroded. This is especially necessary where heavy foot or vehicular traffic is expected, or in areas that may be inundated with water.

Edges can be restrained by using lengths of timber (100 x 25 mm preservative-treated pine) held securely in place by pegs.

ABOVE: The patio surrounding this pool is laid in basket-weave pattern and is bordered by random-shaped paving stones. The soft, mottled colours provide a mellow and traditional look to the area.

BELOW: Bricks can be laid with wet or dry mortar on a sand bed or slab. Alternative edging forms are also shown.

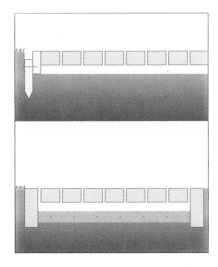

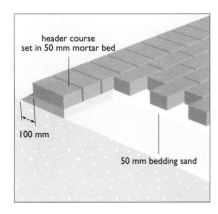

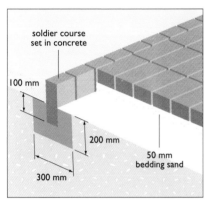

TOP: This paving technique uses a header course set in a 50 mm mortar bed to secure the paved area and avoid the possibility of any movement from the other bricks.

ABOVE: Here, a course of upright bricks set into concrete footings provides an immovable barrier, able to withstand heavy weight and exposure to water seepage.

RIGHT: Tones of red, terracotta and pink predominate in this area of brick paving. The variegated colours will always add a richness, even as the contrasts mellow.

Another method is to lay the edging pavers in mortar (1 part cement to 5 parts sand) with the remainder on a bed of sand. Extend the mortar past the edging pavers and slope it at 45°.

For a really professional finish, dig a trench and push the ends of a row of pavers or bricks 100 mm into a concrete footing, 300 mm wide by 200 mm deep. If you prefer, you can position the top of the concrete footing below ground level and then cover it with soil.

Bedding

Use sand or workable areas of well mixed mortar; spread out the required thickness (minimum 30 mm) and compact. The mortar can be laid dry and lightly hosed after the paving is finished. Alternatively, it can be mixed with water. If so, don't make the mix sloppy – a granular, dryish mixture is best, one that compresses if squeezed in the hand. Periodically, check the bedding for level with a straightedge.

Laying the bricks

Now start laying the bricks, five or ten at a time; work uphill if there is a slope. Tap them down until firm with a rubber mallet or club hammer and a block of soft wood. Maintain a 2–3 mm joint between them (this allows for brick expansion). Check with your straightedge as you go, and pack up any bricks that are too low.

When the bricks have been laid, fill the joints with sand or a dry mortar mix by sweeping it in, then hosing carefully; it may take several applications to fill them completely. The water will make the mortar set, but take care not to wash it out of the joints. Brush off any mortar stains with clean water and hose off immediately.

Maintaining a brick patio

Other than regular sweeping and hosing down, no maintenance should be necessary. Any weeds can either be pulled out or sprayed with a weedkiller.

Concrete paving slabs

Concrete paving slabs have been popular with builders, landscapers and do-it-yourselfers for many years. They come in a variety of sizes, shapes and thicknesses. The texture of concrete paving slabs is much the same for all, being non-skid and fairly coarse, and they can be tinted in many different colours.

Choosing paving slabs

As well as the larger manufacturers whose ranges of concrete paving slabs are extensive, there are also a number of smaller companies that specialise in supplying slabs that have been designed to look like natural paving materials, such as slate, sandstone, granite and marble. The process of manufacturing these paving slabs is different from that of the larger manufacturers, and this will change the character of the slabs.

For instance, when buying mass-produced concrete paving slabs, you should choose a 40-mm-thick slab for pathways and patios, and one between 50 mm and 60 mm thick for driveways. If, however, you buy hand-processed paving slabs, you may be able to use thinner slabs for all purposes. Discuss your requirements with your supplier.

Your local council may also sell off secondhand paving slabs, which is worth investigating.

Shapes and sizes

Massed-produced concrete paving slabs are often made in dimensions based on multiples of 225 mm, and squares and rectangles are common. Other shapes available include hexagons and rounds, which can be used to add visual interest to a project. They are ideal as stepping stones set in gravel, bark chips or grass.

Some concrete paving slabs are available with a finish that resembles individual pavers or stone setts. With a little mortar added to the 'joints', they can look most effective. An attractive way to dress up concrete slabs on a pathway is to surround each with a decorative border of bricks.

Generally speaking, the smaller the concrete slab, the stronger it will be, so it is recommended that driveway slabs should be a smaller size than, say, those used for patios.

Concrete block paving is also available, the blocks resembling brick pavers in size and shape and offering a wide range of colours to choose from. In addition to standard rectangular types, there are special interlocking shapes that pro-

ABOVE: These 'rumbled' concrete pavers match the wall colouring and give this large courtyard a cobblestone look.

BELOW: Large concrete pavers are available in a range of sizes, shapes and finishes. Here concrete pavers have been laid in an irregular geometric pattern to provide a stylish effect. As the pavers weather they often display soft tonings.

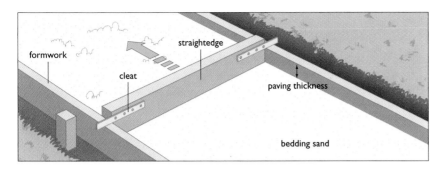

LEFT: When constructing formwork for the paving, check that the slabs fit the width to reduce the amount of cutting. Make the top edge of the formwork the line for the finished paving. Attach cleats to your screed board and slide the straight-edge along the formwork, thus levelling the bed to the correct height for paving.

vide a stable laying pattern. These concrete paving blocks are suitable for all types of paving, whether for pedestrian or vehicular use. Moreover, they are cheaper than more traditional brick pavers.

Buying paving slabs

Paving slabs are usually sold and priced by the square metre, but you can buy them separately and they are very easy to lay. When concrete slabs are delivered, they should be stacked on edge on a hard, dry surface and leaned against a wall or similar firm support.

Laying concrete slabs

Unlike poured concrete, a sub-base is not usually necessary when laying concrete pavers or the slabs, except on clay or soft soils.

However, some paving experts believe that concrete slabs should be laid on mortar. This is a personal choice and will depend a lot on your budget, as it costs more to lay them on mortar than on sand. You should also take into account whether the site you are paving is steep. A driveway, for instance, may need the extra strength of mortar. Your supplier will advise you on the appropriate type of bedding.

If you do use mortar, take care that you don't stain the slabs. To help prevent this, you should wet them thoroughly before laying them on the bedding.

As with any paving, the preparation of the surface to be paved must be thorough (see Preparing for paving on page 76). And it is important to remember that if you're not used to laying concrete slabs, only pave a small, manageable section at a time.

Laying in sand

Spread a bed of sand to a depth of between 40 and 50 mm. To hold the sand in place, construct a kerb of concrete or timber approximately 150 mm wide by the same depth as the slabs. Always use a stringline when laying paving slabs (see diagram, below), and lay them with a joint of approximately 10 mm between each one.

For a patio or other large area, the starting point will depend on the boundaries and the type of laying pattern. If there is an established boundary, such as a wall at one edge, or two fixed boundaries at right angles, start there. Plan the work so that you don't end up with cut slabs or blocks at a step.

To cut a slab, use a bolster and club hammer. Start by scoring along the line to be cut, on both sides, with the corner of the bolster blade, using a straight piece of wood to guide it. Lay the slab on some sand to absorb the hammer blows and work around the slab on the scored line a number of times to deepen it until the slab breaks in two. Edges cut this way tend to be rough, so in order to conceal them it is best to lay them against an edging.

Alternatively, you can hire a hydraulic cutter or a diamond-tipped brick saw, which is perfect for difficult cuts or where your requirements for neatness and accuracy are paramount.

BELOW: Mark out the area to be paved using stringlines. Lay paving slabs on a prepared base. Note the use of timber pieces between slabs to ensure an even pattern.

BOTTOM: Using a bolster, score along the lines to be cut, on both sides. Work around the paving slab on the scored line several times, until it breaks.

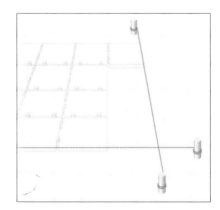

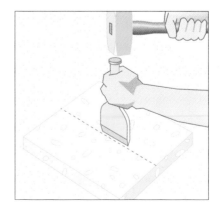

Laying on a mortar bed over a concrete slab

Use a 1:5 cement/sand mortar mix. For easier adjustment of the paving slabs, they could be 'spot bedded' with a small mound of mortar at each corner and in the middle, but this is not as strong as laying slabs in a full mortar bedding. A satisfactory compromise for the non-professional is a box-and-cross bedding (see diagram, below).

Box-and-cross bedding

1 Place strips of mortar with a bricklayer's trowel so that they form a rectangle slightly smaller than the dimensions of the slab, enclosing a cross strip. The cross strip can be omitted for small square slabs, but large rectangular slabs may need to be 'double-crossed'. The mortar strips should be 30 to 50 mm deep.

2 Position the first slab on the mortar bed and tamp it in firmly with a wooden mallet or a length of timber.

3 Repeat with successive slabs (see diagram, bottom), using small pieces of timber as spacers if the paving slabs are large.

4 Check alignment and level against adjoining slabs with a straightedge.

Fill the joints between them with mortar rammed in with a thin piece of wood. Use a very dry mix (just short of crumbly) to avoid staining the surface. Clean off any excess mortar with a wet sponge as soon as possible to prevent staining. Finish the joints to a level 1–2 mm below the paving.

Tips

- Concrete paving is generally more true to size than other types of paver and, therefore, is easier for the home handyperson to lay.
- Concrete is an inexpensive paving material.
- Where staining may occur, such as around barbecue areas or on pool surrounds, it is advisable to treat concrete with a proprietary sealer.
- Concrete is versatile and can be made to look like natural materials such as sandstone, slate, marble and granite.

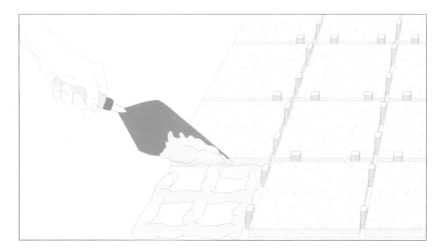

ABOVE LEFT: Lay slabs on a sound box-and-cross bedding of mortar.

LEFT: Position the paving using small pieces of timber for spacers if the slabs are large. Alignment and level should be checked against adjoining slabs.

Pouring a concrete slab

If you're considering doing any concreting, it's as well to realise that large concreting jobs are hard work and it may be better to employ a professional unless you are experienced – and very fit.

Whether you intend to do it your-self or are employing a profes-sional, check that your site is cleared of all vegetation and that there is a suitably firm sub-base for the concrete. Crushed stone or sand is ideal and can be bought from builders' merchants or sand and gravel suppliers.

Note that most sub-base materi-als will lose about 25 per cent of their original volume when com-pacted. Beware of any demolition rubble, too, as this will often con-tain large lumps of masonry that can make it difficult, if not impossi-ble, to compact well enough to pro-duce a stable sub-base.

Estimating quantities

To estimate the quantities of mate-rials you will need for a concreting job, first draw the layout of the area and mark it off in metre or half-metre squares (see diagram, above). Count the squares, averag-ing out the part-squares, and multi-ply the area by the thickness. Remember that for paved areas, the horizontal dimensions will proba-bly be worked out in metres and the thickness in millimetres, so make sure the decimal points are in the right place.

To allow for wastage, order ten per cent more than the amount you have calculated. Always order your materials in advance, but not so far in advance that the cement has time to 'air harden'.

Materials storage

Make sure your storage arrange-ments are complete before delivery. If you have to store materials out-side, use a raised platform and cover tightly with plastic sheeting well weighted or tied down. Where it is necessary to have materials off-loaded on to a footpath or public thoroughfare, you may need coun-cil permission.

Wherever possible, have the materials delivered right on to the site, as moving them is very hard work: each cubic metre will fill 25 to 30 average wheelbarrows.

You will need:

builder's measuring tape
wooden pegs, approximately 25
  x 25 x 250 mm
straightedge
spirit level
club hammer or mallet
cord for stringlines (preferably
  coloured)
50 mm nails
builder's square
steel and wood floats
bricklaying and pointing trowels
shovel
stiff broom
wheelbarrow
pre-mixed concrete
reinforcement
buckets
hose

Formwork

1 All concreting jobs should be properly set out with formwork, pegs and stringlines. The pegs will stay in place throughout the work for checking as you go, and the stringlines can be removed when they get in the way, and then set up again when they are needed.

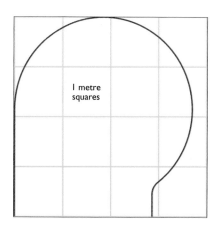

ABOVE: To estimate the quantities of materials needed for an irregular area, count the squares, averaging out the part-squares, and multiply the area by the thickness. Allow an extra ten per cent for wastage.

BELOW: The formwork for this slab uses rigid and flexible edge boards. The curved sections require stakes (pegs) at least every 400 cm to ensure the edging holds its shape under pressure.

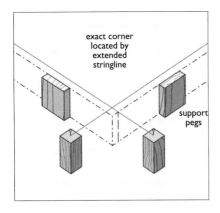

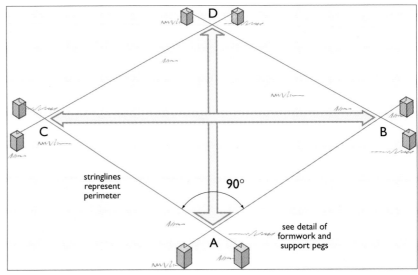

ABOVE: Position support pegs to allow for formwork thickness.

ABOVE RIGHT: Stringlines extend to pegs placed outside the working area. This allows corners to be located exactly, and means the pegs need not be disturbed during subsequent work.

BELOW: Rake concrete down to within 10 mm of the top of the formwork.

2 Following our diagram (above), stretch a stringline along side AB and fix it tautly around nails in the tops of pegs driven in well outside the working area where they won't be disturbed during subsequent work (see diagram, above left). These pegs, with nails driven in the top, allow the corners to be located exactly. Do not fix the stringline to the exact corners (i.e., where string lines cross is the actual corner).

3 Stretch a stringline across A at right angles to line AB (use the builder's square to check the angle), measure along it to locate corner C and drive in a peg with a nail. Anchor the stringline as in previous step.

4 Repeat for side BD, driving in a corner peg at D. Measure side CD; it should be equal to AB. Measure diagonals AD and BC; they should be the same. If measurements are correct, fix a stringline for side CD, again to pegs outside the working area.

5 Set up formwork for the slab. Edge boards made from strong timber are used as the 'frame' for a concrete slab. You can use old fence boards or floorboards, as long as they are at least 20 mm thick. They should also be as smooth as possible so that they free easily from the concrete when it has set. Set the boards up so that their upper edges are level with the finished surface of the concrete and make sure that those edges are straight and undamaged. Use a spirit level to ensure that they are perfectly level. Keep the edge boards firmly in position with pegs driven into the ground, making sure that they don't project above the boards.

Reinforcement

For most domestic paths and patios, a 75 mm layer of concrete over a compacted sub-base will not need additional reinforcement. However, where the concrete will receive heavy traffic or over clay or unstable soils, adding steel reinforcing mesh makes sense.

Mesh is available from builders' merchants and is relatively inexpensive. It can be cut to size with a hacksaw. Make sure that it is supported at least 25 mm below the surface of the finished concrete. The easiest way to do this is to fix it to the tops of wooden pegs with staples.

Mixing and pouring

Concrete is a mixture of cement and various aggregates, such as sand and stone. The proportions of the mix determine its strength. For general-purpose use other than foundations and exposed paving, use a 1:2:3 mix of cement, sand and 20 mm aggregate (1:4 if combined aggregate is ordered); for foundation work, choose a 1:2.5:3.5 mix (1:5 with combined aggregate); and for exposed paving, a 1:1.5:2.5 mix (1:3.5 for combined aggregate).

The key to good concrete is accurate proportioning of materials and thorough mixing. The exact quantities in a batch are not important as long as the proportions are right. Use the same-sized container for measuring all materials; a heavy-duty 15-litre bucket is about right, as a batch based on one bucketful of cement will be an ideal size for hand-mixing or for a small mixer.

Cement bulks up considerably when loose; fill the bucket, tap the side two or three times with the shovel to shake the cement down, then add more to bring it level with the top.

Always use a separate bucket and shovel for cement only, otherwise moisture from the aggregate will cause the cement to cake and build up on the tools.

Add water only to the extent needed for a sufficiently workable mix. Some water will already be present in the aggregate, so the amount added will be a matter of trial and error.

To mix concrete by hand, you must work on a hard, smooth surface, such as a driveway, or on a sheet of plywood or other hard, waterproof material. Mixing by machine is infinitely easier.

Do not let concrete fall more than one metre from a wheelbarrow or bucket when it is being placed. Spread concrete with a shovel and work it into place.

Tamping down

Rake down to within 15 mm of the top of the formwork (see diagram, opposite). The concrete must be tamped down after it has been poured and raked (see diagram, top, page 84). A tamping board is a stout, smooth board of approximately 100 x 50 mm, with a straight edge, about 500 mm longer than the width of the poured concrete. This tamping board is drawn across the concrete, using a sawing action, until the concrete is level with the top edges of the formwork.

Finishing

After tamping, the concrete will have a rippled surface, which can be left as is. Alternatively, a variety of finishes can be applied to smooth the surface or give it more visual appeal, using a broom, a shovel or a steel or wooden float.

A range of finishes

Working across the freshly-tamped concrete with a soft broom will give a finely-textured, lined finish. A stiff broom will produce a 'corduroy-like' texture. Wash the bristles regularly to prevent clogging.

You can use a wooden float to produce a variety of finishes. If you use a clean float on fresh concrete before it has hardened completely, it will give a fine 'sandpaper' texture.

ABOVE: Removing excess concrete by shovel prior to tamping the slab level with the top of the formwork.

A steel float, kept clean, will give a smooth finish to fresh concrete. The tool should be almost literally floated over the surface, otherwise it will leave marks. For a really smooth finish, go over the concrete again after it has 'gone off' slightly.

Aggregate finish

For an exposed-aggregate finish, spread coarse aggregate evenly on the fresh concrete after initial finishing and tamp it firmly into the surface with a float.

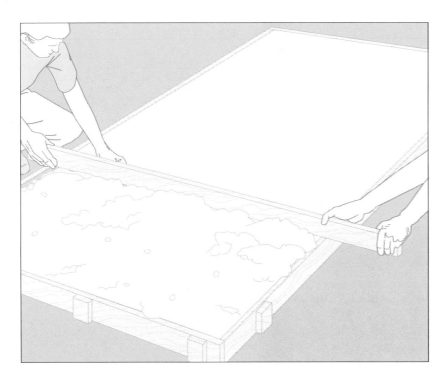

LEFT: Tamp the concrete to level off the surface, using a chopping and sawing action, until the concrete is level with the formwork.

BELOW: Finishing can be done with a soft or hard broom (top left), the latter giving a ribbed texture on fresh concrete. A wood float (top centre) will render a fine sandpaper texture, and a steel float (top right) a smoother finish. An alternative method is to sweep over the concrete using the back of a shovel (below left). An exposed aggregate finish should be sprayed and brushed when hardened, to wash away loose material (below right).

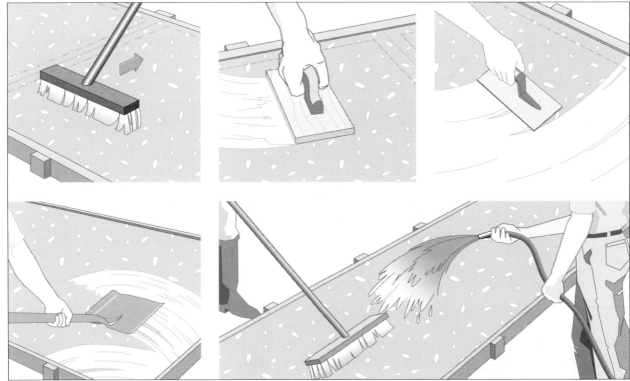

RIGHT: Garden beds and gravel edge this new concrete path. Large concrete areas such as this, require expansion strips to allow for expansion and contraction throughout the year.

When the concrete has hardened to the point where the coarse aggregate won't dislodge easily, gently brush and spray with water to wash away any loose, fine material. This is a particularly attractive finish if specially selected gravel or crushed stone is used. If you intend to do this yourself, practise first, as it needs care.

Curing

As soon as the surface is hard enough to resist spoilage, it must be protected. This process is known as curing. First, cover the concrete with plastic sheeting, ensuring that it is in contact with the entire surface, is free of air pockets and is well secured in place.

Tape the plastic sheeting to the edge boards and cover any lapped joints with sand or bricks. As the concrete must not dry out during the curing period, it is necessary to wet the surface periodically, replacing the plastic sheeting each time.

Curing takes seven days, after which the plastic sheeting is removed and the surface hosed thoroughly. If concrete is not cured properly and dries out too quickly, the surface will be weak and cracks may occur, spoiling the appearance and perhaps reducing the life of the concrete. Protect particularly from sun and wind, as they speed up evaporation and the concrete will dry out too soon.

The method for curing coloured concrete is different, as water-curing with plastic sheets can produce bad results. Check with your supplier for the appropriate method.

Concrete cleaning tips

Look after tools

Wet cement and concrete will stick to most other materials, particularly metal tools you may use when mixing. This will encourage a further build-up if allowed to harden. Keep tools clean while you are working by hosing and brushing them off regularly, and after use. Any concrete that has hardened on shovels or wheelbarrows should be removed by wire brushing. Rubbing tools down with a piece of brick prior to wire brushing will also help.

If using a concrete mixer, put half the aggregate and some water in it – but no cement – after the drum has been emptied and run it while you are placing the first load. This will help prevent a build-up of concrete on the blades and interior of the drum. Do the same before turning off the mixer at the end of the day. Then clean it out carefully by hand.

Cleaning concrete

Proprietary cleaning agents are available for removing a wide variety of stains from concrete and they should always be used in accordance with the manufacturer's instructions.

Spilled paint should be treated with paint stripper, which should be stippled into the surface with a stiff brush. The softened paint can be removed with a scraper and wire brush, after which the surface should be hosed down to remove all traces of the paint and stripper.

Any mould growth should be scraped and brushed off, then the concrete treated with a solution of 1 part bleach and 4 parts water. Leave this for a couple of days before hosing the concrete down and going over it with a scrubbing brush. A second application may be required for particularly bad growths.

To remove oil or grease stains from a concrete drive or garage floor, first sprinkle on sand to absorb any surface liquid. Brush this up and remove it. Then tackle the stain by applying white spirit or a proprietary degreasant, working it into the stain with a stiff-bristled brush. Finally, hose the area down completely.

If there is a large area of staining to be dealt with, it may pay you to hire a high-pressure steam cleaner, which is very effective at removing a wide variety of stains from concrete and other forms of paving surfaces.

BELOW: An elegant formal area has been created by setting large slate slabs in concrete. Prepare the area as described for paths but use a 25 mm thick layer of concrete instead of sand. Set the stones in place and fill the interstices with more concrete.

Slate paving

Slate can look extremely attractive both inside and outside a house. However, dark slate tends to absorb the heat and on hot days it can be uncomfortable to walk on. Choose one of the light-coloured slates if you are paving a patio or courtyard. Think carefully about choosing slate for a pool surround, as it will get hotter than many other paving materials.

Random slate set in grass or gravel and shaded by trees and shrubs is particularly attractive. It comes in rough shapes like crazy paving stone and looks good in garden areas; it is usually available from landscape garden suppliers.

There are four different edges on slate tiles. The sawn edge is a neat, cut edge; the hand-cut edge is pop-ular for outdoor paving, as it looks rustic; the chipped edge also looks rustic; the guillotined edge is a neater form of chipped edge. Although some types are cheaper than others, all slate is expensive.

Types of slate

In the UK, slate is more commonly used as a roofing material than for

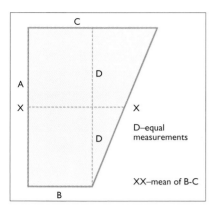

D—equal measurements

XX—mean of B-C

ABOVE: Calculate the area to be tiled by measuring the length and width, and multiplying. To calculate an irregular area, take a mean measurement – the length by the mean of two different width measurements.

Tips

- Slate is a natural material that has a tough, hardwearing surface and low porosity, so it is unlikely to stain.
- Choose lighter slate for outdoor areas, as dark slate absorbs heat and can become very hot.
- Don't seal slate that is laid outside, as the sun may blister the sealant, and rainwater and grit will also damage it.

paving or flooring and, as a result, much that is offered is in the form of thin roofing tiles. Invariably, it comes from Wales where it is mined. However, thicker sections of slate suitable for paving use may be ordered from specialist suppliers.

Some companies also import slate from countries such as Africa, India and China, and these sources are the most popular for paving slate, since they offer a wider range of colours than the native Welsh slate, which invariably is a soft grey. South African slate has long been regarded as the best quality slate, mainly because only the best slate is exported from that country, whereas that from India and China may be of poorer quality. In fact, the better grades of Indian and Chinese slate are just as good as African slate. Most slate from these countries is cut into tiles.

African slate is smooth and has a black base, so usually it is not suitable for exterior paving. Chinese slate is lighter in colour, with tonings of khaki, burnt orange and rusty brown, and has a slightly rough texture on the surface, which makes it ideal for outdoor use. Indian slate has a silvery-grey base with tonings of pink, burgundy and tan, and is also suitable for outdoor paving. Note that salt water will damage these slates.

Like any type of natural stone, the price of slate is likely to vary depending on how close you live to the source of supply. If you live near where it is mined or stocked, the cost of transporting it to you will be considerably less than if you live some distance away. Consequently, this may restrict your choice of paving. Enquire at builders' merchants, stone merchants or check the Yellow Pages for suppliers.

Ordering slate

Slate tiles can be bought in sizes that range from 150 x 150 mm to 600 x 300 mm. They vary in thickness from 8 to 20 mm; the average

thickness is around 13 mm. Slate tiles under 6 mm in thickness are not recommended for external use. The thinner slates of 6 mm or less need more care in laying than do the thicker varieties.

To calculate the area to be tiled, measure the length and width, and multiply the two. If the area is irregular in shape, take an average measurement: for example, the length by the mean of the two different width measurements (see diagram).

Always order five per cent over and above the measured area to allow for wastage and cutting.

When ordering slate, tell the supplier what surface you will be laying it on. If laying on timber, you will need hessian and a cold-pour bitumen (membrane liquid), available from your slate supplier.

You can cut tiles with a diamond-tipped saw, which can be hired, or with a silicon carbide/carborundum masonry disc on an angle grinder. Slate can also be cut with a hacksaw fitted with a carborundum blade, but this can be time-consuming.

Alternatively, the slate supplier may offer a tile-cutting service, and this is probably the most practical and economical solution.

When planning a patio, estimate that the slate will raise the floor level by approximately 18–20 mm.

Laying slate tiles on concrete

You will need:

slate tiles
cement-based slate adhesive
straightedge, approximately 2–2.5m long
spirit level
square
mixing board or barrow
12 x 12 mm notched trowel
rubber mallet
tape measure or rule
steel wool
buckets
broom

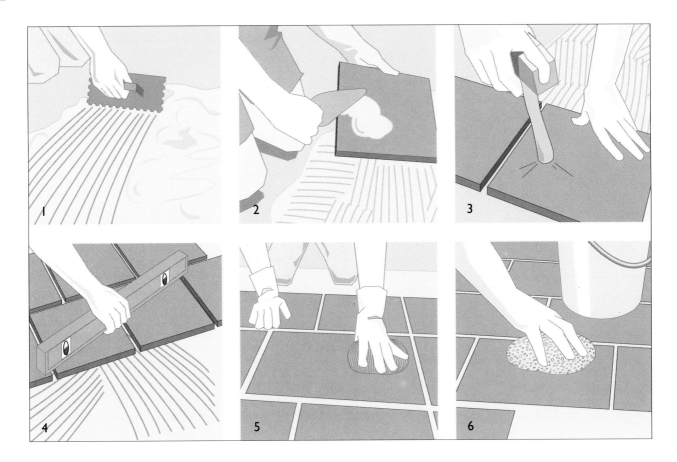

1 Apply a layer of adhesive to the surface to be tiled.

2 Coat the back of the tile with the adhesive, then settle it into the bed.

3 Tap the bedded tile gently into position.

4 Level tile with a straightedge or spirit level.

5 Thoroughly clean the area with water and a nylon scouring pad or dry steel wool.

6 Remove all excess grout with sponge and water.

Slate should never be laid outside in extremely hot or wet weather. It should be laid on a clean concrete slab, using a recommended sand and cement-based slate tile adhesive applied with a notched trowel. If concrete has a steel-trowelled finish, acid etching or chipping may be necessary to provide a key for the adhesive.

Before laying, grade your tiles into thick, medium and thin pieces. Starting nearest the house, lay the thicker tiles first, then the medium ones and finally the thinnest ones.

The natural fall of the surface will often accommodate the different thicknesses in the tiles, but where it is necessary to adjust the level so that tiles are flush, simply build up the adhesive accordingly. The adhesive can be built up to a depth of 6 mm if necessary. Tile only a small area at a time.

If the concrete surface on which the slate tiles will be laid is rough and uneven, a screed of sand/cement

mortar will be necessary to level it. Unless you are experienced at this sort of work, this could be the time to call in the professionals.

Prepare the site thoroughly and check the fall for correct water run-off – it should be about 10 mm for every metre.

Sweep the surface to be tiled to remove all dust and debris. Mix adhesive with water until you obtain a smooth and heavy paste. Let the mixture stand for at least five minutes before re-stirring.

Apply adhesive to concrete

Using a 12 x 12 mm notched trowel, apply a layer of adhesive to the surface to be tiled. Do not cover an area any larger than can be completely tiled within ten minutes. Err on the side of caution in this respect.

Apply adhesive to tile

Coat the back of the slate tile with a thin coat of adhesive, then using a sliding and twisting action, press the slate over the freshly-spread adhesive on the floor and settle it into the bed with a backward and forward motion. This should squeeze out most of the air pockets from under the slate.

Bed the tile

With the rubber mallet close to the centre of the tile, tap the bedded tile into position. Pressure on the tile near the edge will loosen the bond on the opposite side, and eventually the tile may begin to separate from the surface below and crack. The tapping operation should squeeze out most of the remaining air pockets trapped under the slate, and helps to level it with the surrounding tiles.

Continue to lay tiles

Proceed with the other tiles, leaving a 5–15 mm joint between them and lining them up with a stringline or straightedge. Also, use the straightedge to ensure that the tiles, faces are all flush and do not 'lift' at the edges. As you work, clean surplus adhesive away from the face of the tiles with a clean, damp sponge. It is very difficult to remove when it is dry.

Finish by cleaning and grouting

When you have finished laying slate tiles, simply wash thoroughly with warm water. Do not use any product that contains solvent or abrasives, and make sure that you do not walk on the slate for at least 24 hours after it has been laid because you might damage it.

After this time, you should grout the joints between your tiles with neutral grey or charcoal grout. Wash excess grout from the surface of the slate straight away with a large sponge and plenty of clean water. If necessary, spot clean with dry steel wool.

Keep washing and cleaning newly-laid slate tiles for at least four days.

Maintaining a slate patio

Slate, which is metamorphic rock that has been formed over millions of years, has a low porosity, so is unlikely to stain, except where there is oil and grease spillage around areas such as barbecues.

Slate should be sealed when laid inside, but it is not advisable to seal it outside because the ultraviolet rays of the sun will attack the sealant and may cause it to blister. The minerals from rainwater can also be harmful, while any grit walked into a sealed surface can act like sandpaper and wear the surface away. A sealed surface will also tend to be more slippery than an unsealed one. Never apply sealer to warm or hot slates.

To keep a slate surface clean and scratch-free, it is essential to sweep it regularly with a soft broom and wash it with clean water or a slate shampoo. Slate can be spot-cleaned by rubbing it with dry steel wool, but not if it has been laid around a pool, as the steel wool fibres will cause rust spots if washed into the pool. No slate of any type should be sealed unless absolutely clean and dry beforehand.

Quartzite

Like slate, quartzite is a natural material that has been formed over millions of years. Slightly harder and thicker than slate, it comes mainly from India and China and contains silica, which gives its surface a glitter.

Although it is not a slate, quartzite splits like slate. Quartzite tiles come in similar sizes to slate, the most popular sizes being 300 x 200 mm, 300 x 300 mm and 600 x 300 mm. Thicknesses range from 12 mm to 18 mm.

Laid in exactly the same way as slate, quartzite is even more expensive, but is extremely suitable for exterior paving because of its lighter colours and roughish texture, which makes it non-skid.

Popular colours are salmon pink, dark emerald green with a grey glitter and white, all of which come from India. There is also a dark green/grey quartzite from Norway, but this is more expensive still.

Because quartzite is a harder material than slate, it can be cut to size and shape only with a special masonry disc on an angle grinder or a diamond-tipped saw. Like slate, quartzite should not be sealed when it has been laid outdoors.

Slate-finished sandstone tiles are non-slip and extremely hardwearing. They are ideally suited for pool surrounds and traffic areas.

BELOW: Slate tiles, with their green-grey and blue-grey tones, provide timeless charm and are a highlight of this stylish garden. Their use on pathways, fountain and pool surrounds gives a pleasing uniformity to the overall design.

ABOVE: The texture and tones of sandstone provide warmth to any outdoor area and set it apart from other paving materials.

Sandstone paving

Sandstone looks wonderful anywhere. It is just as attractive on wide steps sweeping down to a patio as it is on narrow pathways snaking around haphazard clumps of flowers.

Sandstone paving is also extremely popular for swimming-pool surrounds, giving a mellow surface that complements the crispness of the pool's tiling.

Old sandstone is often in demand, as its weathered look is more likely to suit an established house and garden. You may have trouble tracking down weathered sandstone, so try scouring demolition sites or talk to paving contractors.

If all else fails, there is an extremely easy way to age new sandstone. Simply make up a mixture of tomato plant food, to the same formula as used for plants and apply it to the sandstone. You may need to make three or four applications over a period of about two weeks to complete the aging process. Remember, it is possible that dark staining may occur on sandstone underneath pot plants fertilised with tomato food.

There are many different colours and markings in new sandstone, and while it is a heavy material (about 2.3 tonnes per cubic metre), it is reasonably soft, so it is easy for the handyperson to cut and lay.

Shapes and sizes

Sandstone is usually 50 mm thick and is sold in sheets of 3 x 2 m, in rectangular blocks of 800 x 400 mm and in random shapes for crazy paving. The 3 x 2 m sheets have to be cut before laying, and this can be done quite easily with a hammer and bolster, an angle grinder or a circular saw, but it takes time and effort. On the other hand, the 800 x 400 mm blocks can be laid with the minimum of effort. They can also be butted together without grouting if bedded in a moist slurry of sand and cement.

Laying sandstone

Sandstone can be laid in a 50-mm-deep bed of 1:6 cement and sand mixture, but ideally it should be laid in a slurry (almost 1:4 cement and sand mix) on a 100-mm-deep concrete base. (See page 81 for details of constructing a concrete base.) The surface of the slab should be treated with a PVA sealer solution before laying the slurry. When laying the sandstone, it should be firmly, but gently, tapped down with a rubber mallet.

A most important consideration when laying sandstone is to make sure there is support for the slabs around the perimeter. The best way to provide extra strength to a sandstone-paved area is to construct a concrete edge.

When laying crazy paving, always lay the large pieces first,

RIGHT: Paving styles such as these may be varied to suit the dimensions of your pavers, be they irregular sandstone blocks or sawn pieces.

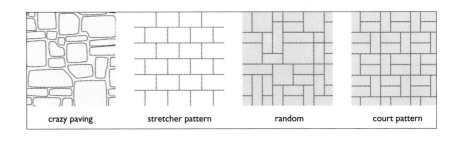

crazy paving   stretcher pattern   random   court pattern

RIGHT: This fascinating mixture of stone slabs provides a decorative crazy paving patio. The rich sandstone hues complement the cream-painted walls as well as the traditional iron-work furniture.

then go back and fill in with the small pieces. Use a 1:4 cement and sand mix to grout between the irregular pieces. When marking sandstone for cutting, it is best to use a scriber with a tungsten tip to avoid any staining.

Cleaning sandstone

When laying sandstone, it is important to keep wiping away any dirt with a clean sponge and clean water. This way, there should be no surface dirt left on the sandstone when the job is finished. If dirt remains, clean it off with fresh water and a wire brush.

Be very careful when using agents containing acid to clean sandstone. In fact, this job is best left to the professionals, who will know the best way to approach the task.

A very good way to clean sandstone is to fill a bucket with water,

add two cups of chlorine bleach, mix well and pour on to the sandstone, spreading it around with a broom. When the sun comes out, the sandstone will be beautifully clean and fresh looking.

You can usually remove moss and stains left by spilled drinks, bird droppings and berries from trees and shrubs with a mixture of two parts water to one part domestic bleach. Simply pour on to the sandstone and sweep it over with a soft broom.

You can seal sandstone paving to protect it from staining, but only if the sandstone is laid on concrete. If laid on sand, rising damp may stain the paving and it will not be possible to penetrate the sealant to clean the sandstone.

Artificial sandstone

Artificial sandstone is in great demand. Little wonder, when it

costs around half the price of the real thing.

The surface of artificial sandstone is non-skid and smooth, but it does not have the grain that is representative of real sandstone. A homogeneous product, made from cement with aggregates or reconstituted stone, it doesn't break down like

Tips

- Sandstone is heavy, but is a relatively soft material, so it is easy for the home handyperson to cut and lay.
- New sandstone can be instantly aged with a mixture of tomato plant food and water.
- Don't seal sandstone laid on sand in case rising damp causes staining.

real sandstone, and manufacturers claim it becomes harder as it ages. It can be made in a variety of different colours, but the most popular choice is that nearest the natural sandstone colour.

Depending on the manufacturer, there are a variety of paving slab sizes to choose from. Typically, these range from 250 x 250 mm to 675 x 450 mm, each 40 mm thick. Bullnose pavers are available, as are special shapes.

Artificial sandstone is laid in the same way as real sandstone, on a mortar bed on top of a concrete slab. However, it is also possible to lay it on a 50-mm bed of sand over a 75-mm layer of compacted hardcore or crushed stone. Joints should be filled with sand or pointed with mortar.

Artificial sandstone can be sealed with a silicone or hydrocarbon-based sealer. The same cleaning techniques as those recommended for sandstone apply to artificial sandstone.

ABOVE: Sandstone flagging gives a formal style to this elegant courtyard. Its subtle colour range will always work well against the rich green shrubbery.

BELOW: Artificial sandstone tiles are non-skid, but don't have the interesting grain of the real thing. Artificial sandstone can be made in a variety of colours.

Ceramic tiles

Ceramic tiles have always been popular as a paving material, and today there's a huge range of colours to suit any situation. Use unglazed tiles outside, as glazed tiles can become slippery. All tiles are ceramic – that is, they are made of clay – but it is how they are manufactured that makes the difference.

Tiles that have been fired at very high temperatures become vitrified, which means they have a surface as hard as glass and will absorb up to only three per cent moisture. Vitrified tiles are available glazed or unglazed. The tessellated tile is a perfect example of the unglazed vitrified tile. Terracotta tiles are more porous. They vary in density, depending on the temperature at which they have been fired, but most will absorb more than seven per cent moisture, so they can be susceptible to staining. However, the very nature of the rougher surface of terracotta tiles makes them ideal for exterior use, sealed or unsealed, as well as being very much in demand for interiors. Terracotta simply means 'baked earth', and the term is also used to describe what are generally known as quarry tiles.

Terracotta tiles

Terracotta, or quarry, tiles are earthenware tiles that are rough, extruded, irregular tiles often manufactured with a ribbed back.

Terracotta tiles vary in colour because it is the colour of the clay that dictates the colour of the tile.

ABOVE: An elegant pathway leads on to a tiled courtyard. The small vitrified tiles on the path are laid diamond-style among the terracotta tiles, creating a striking pattern. Dark grey slate is used for the steps and edges.

BELOW: Terracotta steps and sandstone combine well.

Being a natural material, the colour of terracotta will not fade. In fact, it often improves with age. There is a large range of terracotta tiles to choose from, many of them imported from France (pink), Italy (red/brown), Spain (peach), Mexico (beige to peach) and China (ox-blood red). Most terracotta tiles are extremely porous, although their density and, therefore, porosity does vary. Your supplier will be able to advise you in this respect.

Tile sizes available are 210 x 100 mm, 150 x 150 mm, 200 x 200 mm, 300 x 300 mm and 400 x 400 mm (for a handmade Spanish tile). The thickness of the tiles ranges from 10 mm to 25 mm.

Soaking tiles

Before laying the more porous terracotta tiles from France, Mexico and Spain, they should be soaked in water for at least half an hour. This is because terracotta tiles are like a sponge and, as such, they will suck all the water out of the sand and cement mixture, weakening it and loosening the tiles.

Italian terracotta tiles are less porous and don't need soaking, but it won't do them any harm. Again, your supplier will be able to advise you if soaking is necessary for the tiles you choose.

Laying tiles

Terracotta tiles can be difficult to lay; they are often handmade, so they are not always even. You will need a lot of patience if you intend laying them yourself.

Remember, the average terracotta tile is 15 mm thick. In comparison, house bricks are 65 mm thick, clay pavers 50 mm thick and concrete pavers range from 40 to 80 mm thick. Being much more fragile than these other kinds of paving, terracotta tiles should preferably be laid on a rigid surface, such as a concrete slab, which will ensure there is no movement.

Laying tiles on timber

Make sure you understand what's involved if you decide to put terracotta tiles over, say, an old timber deck or veranda. You have to allow for the fact that timber moves, which could cause tiles to crack, and is also subject to water penetration.

One method is to put down sheets of exterior-grade plywood to provide a firm base, and lay the tiles on top of them.

There is also a product available that can be trowelled on to the timber and left for 24 hours, by which time it becomes a rubber-like film that acts as a shock absorber should the floor beneath the tiles move. If you use this method, you will also need to consider incorporating a waterproofing system, as well as flexible grouting.

Do seek advice from a professional before you tackle tiling over timber; it could help prevent problems later on.

Laying tiles on concrete

If you are starting from scratch, the best surface for a courtyard is a concrete base of around 100 mm in depth (see page 81). On this you would spread a 1:4 cement and sand mix between 15 and 20 mm thick. This thickness can vary a little, depending on the fall of the surface to be tiled. In some cases, you may have a depth of between 30 and 35 mm and gradually reduce this to as little as 15 mm to accommodate the fall.

Although tile adhesive is stronger than a cement and sand mortar mix, many professionals prefer to use the latter rather than an adhesive to lay tiles, as it is far more difficult to level out an adhesive in order to overcome irregularities.

Don't attempt to tile too large an area in one go, as the mortar mix can stiffen up quite quickly, providing a poor bond with the tiles. For the do-it-yourselfer, it is sensible to make sure the cement and sand mortar mix is used within a couple of hours of mixing, so with this as a guide, it is probably better to attempt an area of no more than 3–4 square metres at any one time.

In the course of laying terracotta tiles, it is important to keep them as clean as possible. While work is in progress, cover them with a natural, 'breathing' material, such as medium-weight canvas, calico or painters' dust sheets. Do not cover the tiles with plastic, newspaper, aluminium foil or tar paper.

When laying a pool surround with terracotta tiles, start first with the bullnose tiles that are laid on the pool edge to prevent water from splashing on to the surrounds.

Cutting tiles

When laying tiles on a patio, start from the edge of the base opposite a wall and work towards the wall. By doing this, any tiles that need cutting will be against the wall, so they will not be obvious.

Provided the terracotta tiles aren't too thick, you can cut them with a tile cutter, but professionals prefer to use a diamond-tipped saw or an angle grinder, both of which can be hired. Don't try cutting with a bolster and hammer, as you may shatter the tiles.

When marking terracotta tiles for cutting, always make the mark on the reverse side of the tile, as pencil or any marking pen can permanently mark the tile. If you are employing a professional tiler, make sure he understands that any damage of this sort to the tiles will be his responsibility and he will either have to remove marks or replace the tile.

Grouting

Tiles are best laid with a space of around 3–6 mm between them; it is advisable to grout tiles as you go, washing away any residue with clean water immediately. When grouting terracotta tiles, it is better not to use coloured oxides, as they may discolour the tiles. If you do colour the grout, make sure that you are familiar with the process

and that the oxide, sand and cement are mixed without leaving dry lumps of oxide in the grout.

Make sure you note the mixing ratio of all the dry materials that are used in the grout, so that if you find that you have to make running repairs in the future, the new grout will resemble the old.

Sealing and cleaning

Sealing porous terracotta tiles to protect them is a job best left to the professionals. The type of tile you use, and how and where it is laid can all affect how the sealant performs. Sadly, a beautiful tiling job can be ruined by inexpert sealing procedures.

The trick to sealing terracotta tiles is to use a water-viscous silicone, which has the consistency of water, whereas other silicones have the consistency of honey. The water-viscous silicone seals the subsurface, while other silicones will sit on the surface.

It is not necessary to seal all terracotta tiles, as nature will take care of most stains. However, where there may be a problem with grease and oil, such as in a barbecue area, sealing is recommended.

You can clean terracotta tiles with an alkaline detergent and a scrubbing brush, but basically outdoor tiles will look after themselves. If tiles are particularly dirty, it is possible to give them a pressure wash. However, this should be done very infrequently and very carefully, as pressure washing can sometimes disturb and loosen the grouting between the tiles.

Freshly-laid terracotta tiles can be washed with water and detergent, but don't use too much water, as the grout will not be capable of withstanding a heavy soaking for at least a fortnight.

New terracotta paving may be affected by the appearance of salts on the tiled surface. This is known as efflorescence and is usually temporary, lasting for about six weeks. If the efflorescence is 'frothy', it is a

ABOVE: The rich hues of terracotta shown here at their best against the lush greenery of a courtyard, with a classic urn as a beautiful centrepiece.

good idea to sweep it off with a broom before washing down the tiles with water.

After this dry sweep, a regular washing down with warm water containing a splash of vinegar should help to get rid of it. The more you wash the tiles down, the quicker the efflorescence will go.

Vitrified tiles

Unlike terracotta tiles, vitrified tiles are fired at very high temperatures, making them extremely hard and non-porous. The colour in vitrified tiles is permanent, as it is fired with the clay. Vitrified tiles are also more regular in size than terracotta tiles and they have a lattice design on the back, which greatly improves adhesion. Standard vitrified tiles are approximately 10 mm thick and come in a variety of sizes, the most popular 200 x 100 mm, 200 x 200 mm, 300 x 200 mm and 300 x 300 mm.

Vitrified tiles may be glazed or unglazed, but for safety reasons, unglazed vitrified tiles are recommended for outdoor use. In the range of standard mass-produced vitrified tiles for external use, there is a plain finish and a slate finish.

The plain finish gives a smooth look, and this can sometimes become slippery when wet. The slate finish, on the other hand, has a rippled surface that provides an effective non-slip texture, so it is commonly used for swimming-pool surrounds and patios.

Vitrified tiles are laid in the same way as terracotta tiles, but are laid closer together, needing only a 2–5 mm joint between tiles. This joint can be grouted with a cement/sand mortar or with a coloured tile grout. Vitrified tiles need no sealing and are easily cleaned with detergent and water.

Tessellated tiles

Vitrified (porcelain) tiles that are cut into different sizes and shapes to form a mosaic are known as tessellated tiles.

Apart from their decorative use inside a house, tessellated tiles can also be laid on patios and in courtyards, and on steps and swimming-pool surrounds. The sizes and shapes vary, from a 25 mm square to a 70 x 50 mm triangle, a 200 x 25 mm strip and a 100 mm square. All are 10 mm thick.

Tessellated tiles are manufactured by applying hard pressure to the coloured clay and pressing into a mould of the required shape and size. The tile is then fired at very high temperatures to become fully vitrified. This gives it the advantage of being permanently coloured and water-resistant, making it highly suitable for outdoor use.

Laying tessellated tiles is time consuming, and the accuracy required more often that not calls for a professional. But it is now possible for the home handyperson to buy paper-faced, do-it-yourself panels in a chosen design. This sheet of tessellated tiles is simply laid on the prepared surface and the paper facing is carefully peeled away from the tiles after wetting.

A tessellated tiled patio

If you would like the traditional look of tessellated tiles, the following project will challenge you.

You will need:

tessellated tiles

tile cutter or cutting machine

notched 6 x 6 mm trowel

straightedge

50 mm nail

scriber

ceramic primer (if tiling on timber)

ceramic tile adhesive or sand/cement mix

grout

Preparation of the surface

The first step is to make sure the base is firm. Ideally, it should be a concrete slab (see Pouring a concrete slab, page 81).

The concrete must be clean and free from any dust, oil, paint or other material. If the concrete is uneven, it will have to be screeded with a 1:3 cement/sand mortar mixture to make it level, or true to fall. If the surface has any dents or ridges it is best to fill these first, using the same cement/sand mortar mix and allow to dry before applying the main coat. A cement-based ceramic tile adhesive can be used when the screeding mix has hardened.

Setting out the tiles

Start at the centre of the area to be tiled and work outwards (see diagram, opposite). To find the centre,

ABOVE: A narrow courtyard beautifully finished with terracotta tiles and edging. A classic outdoor surface, terracotta flatters all the greenery in this small setting.

mark the surface between the centre points of the outside edges of the patio area and lay a straight-edge along the first line marked.

The trick is to break the area into four quarters and to tile each quarter separately. With the first quarter laid correctly, the others will be parallel and square. Lay the tiles loosely along each line from the centre, making allowance for the border and what is known as the in-fill tile.

Unlike most tiling, the border of tessellated tiles is not laid flush against the edge. Instead, it is out from the edge with an in-fill tile laid flush against the edge. The reason for this is that if a pattern has to be cut, it will look lopsided if it is against the edge, whereas you can get away with a plain tile cut slightly differently from its neighbour.

Laying the tiles

Lay the loose tiles from the centre to the edge of the area to be tiled, measuring carefully as you go (see diagram, below).

Continue tiling outwards, using the lines as guides to keep the tiling square to the edges. Tile only one square metre at a time, pressing each tile firmly into the mortar or adhesive bed. Spacing between tiles is usually somewhere between 1 and 2 mm. Clean off any surplus adhesive from the face of the tiles as you go.

Make sure the in-fill tile is approximately half the size of the standard full tile used on the patio.

Cutting tiles

Lay the tile on a flat, firm surface. Score the face of the tile along the mark with a tile cutter or glass cutter. Break the tile by placing a nail under the scored line and pressing down on both sides of the tile.

Alternatively, use a tile-cutting machine, which you can hire.

Grouting and cleaning

As soon as the tiles are rigid, grout the joints with a grey pre-mixed grout or a sloppy mortar mix.

When tiling is complete, leave the patio for three or four days for the grout to harden, then clean it with a solution of detergent and water. Rinse it off thoroughly with clean water.

ABOVE: Another view of the terracotta courtyard. Notice how effective the slate is in providing a contrasting border to the tiles.

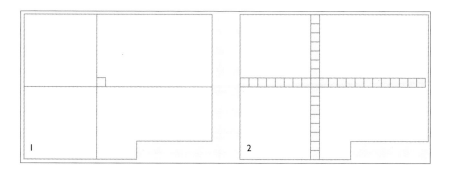

LEFT:

1 To find the centre, mark the floor between the centre points of the opposite walls or outside edges. Break the area up into four quarters.

2 Lay tiles from the centre to the edge of the area to be tiled. Tile each quarter separately.

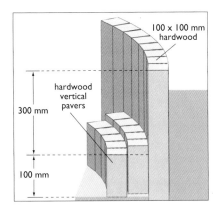

ABOVE: Using vertical timber sections to construct a retaining wall.

A sunken courtyard

You can make your garden more interesting by providing occasional changes in level. By raising a garden or lowering a paved area, you can create small enclosures that are ideal as sheltered, outdoor living spaces, especially when a retaining wall can double as bench seating. On the other hand, you may want to create a sunken haven for shade-loving plants or an elevated patch of lawn to act as a sun trap.

Planning the levels

Start by taking note of the shape of the garden, the position of the house and large trees, and especially the existing contours of the land. Then decide which areas could be lowered or effectively raised, and whether the shape should be circular, square or irregular.

The basis of any raised or sunken garden is a retaining wall. There are various types of retaining wall and these are described in Chapter 2 on pages 29–36. A simple timber wall, where the logs are set vertically, is another option.

Vertical timber wall

Narrow timber logs set into the ground can be used to make a retaining wall for curved shapes as well as straight ones. As long as they are properly set into the soil, vertical logs, either circular or square, will withstand any amount of stress from the soil and the moisture it contains, especially if you combine them with wooden paving to keep the logs in place.

For a 300–350 mm high wall, you should allow 150 mm of log below ground level. You can make the paving in a similar manner from shorter logs. To be solid and stable, they should be at least 100 mm long and tightly packed. Lay the paving first, and then use the deeper wall logs to wedge the pavers in place. Build up the soil behind the retainers. To be large enough for several people to lounge in comfortably, a circular sunken courtyard should have a diameter of three metres.

RIGHT: Timber verticals and paving create an unusual sitting area, sunk into the surrounding slope. Drainage of such an area needs to be carefully planned.

Patio planting

Groups of pots in a variety of shapes look wonderful on patios and in courtyards. Shrubs or trees trained as standards, with tall stems and ball-like foliage, go beautifully in square pots, alongside round pots containing arum lilies or hydrangeas, and shallow dishes brimming over with fast-growing plants like white *Impatiens* and *Alyssum*.

ABOVE: Our pot is planted with pretty lobelia, but any small to medium-size annuals will do, as long as they suit your site. Choose small or trailing types such as alyssum, bedding begonia or portulaca for the pockets, and more upright but still petite plants for the top.

Pots and planters

You can underplant the standard trees with groundcovers, such as violets, *Campanula* or *Erigeron*, for a lush effect. Groupings of pots containing herbs are also most attractive. A standard bay tree, underplanted with oregano in a square pot, with a rosemary plant in a round pot and a shallow dish filled with parsley, chives and mint will not only add fragrance, but will also be useful in the kitchen.

Clusters of pots and planter boxes spilling over with colourful flowers, such as petunias in summer or pansies in winter, can be added in abundance. One important point to remember is that plants in pots need constant watering and, therefore, are more labour-intensive than those planted in open gardens.

You can have pots of colour wherever you choose with flourishing container plants. Mass them for greater appeal.

Building a large planter
To make real impact, a planter needs to be larger than commonly available pots and tubs.

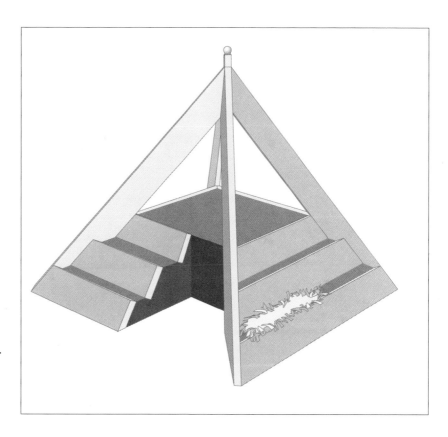

RIGHT: A pyramid planter allows for creative planting, with cascading greenery around the perimeter an attractive option.

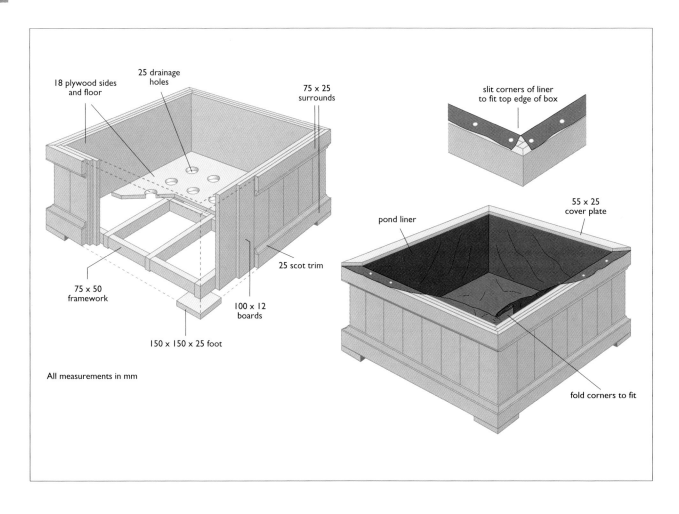

18 plywood sides
and floor

25 drainage
holes

75 x 25
surrounds

slit corners of liner
to fit top edge of box

75 x 50
framework

25 scot trim

100 x 12
boards

150 x 150 x 25 foot

All measurements in mm

pond liner

55 x 25
cover plate

fold corners to fit

ABOVE: Constructing a large planter. Flexible pond lining material protects the wood from moisture, but is pierced above the drainage holes in the wooden floor to prevent the plants from becoming waterlogged.

The planter above measures 1100 x 1100 mm and is 500 mm high. Although using exterior-grade plywood for the sides will give more strength against soil pressure, if you have a source of suitable timber boards (recycled perhaps), you can adapt the design by forming internal perimeter frames for the sides.

The interior of the box is lined with PVC pond liner. This will prevent moisture from the soil from soaking into the wood and rotting it. However, to make sure there is sufficient drainage, it will be necessary to bore a series of holes in the floor of the box and pierce corresponding holes in the PVC pond liner.

A layer of coarse gravel should also be laid in the bottom of the planter before adding the soil. This will allow efficient drainage and will prevent the roots of your plants from becoming waterlogged.

Construction method

1 Cut out two 1100 x 475 mm and two 1066 x 475 mm sides from 18 mm exterior-grade plywood.

2 Make the 1066-mm-square floor frame from 75 x 50 mm timber. Then cut a sheet of 18 mm plywood to the same size. Nail this to the floor frame with galvanised nails, then bore a series of 13 mm holes for drainage.

3 Drill clearance holes in the plywood side panels and screw them to the floor frame and to each other down the four corners.

4 Clad the outside of the planter box with 100 x 12 mm V-jointed tongued-and-grooved boards, using waterproof glue and nailing through the board tongues.

5 Trim around the top edge and bottom of the box with 75 x 25 mm boards, adding scotia moulding. Then add the feet.

Courtyard planting ideas

Shade-lovers

Arum lily (*Zantedeschia aethiopica*)
Aucuba
Begonias
Busy lizzie (*Impatiens*)
Camellia japonica
Canterbury bells
    (*Campanula medium*)
Fuchsias
Geraniums
Glechoma hederacea
Hostas
Ivies
Japanese aralia (*Fatsia japonica*)
Mexican orange blossom
    (*Choisya ternata*)
Mimulus
Pansies
Pieris
Plentranthus coleoides
Sarcococca
Skimmia
Viola

Sun lovers

Abutilon megapotamicum
Agave
Cabbage palm (*Cordyline australis*)
Chamaerops humilis
Chusan palm
    (*Trachycarpus fortunei*)
Cistus
Dogwood (*Cornus florida*)
Jasmine
Laburnum
Lavender
Marigolds
Nasturtiums
Palm lily (*Yucca gloriosa*)
Pelargoniums
Phoenix canariensis
Phormium
Pinus mugo
Pittosporum
Rosemary
Tamarisk
Yew (*Taxus*)

6   Measure and cut the liner. Make it the length of the box plus double the depth and the width of the box plus double the depth, add ten per cent on each side.

7   Lay the liner in the box, pressing it into the angles, folding it in the vertical corners for a neat fit. Fold the liner over the top edges of the sides and pin it with galvanised clout nails. Trim the liner just short of the outer edges. Add the cover plate to conceal the edge of the liner.

8   Feel the bottom of the liner for the drainage holes and pierce the liner above each hole.

TOP: A bench seat among the rich colours and scents of the garden offers an alluring retreat.

ABOVE: A large planter such as this can be stained or painted to match your outdoor furniture or finishings. The small feet beneath the box ensure it sits well above any surface water, thus extending its life.

TOP: Two-tiered hardwood sleepers make an attractive border to this patio, well-suited to the tumbling greenery and colourful annuals around the edge.

ABOVE: Large pots, a coopered barrel and hanging baskets show some imaginative options for dressing up a patio.

LEFT: The plan here was to use small trees along the fence line to create privacy without excessive bulk. Dense shrubs were used both to fill in the gaps and to provide food and shelter for birds.

LEFT AND BELOW: The plants in these two courtyards show how large pots are an effective way of bringing colour and decoration into your outdoor living areas. The flowers and shrubs can be selected to complement the colours of your nearby garden beds.

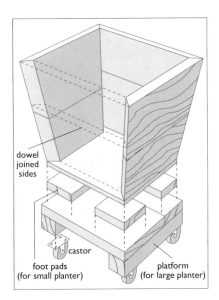

ABOVE: Construct a simple timber planter, either on foot pads or a moveable base with castors.

BELOW: These two useful wooden planters can be easily built and finished in a style to match your courtyard.

Building a small planter

The handsome wooden planters shown below will go a long way towards improving the look of a patio arrangement. When built, they will be 300 mm high and 350 mm square (at top) and 350 mm high and 400 mm square (at top).

To make the sides, dowel-join, glue and clamp the 100 x 25 mm sides to the 200 x 25 mm sides, and the 150 x 25 mm sides to the 200 x 25 mm sides. Join the pieces for the platform base in the same way. Sand or plane the edges before joining.

Mark out each trapezoidal side so that the bottom edge is 120 mm shorter than the top; cut the sides to size with a circular saw set at a 45° angle. Clamp a straightedge (or straight piece of timber) to the work as a guide for the saw. Glue and nail the sides together with 40 mm nails, level the bottom edges with a plane, then nail the base to the sides with 40 mm nails.

Nail foot pads to the corners of the small planter with 40 mm nails. Drill a few 10-mm-diameter drain holes in the bottom.

Finishing the planters

To make the platform for the large planter, nail two supports to the base with 40 mm nails and screw castors to the supports.

Paint timber with an appropriate natural or solid-stain wood preservative. Line the insides with polythene sheet. Punch through the plastic liner to the corresponding drain holes in the bottom of the planter.

ITEM	MATERIALS	LENGTH OR SIZE IN MM	No. REQ'D
Small planter side	100 x 25 mm sawn treated timber	350	4
Small planter side	200 x 25 mm sawn treated timber	350	4
Small planter base	18 mm exterior ply	230 x 230	1
Foot pads	100 x 25 mm sawn treated timber	100	4
Large planter side	150 x 25 mm sawn durable timber	400	4
Large planter side	200 x 25 mm sawn treated timber	400	4
Large planter base	18 mm exterior ply	280 x 280	1
Platform base	100 x 25 mm sawn treated timber	300	1
Platform base	200 x 25 mm sawn treated timber	300	1
Platform supports	50 x 50 mm sawn treated timber	300	2

Fixings and fasteners. 1.2 m of 10-mm-diameter dowel (24 of 50-mm-long pieces); 130 of 40 mm galvanised nails; 4 of 31-mm plate-fixing castors; 2 m of thick polythene sheet; suitable wood preservative.

Order quantities for sawn, preservative-treated timber. 2.1 m of 100 x 25 mm; 3.3 m of 200 x 25 mm; 1.6 m of 150 x 25 mm; 600 mm of 50 x 50 mm; plus 230 x 230 mm and 280 x 280 mm of 18 mm exterior-grade plywood.

RIGHT: There are many benefits of creating a centrepiece in your patio: the paving options – as here – can be striking, as you spread out from the centre. Also, the circular garden bed allows for elegant plantings with more formal touches.

BELOW: These planter boxes surround pergola posts and are an attractive way to display a selection of showy flowers. The boxes have been finished in a natural timber style to match the pergola.

Fences, Screens and Gates

With careful planning and the use of appropriate materials, fences and screens can become integral features of your garden. You can choose different fences to match your garden style and needs (for such uses as patio surrounds, driveways and boundaries). The available materials are more extensive than ever and include galvanised metals, pre-painted cast alloys, wire mesh, plastic and, of course, timber of all sorts. Gates can be constructed in materials and styles to suit your fences and screens.

A range of timber fence styles and materials is examined on the following pages, and instructions are given for two simple projects: constructing a fence and building a gate.

Screens can be used as protection from wind, to provide privacy and shade and to create separate, defined areas in your garden. They also have other practical uses, such as concealing utility areas and unsightly features. They can be constructed of similar materials to fences. However, possibly the most inexpensive and attractive method is to use trellis panels. Trellis screens have a number of advantages, as they allow air movement and light, and are suited to climbers. On the following pages, we look at constructing and erecting trellis screens, as well as ideas for using them in your garden.

Fences need not hem you in – especially if the view beyond is worth framing, as in this case. An aged post-and-rail fence, draped with abundant hydrangeas, gives this garden a striking boundary and extends the lawn into the meadow beyond.

Fences and fence styles

Fences can provide various degrees of privacy and architectural interest, but they may also cut off light and breezes. Select a fence style that will satisfy your needs: a louvre or trellis will let in breezes; a panel or vertical-board fence will offer privacy. Or combine two styles: for example, a solid one below with an open style above.

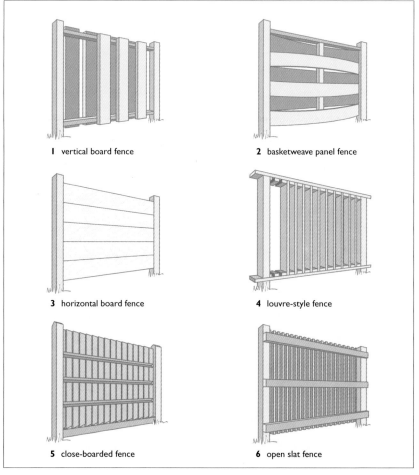

1 vertical board fence

2 basketweave panel fence

3 horizontal board fence

4 louvre-style fence

5 close-boarded fence

6 open slat fence

ABOVE: Trellis-style fencing provides privacy while giving a more open feel to the garden.

ABOVE RIGHT: Selecting a fencing style – some of the options.

1 Vertical-board fences and screens are popular and easy to construct. By nailing boards to both sides of the rails, you will allow breezes in, but maintain privacy.

2 Basketweave panels can be purchased from DIY stores and garden centres. They will also sell suitable posts, post spikes and galvanised brackets for attaching the panels. You can use grooved concrete posts, too.

3 Grooved posts work well with a horizontal-board design. As an alternative, you can nail boards to the posts and to 100 x 50 mm rails top and bottom.

4 Louvre-style fences and screens are attractive and allow ventilation. The verticals – 150 x 25 or 200 x 25 mm – are angled and overlapped slightly. The degree of the angle determines the amount of privacy provided.

5 Vertically-boarded panels, using feather-edge boards, can be constructed or bought. A gravel board at the bottom and capping top will protect the end grain.

6 For an open slat design, space 75 x 25 mm timber boards their own width apart. Secure the boards at top, bottom and middle with rails of larger timber.

ABOVE LEFT: This impressive rear fence is topped with timber slats. A full-height gate fits flush, offering complete privacy and security.

BELOW LEFT: Lattice panels are used here to top a rendered wall and provide privacy and elegance.

BELOW: Some classic wrought-iron fencing styles are now available in lightweight alloys.

Building a timber fence

Putting up a timber fence is a satisfying project that does not require any special skills or tools. The hardest part is digging the holes; after that, the structure takes shape quickly. You may need to rent a post-hole digger, but otherwise will require only a circular saw and ordinary carpentry tools.

Designs vary widely, but just about all fences consist of the same basic elements: a series of posts sunk into the ground and connected by rails at the top, bottom and possibly middle as well, and palings or panels that are nailed to the rails to fill the spaces between posts. Most fences require 100 x 100 mm posts, but the rails and fencing material can be almost any size. It is possible to buy prefabricated fence panels, but purpose-designed and built versions will give a better result. See page 108 for typical fence styles.

Before beginning, check with your local council. You may need planning permission for a tall fence or one on the property's boundary. In a conservation area, there may be restrictions on material and style.

Preparing the site

Once you have chosen a design and established a location, stake out and measure the site. Plot post spacing for the most efficient use of timber. Spans of about two metres work well; to keep the fence fairly

Below: Building a timber fence

1 Lay out the site, dig holes and set posts in concrete or post spikes (see 'Building resources guide'), starting with the end posts. Check each post for plumb by holding a level to two adjacent faces; nail braces to hold the posts upright. Check, too, that posts are aligned by tying string from end post to end post.

2 As you shovel concrete into the holes, have a helper tamp the concrete to remove bubbles. Round off the concrete so that water will drain away from the posts. After the concrete cures, cut the posts to a uniform height, if necessary. Shape the post tops so that they will shed water.

3 Attach the rails to the posts. We used galvanised rail clips, but see the 'Building resources guide' for other techniques. Traditionally, mortice-and-tenon joints are used for fence construction. A line level and combination square ensure that each rail is level and square with the posts.

4 Measure carefully and use a square to mark locations on the rails for each fencing board. Wood blocks squeezed between the boards will maintain uniform spacing. Have a helper align the boards – in this case, flush with the bottom – while you nail them to the rails. This is not an easy job for one person.

1

2

3

4

LEFT: A new hardwood fence, which can now be stained or painted to suit. Left in its natural state the timber will soon age into a soft, silvery grey.

rigid never set posts for a paling or panel fence more than 2.4 m apart.

If you are building your fence on a slope, plan to step the fence down the hill, setting each section lower than the one preceding it. Build the fence to follow the contour only if the slope is very slight. Whichever way you decide to construct the fence, be sure to set the posts vertically, otherwise the fence will look as though it is falling down the hill.

Materials

Always use preservative-treated timber for all posts, rails, boards and panels. To minimise rust, buy only galvanised nails and fittings. To preserve posts, let them stand in a bucket of preservative overnight.

If you want to stain or paint your fence, apply the finish to posts, rails and panels before you nail up the fencing. Besides saving time, this will provide better coverage.

LEFT: This solid, timber fence provides total privacy. The palings are raised off the ground to avoid rot.

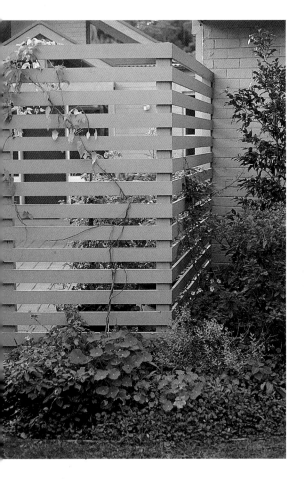

Garden screens

A garden screen is both handy and attractive. It can provide privacy from neighbours or passers-by, conceal unsightly gardening materials, give shelter from winds and enhance the appearance of the garden. Design your garden screen to do just what you want it to, remembering that an L-shaped screen is more stable than a straight one.

Making an L-shaped screen

This project is simple, even for the beginner. Use planed, preservative-treated pine, stained or painted to match your house style, for an effective result.

1 Dig three holes for post footings, each 300 x 300 x 300 mm. Fill each hole with concrete, levelling the surface carefully and allow to set.

2 When the concrete has hardened, use a bolt-down post bracket to mark out the positions of the bolt holes on each concrete footing. Drill holes for expansion bolts.

3 Bolt the brackets to the concrete footings with expansion bolts. Then push the posts into the bracket sockets and tighten the clamp bolts, making sure the posts are completely vertical with a spirit level.

4 Use 100 x 19 mm horizontals and position them on the posts with 70-mm gaps. Fasten each horizontal with two 40-mm countersunk screws (brass are best as they won't stain the timber) at each end. Finish with stain, if desired.

ABOVE: Vertical posts and horizontal slats make an effective screen, increasing the privacy of the courtyard. The screen can also support climbing plants.

RIGHT: An easy-to-build and functional L-shaped screen, with an attractive use of timber slats.

1 Bolt post brackets to footing pads.

2 Stand posts in brackets.

3 Screw horizontals to posts.

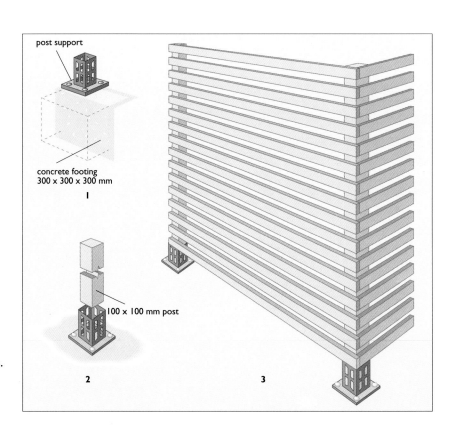

post support

concrete footing
300 x 300 x 300 mm

1

100 x 100 mm post

2

3

Materials

- three 100 x 100 mm timber posts 2.5 m long;
- 15 horizontals, 100 x 19 mm x 2 m long, and 15 similar 1-m-long horizontals (adjust the length to fit your site);
- two 25-kg bags of pre-mixed concrete;
- three bolt-down post brackets;
- 12 expansion bolts to fit brackets
- 120 countersunk 40-mm brass screws.

Building a garden tidy

A simple and effective way to improve the appearance of your house is to build a tidy such as the one shown below. The low screen and shelf for pot plants will conceal your dustbins, while the prefabricated louvred-door panels allow air to circulate around the bins. We built an L-shaped screen against the house, but it is easy to add another end if a freestanding structure will suit you better. If you have a large, wheeled bin, enlarge the tidy so that it is high enough and deep enough to accommodate the bin.

1 Starting from the prefabricated louvre panels, calculate the finished dimensions of the screen you require. We used 1000 x 520 mm panel, so the frame is 520 mm deep, 1040 mm long and 1000 mm in height.

2 Erect the sides, using uprights between each louvred panel, and inserting between the end uprights a shelf support 250 mm down from the top. Fix a corresponding support to the wall of the building.

3 Nail the shelf slats to the supports, spacing them evenly apart to allow for drainage.

4 Add external corner battens as shown in the diagram. Add a top trim, mitred at the corner and nailed to the tops of the uprights as well as to the louvred screens.

5 Finish by painting or staining the screen so that it fits the style of the house and is well protected from any bad weather.

Materials for garden tidy			
Component	Size (mm)	Length (mm)	No.
Louvre panel	1000 x 520		3
Frame uprights	50 x 50	1000	4
Shelf support	50 x 50	520	2
Shelf slats	75 x 12	1040	
Top trim	75 x 12	1040	1
	75 x 12	520	1
Corner battens	30 x 30	1000	1

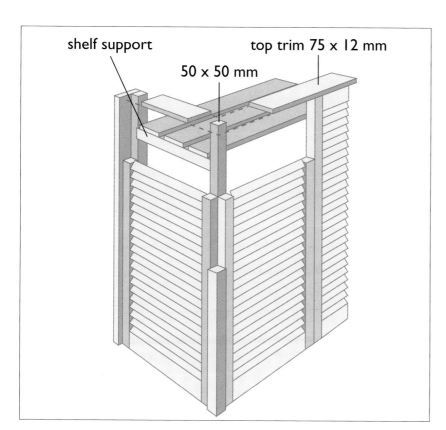

shelf support   top trim 75 x 12 mm

50 x 50 mm

LEFT: The basis of this garden tidy is a simple timber frame which is then covered in prefabricated louvre panels. Adjust the size of your framework to suit the available panels.

Trellis screens

Designs for screens can be varied, but for a really striking effect, consider trellis screens, which provide a degree of privacy without blocking summer breezes. Trellis screens also offer sound support for climbing plants, which increase privacy even more. Trellis is not expensive and demands no special expertise to build – you can install it with only simple hand tools and an electric drill.

Trellis styles

The term 'trellis' refers to any decorative pattern made with narrow, thin strips of timber. Trellis designed mainly for privacy has 38 mm openings; for climbing plants, the openings may be 150 mm or more wide. If you are using trellis to roof an arbour, it will need to be stronger than usual; use 50 x 25 mm battens instead of laths.

Trellis lends itself to a variety of decorative effects. Choose a style that suits your home and the purpose to which you will put it – privacy screen, support for climbing plants or as a windbreak. Then varnish or paint it, as desired.

1 Provide a contrast of round and square openings by boring holes at the points where the timber strips intersect.

2 Vertical and horizontal strips make a strong grid pattern, which can be emphasised by using laths with a rough texture and variations in thickness. Roofing laths, used for hanging tiles on roofs, are ideal for trellis and come ready treated with preservative.

3 Notched trellis strips create an interesting and decorative design. Use wide slats and cut 90° V-shaped notches in them with a tenon saw or jigsaw.

ABOVE: These trellis panels are attached to the eaves, shading the wall from the afternoon sun and supporting climbing plants.

RIGHT: Four decorative trellis styles.

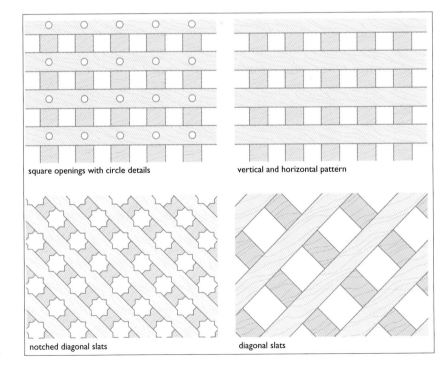

square openings with circle details

vertical and horizontal pattern

notched diagonal slats

diagonal slats

ABOVE: The lattice screen on this deck contributes elegance as well as privacy. Notice how well it integrates with the railing and employs finials to give it a certain class and continue a theme.

LEFT: This lattice screen, designed to suit the era of the house, serves as a useful divider of sections of the garden.

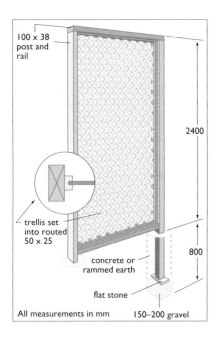

100 x 38
post and
rail

2400

trellis set
into routed
50 x 25

concrete or
rammed earth

flat stone

800

All measurements in mm   150–200 gravel

ABOVE: Framing and erecting a screen.

1 Use your router to cut a 12 mm-deep rebate (wide enough to accommodate purchased trellis) in 50 x 25 mm timber. Use this to frame your trellis panel.

2 Set two 100 x 38 mm posts in the ground, using our diagram as a guide. Position them 1025 mm apart and use a crowbar to ram them firmly in place.

3 Position a 1025 mm horizontal length of 100 x 38 mm timber running between the posts, 75 mm from ground level. Nail through the posts into the ends of timber.

4 Sit the framed screen in place on the horizontal length and nail through the rebated frame at the sides and bottom.

5 Nail the top horizontal in place last, nailing through it into the top of the posts as well as the top of the screen.

4 Trellis for supporting plants can be more open than trellis designed to provide a degree of privacy (see page 114). It doesn't provide much cover until climbing plants begin to flourish, but it is effective.

Prefabricated trellis panels

Most major DIY stores and garden centres sell prefabricated trellis panels at a price that is often less than that of the slats alone. These are easy to install because the cutting and nailing have been done.

Inspect the panels carefully before you buy. Cheaper varieties are often made from laths that are much thinner than those you would buy separately, and the staples holding cheap trellis together may be thin and dislodge easily. Although most are made from treated pine and will resist moisture, they may not have a long life.

Making trellis panels

1 Build the frame as described opposite, on page 117, and, if desired, paint or stain the frame and the strips of lath. If you prefer a natural wood finish, coat it with wood preservative.

2 Lay the laths against the frame diagonally, placing the strips so that each touches the next to form a solid screen. Nail every second strip (or every third for plant-supporting trellis) and then remove the pieces not nailed. To avoid splitting the thin strips, blunt the tips of nails by pounding on them with a hammer before using them.

3 Repeat this process for the second layer of trellis, starting at the opposite corner.

4 Trim the ends with a cross-cut or circular saw.

Erecting a single-panel screen

Freestanding single-panel screens like those shown below can be used in clusters or lines. Choose your own configuration for the degree of privacy you require. Those illustrated are made with 1000-mm-wide, 2300-mm-high trellis panels.

Making your own lattice screen

I

2

3

4

5

6

I After you have set the posts, measure the distance between them and build a frame from 100 x 50 mm timber. Square each corner, using temporary wood braces to hold the corners square. Then nail the frame together at each corner.

2 Remove the braces one by one, check each corner again with a

LEFT: As well as creating privacy without the solid presence of a fence, screens can provide shady spots and dappled light in the garden.

square, and secure the joint with a metal strip or angle. As with all outdoor work, use only galvanised screws and hardware to avoid rust and staining of the wood.

3 Now attach the first stop of 25 x 25 mm timber to the inner side of the frame. Align it with one edge. Predrill holes at intervals of 300 mm or so, and drive screws through the 25 x 25 mm timber and into the frame itself.

4 Take a prefabricated panel or make your own trellis as described above. Make sure it fits precisely into the frame, trimming the edges as necessary to

fit. If you have not yet done so, paint or stain the trellis and frame.

5 After the paint dries, lay the panel atop the frame's first stop, then install a second stop on top of the panel. If desired, attach the trellis to the first stop with a staple gun before adding the second stop. This makes for easier handling.

6 Fasten the frame to the posts with coach screws spaced about 300 mm apart. Predrill holes and, for a neater appearance, counter-sink them as well. Fit each coach screw with a washer before driving it. Touch up paint.

RIGHT: The arch in this screen adds distinction to the garden. Although it takes quite a deal of careful construction (see details, below), it is certainly worth the effort.

BELOW RIGHT: Constructing an arched screen.

1 Make the arch as described and join it to 100 x 75 mm posts, 1550 mm long. You will have to cut rebates in the front and back of the posts to enable them to slot into the ends of the arch. Rout grooves out of the straight sides of the arch-supporting posts to take the trellis panels.

2 Cut the arched shape out of trellis panel and fit the trellis into the grooved arch. Nail them together.

3 Stand three posts in the ground (see diagram) using concrete or rammed earth, and attach the 100 x 38 mm top and bottom horizontals to the structure.

4 An alternative to routing grooves into an inner frame to hold the trellis (as for single partitions) is to nail frames of 25 x 25 mm battening inside posts and horizontals, nail trellis to these and nail battening to other side.

5 Finish the arched panel with 125 mm-long horizontals between the arch and the posts, 75 mm from the ground.

Making an arch

A screen at the side of your house will separate the garden facing the street from the private areas.

To make an arch, cut five semi-circular bands from a sheet of 19-mm exterior-grade plywood, and glue and nail them together. The centre piece should be only 25 mm wide, with an inner radius of 400 mm and an outer of 425 mm, to form a recess for the trellis. The other four pieces should be 75 mm wide, with radii of 375 mm and 450 mm. When you assemble the arch frame, you will notice that the two outermost layers of the arch project an extra 100 mm to join the post. This projection should be straight, not a continuation of the curve.

The following pages show the making of an arched gate, a simple gate and a ledged-and-braced gate.

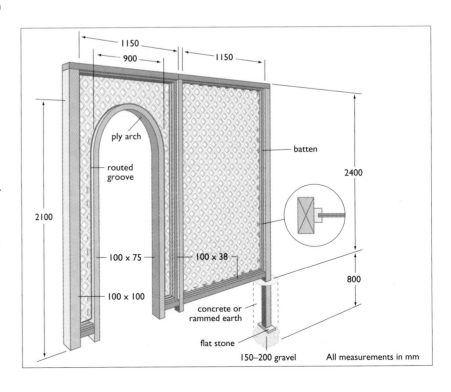

LEFT: The low height and lightweight timbers used in this picket fence have allowed for a very simple gate construction. The palings are fixed to two rails, with extra blocks added below the rails at one end to take the hinges.

1 Build a frame 10 mm narrower than the gap in the fence. Square the frame, secure corners with angle brackets and install a brace from the bottom of the hinge side to the top of the latch side.

2 Add finish boards to match the fencing. Measure carefully and install hinges, taking care that they are square with the edge. All but very lightweight gates should have three hinges.

3 Prop the gate into position on blocks. Plumb it and have a helper mark each hinge position. Remove the gate, drill holes and hang the gate. Finally, install your latch hardware.

Gates

When a gate is needed, your paths, fences and screens will affect what is possible. Usually it is best to keep to your existing fencing or screen materials (be they solid timber, trellis or metal) and install a gate to suit. In some cases, however, you may decide to vary your gate style. In the case of a trellis screen on each side of a pathway, you may prefer to have a solid gate for purposes of privacy. Often, in the case of a gate next to a carport or as a garden entrance, a metal security gate may be required.

Building a simple gate

1

2

3

An arched gate

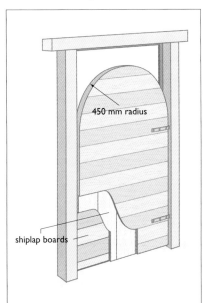

By giving a contemporary gate an arched top, you will add a touch of elegance. An easy way to do this without building curved frames is to construct the gate from three layers of preservative-treated, 13 mm tongued-and-grooved boards. These create a solid, self-supporting, weather-resistant slab of timber that can be cut to any shape you wish.

Our gate is 1830 x 900 mm (the height being to the top of the arch). Make the middle layer of vertical boards first, and glue and nail the horizontal outer layers to each face. You will waste less timber if you establish the shaped top first and keep to it when adding the outer layers. Use heavy 200 mm hinges to hang the gate from its posts.

RIGHT: A bold and handsome gate, using a theme of stained timber to connect all elements.

A ledged-and-braced gate

This gate is made from preservative-treated, tongued-and-grooved pine boards, which are fixed to the rails by nails or screws. The rails are 150 x 25 mm (10 mm less than the width of the finished gate). When nailing the boards to the rails, use two nails each time and punch them in. Keep the boards tightly clamped and place blocks underneath while attaching the rails. The notched brace is fitted last and adds rigidity. A picket fence can be made using these same principles.

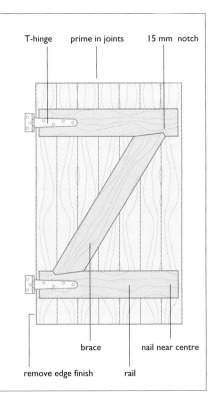

ABOVE: This is *Clematis x jackmanii*, a large-flowered hybrid that has produced numerous, equally desirable, but differently coloured cultivars. Some of these bloom in spring, others as late as autumn. Clematis grow from 2–4 m in sun or dappled shade. Plant so that the roots are always shaded. Keep moist year round.

Climbing plants

Climbers produce some of the most magnificent floral displays of any plants. They can cover bare walls, fences, trellises and pergolas with sheets of bloom in every colour in nature's range. Yet even the largest and most rampant takes up an area of ground only the size of its trunk. Because climbers grow up first, then spread out, they actually expand the garden by growing on to otherwise blank walls or other suitable supports, leaving the beds free for non-climbing plants.

Beautiful wall coverings

Climbing plants will transform a bare wall and form a beautiful backdrop for your garden.

Some climbers cling with suckers or aerial roots and need no support. Virginia creeper and Boston ivy are sucker plants. Common ivy (take to it with the secateurs occasionally, otherwise it might raise the roof) and the spectacular trumpet vine, with its brightly coloured trumpet-like flowers, have aerial roots. Some climbers twine their stems around a support and need a trellis or strong wire-mesh support. Examples are wisteria and the gloriously-scented *Jasminum polyanthum* (like common ivy, both need to be kept in check). Many plants with long, arching stems, such as climbing roses, can be grown to cover a wall, but as they aren't strictly climbers, they

BELOW RIGHT: How vines attach themselves. Suitable supports include string, wire and trellis.

1 Clinging tendrils
Tendrils grow from stem to coil around supports. Clematis, *Passiflora* and *Pyrostegia* all have tendrils.

2 Twining
The vine stem itself twines around a support. *Clerodendron* and wisteria climb by this method.
Attach to smooth surfaces such as walls or timber.

3 Adhesive pads
These resemble small suction pads and attach directly to vertical surfaces. *Parthenocissus* has pads.

4 Aerial roots
These grow directly from the stems and adhere the vine to any surface. Ivy and trumpet vine have aerial roots.

will need training and support. Decide whether you want a light cover or a heavy disguise. Some climbers such as parrot's bill feel their way delicately; others, Russian vine for instance, scramble over everything in sight. Most climbers are easily trained and generally grow fast so, whatever your choice, you're sure to have a beautiful wall cover in a season or two.

A large brick or stone wall can create an ideal microclimate for plants by excluding cold and strong winds, and radiating heat from the sun. Soften it with a partial covering.

Perfect in limited space

Climbers are a godsend for tiny gardens and courtyards, providing colour and sometimes fragrance without intruding on the limited ground space. In any garden there can be awkward corners or passageways too narrow for shrubs. As the climber grows up and spreads over a wall, it will visually extend your garden.

Privacy and shelter

Climbers are more than just decorative, they're practical, too. If you want more privacy or shelter from wind, a simple trellis could soon become a leafy screen and a sensational cascade of blooms. If summer shade is a priority, a climber-covered pergola makes a cool retreat – but choose deciduous types if you want winter sunshine. With support, climbers will grow up and shade a hot, bare wall, cooling the interior noticeably. Some, such as Boston ivy and Virginia creeper, will climb walls without additional support and they're deciduous, too, so you won't miss out on winter warmth. Even if you want none of these things, you're still bound to have a fence that needs hiding.

Year-round display

Most climbers flower in the warmer months, but there are winter bloomers, too, making dramatic displays possible all year. A very

BELOW LEFT: Sweet-smelling honeysuckle (*lonicera*) is a great climbing plant that grows best in a sunny position in well-drained soil.

BELOW: The passion flower (*Passiflora coccinea*), with its distinctive scarlet flowers, will brighten up any garden wall. Grow in well-drained soil, in full sun or partial shade.

ABOVE: A high red-brick wall is home to Virginia creeper. In cooler gardens this clinging vine produces magnificent autumn tones. A patch of creeping fig can also be seen, though we'd suggest using one or the other.

RIGHT: These climbing roses have been trained on to stout wires attached to the wall in an intertwining zigzag pattern. As the stems grow, they are fastened to the wires with plant rings or garden twine and all lateral growths are removed so that the finished result is a pattern of flowers and foliage flat against the wall.

LEFT: A stunning climbing rose in full bloom transforms this patio.

ABOVE: Graceful and fragrant wisteria is an old-time favourite. Grow this elegant, deciduous vine over a pergola or a stout fence, but remember, it's extremely rampant and needs strong support and yearly pruning to keep it within bounds. Wisterias are not recommended for tropical or sub-tropical areas.

LEFT: Any outdoor structure can be enhanced by the softness, colours and texture of climbing plants and vines.

Tips

- Check support ties from time to time to make sure they're not cutting into the stems as the plant grows and thickens.
- If a climber requires staking, do it at the time of planting to avoid disturbing or damaging the roots. Drive stakes firmly into the ground and attach stems with soft garden twine.
- If you need to get at your walls occasionally for maintenance, create a plant 'screen' that's removable. One way is to suspend baskets planted with some of the smaller, less vigorous species from the eaves and wall. Another is to staple wire mesh to a wooden frame, bracket the frame to the wall and plant a twining climber in a long planter at its base. To gain access to the wall, remove the brackets, tilt the frame outwards and rest it on temporary supports, or rope in some helpers and move both frame and planter completely away from the wall.
- Twining plants must be able to wrap their tendrils securely. Use wire mesh, plastic-coated wire or narrow timber for supports.
- Grow a deciduous climber on a western wall to help cool the house in summer. There'll be no foliage to block winter sunshine.

long show can be had by planting together a number of climbers that flower at different times. Choose plants of similar vigour that grow to about the same size, and include a couple of deciduous types. They will all intertwine and flower one after the other. Take a look at the climbers on the previous pages, then consider your garden. Haven't you a wall or a fence that would look better in bloom?

Espalier

Espaliers look wonderful against walls. Choose a plant that produces a lovely show, such as jasmine or a climbing rose. Or get away from climbers altogether and train a shrub or fruit tree.

Green-thumb ground rules

Position Generally, full sun suits most climbers and gives the best display. However, during hot spells, dappled shade will keep flowers looking good for longer. In cold areas, give evergreen climbers a sheltered, warm south-facing spot.

Soil Good, well-drained garden soil that has been enriched with compost or well-rotted manure gives good results.

Watering Many established climbers can usually get by on rainfall if they are not sheltered by the eaves of the house. Evergreens should be kept moist all year round, while deciduous climbers can withstand drier conditions when dormant.

Feeding Plant in rich, fertile soil. Mulch annually with well-rotted manure or give a ration of complete plant food in spring.

Pruning Most climbers need annual pruning to keep them in their allotted space. Prune evergreens and deciduous plants that flower in spring after flowering. Deciduous climbers that flower in summer or autumn should be pruned in winter.

ABOVE: A splendid example of an espaliered apple tree, which here is grown as a screen rather than flat against a wall as is more usual.

LEFT: There's no rule that says you must use a climber to cover a wall or fence. This magnificent *Pyracantha coccinea*, commonly known as firethorn, is a shrub – not a climber – and has been beautifully trained into this fan shape. The high, sturdy fence makes a flattering backdrop for the superb display of scarlet berries which almost completely cover the plant for nearly half the year, from late summer to midwinter.

Decks and Steps

A deck provides a perfect means of extending your house into the garden and giving you the opportunity to enjoy an indoor/outdoor lifestyle. By linking the house with the garden, your deck becomes an additional outdoor entertaining and leisure area.

Ground-level and raised decks can be built to suit your site and connect with pathway, garden, carport and patio. On the following pages are step-by-step projects for building both a ground-level and a raised deck. As decks are load-bearing and exposed to the elements, careful thought needs to be given to the selection of timber for the bearers and joists, as well as for the decking itself.

Various decking board styles can be chosen, from herringbone to diagonal and parquet. Railings can be made of timber boards or panels (trellis, wired safety glass or exterior-grade plywood) and be designed to screen out winds, offer privacy or provide safety for young children.

When you choose a railing style that complements your house and garden, it can be extended into the design of your pergola and steps (in the case of a raised deck). Selecting one type of timber (say, for handrails and pergola posts) provides a pleasing harmony.

The design of the steps will also be important, especially when a deck opens on to a patio or larger garden area. Narrow steps restrict, whereas a broad flight of steps gives a generous feeling, opening your deck out into the rest of the garden.

As with your deck design, remember to leave plenty of room on the steps for pot plants – and people.

This elegant deck combines good design, workmanship and materials to add a stylish living area to the house. Distinctive railings and the lattice skirt further indicate a well-finished job.

Ground-level decks

A deck that stands on its own just a few centimetres above the ground is considerably easier to build than a raised deck. The simple design of a ground-level deck spares you the intricacies of constructing steps, railings and structural bracing. And a freestanding, ground-level deck does not need to be securely attached to the structure of the house.

ABOVE: Decks need not be large, flat expanses of timber. Here a series of low decks step down a gentle slope, acting both as pathways and as areas for sitting and entertaining. The different shapes add interest to the garden landscape.

A ground-level deck can be situated just about anywhere adjacent to the house, or anywhere else in the garden that you would like to sit. Build one over an existing patio, or step two or more down a gentle slope. Like any deck, a ground-level structure can be dressed up with railings, benches and a pergola.

Planning the materials

A successful deck begins with a sound plan and good-quality timber. Sketch out the plan you want and use the information contained in this chapter to determine the dimensions of the timber you will need to use, and also to ensure that you have spaced the bearers and joists properly.

Suitable timber

Although hardwoods such as oak, cedar or teak would be ideal for a deck, they're expensive, so preservative-treated pine can be used. Calculate the lengths required, adding ten per cent for waste.

When selecting timber, examine each piece and reject any that are split or badly twisted. Boards with

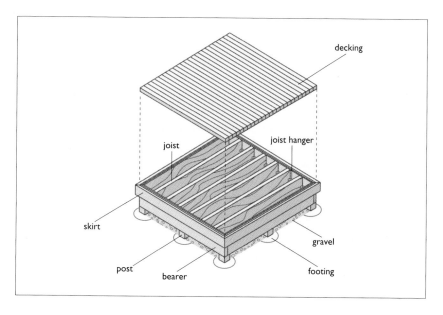

LEFT: Anatomy of a ground-level deck. The posts can be covered by a skirting board around the perimeter.

BELOW: An easy-build deck. On flat ground, the bearers can rest directly on the ground, but be sure to use timber treated with preservative to prevent rotting.

only minor warping or cupping, however, will straighten out as they are nailed in place.

A ground-level deck is supported by posts set in brackets bolted to concrete footings (see 'Building resource guide' for erecting posts) or by wooden piers. Bearers rest on the posts and metal hangers connect joists to the bearers. Decking

Easy-build deck

This deck sits on timber beams that rest on the ground and can be built around a favourite tree or large sheltering shrub.

1 Select your site carefully, as the correct position for your deck is all-important.

2 Lay out the timbers so that you can easily visualise the finished project.

3 Position the 100 x 100 mm bearers (see diagram). If you are building on level ground, only two bearers are needed. Use oak or treated pine for beams that touch the ground.

4 Construct the frame from 150 x 50 mm sections of timber.

5 Lay decking boards. You can fit them closely around tree trunks, but do not attach them directly to the trees.

6 Stain or apply preservative.

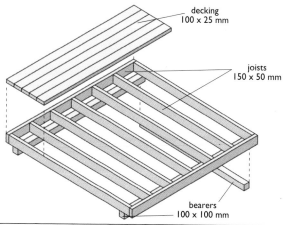

boards are nailed to the joists. If desired, a toe board can be added around the edge of the decking to create a neat finish for the deck.

Fasteners

Decks seem to eat nails. For every square metre of deck, you'll need 125 g of 100 mm nails (for joists) and 250 g of 50 mm lost-head nails (for decking). Use only galvanised nails; ordinary steel rusts and will stain the timber.

For the same reason, bolts, nuts, washers and screws also should be galvanised. Bolts should be as long as the total thickness of the materials being joined, plus 20 mm. Screws should be long enough to ensure that two-thirds of their length enters the piece of timber to which you are fastening.

1   For a preview of how your deck will look, test-assemble a section. This also gives you a chance to identify your straightest timber. Cut scraps of 10 mm thick timber to serve as spacers between boards.

2   Lay out the site with stakes and string. Here we're marking the location of an intermediate post. Measure diagonals to ensure that corners are square and fix them by erecting batter boards.

3   Excavate so that the deck will sit just above ground level. A marked board indicates the combined height of the deck materials (top), the ground level

and height of the posts above the excavated level.

4   Dig post holes, pour 50 mm of gravel into the bottom, and set posts in place. Plumb and brace each post and shovel in concrete. Bevel the top of the concrete so that water drains away from the post.

5   Let the concrete cure for a day or two; then mark the tops of posts (use a spirit level and straightedge) on all four faces and cut them off with a circular saw, making them all the same height.

6   Clear the excavated area of vegetation; then, to inhibit

Building a ground-level deck

1

2

3

4

5

6

vegetation growth, spread a polyethylene sheet over the area the deck will cover. Top this with crushed rocks or gravel. Omit the plastic if desired.

7 Construct bearers by nailing two 200 x 50 mm timbers together. Lay the bearers on top of the posts, and check that they are horizontal with a spirit level. Attach with galvanised connector plates and nails.

8 Position the joists. Use a scrap of timber to adjust the placement of the joist hangers on the bearers so that the joist tops will fit flush with the bearer tops. Nail the hangers onto the bearers.

9 Cut joists to length. Before installing them, sight along each and determine which edge has a bow. Nail joists in place, bowed side up; the weight of the decking will flatten them out.

10 Also nail decking boards to the joists bowed face up. Skew-nail at least two nails into each joist, maintaining uniform gaps between boards with spacers. Make sure that you stagger end-to-end joints.

11 Once all the boards are installed, snap a chalk line along the deck's edge, tack down a timber strip to serve as a guide for the circular saw's table, and cut the boards flush.

12 A board covers the ends of the deck boards and adds a decorative touch. We shaped the top edge of this one with a router, and used a saw to mitre joints at corners and scarfs.

7

8

9

10

11

12

Raised decks

Although more challenging to construct than ground-level decks, raised decks can be built by a do-it-yourselfer equipped with a hammer, circular saw, electric drill and set of spanners. The spanners are needed for tightening bolts, which provide more strength than nails and are used at critical points of the structure.

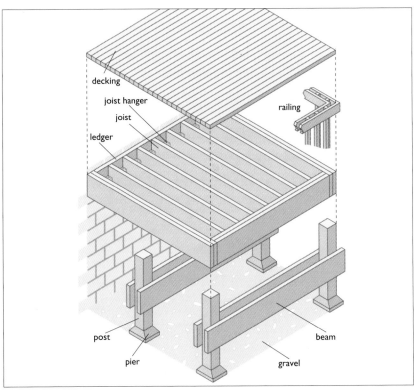

ABOVE: A narrow house benefits through the addition of a raised deck, which extends across uneven ground to encircle a nearby tree.

ABOVE RIGHT: The structure of a raised deck. The key to its success is ensuring the wall plate is level and attached firmly to the house.

RIGHT: The dimensions of stairs need to be calculated to a strict formula.

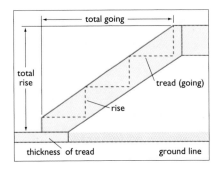

One of these critical points is the wall plate that fastens the deck to your house and serves as the structure's starting point. This board must be absolutely level and securely fastened to the wall with expansion bolts spaced 600 mm apart. With a timber-framed/clad building, it should be secured to the framing with 150 mm coach screws.

If you intend to cover your deck with a pergola, consider extending the deck posts. For another method, refer to the illustration on page 152.

Steps and railings

Steps are necessary for any deck that is more than 200 mm above the ground. If the deck is more than a metre high, you should also surround it with a handrail at least 865 mm high, with no more than

200 mm between horizontal rails or vertical balusters. Generally, a flight of steps consists of a number of treads. The vertical height of each tread is the 'rise' and the horizontal dimension is the 'going'. To ensure that steps are safe, the relationship between the rise and the going should conform to the formula: two rises plus one going = 585–700 mm. The average rise should be between 150 and 180 mm (see Timber steps on pages 142–5). If the risers vary in height by more than about 5 mm, people may stumble on them.

Measure the total rise and calculate a suitable rise and going for the steps, then determine the total going – that there will always be one less going than there are rises. If there are restrictions on space, adjust the rise and going, but keep within the formula. If there are more than 18 treads, you will need to construct a landing.

To attach railings, extend the posts above the decking or bolt verticals to the deck beams (see Railing styles, pages 139–41).

ABOVE: An impressive, large deck leads down to a paved patio. Notice the solid yet airy style of the railings.

LEFT: This garden retreat centres around a raised deck area to create a beautifully integrated living area in the outdoors. Timber is the overriding theme, allowing for a delightful range of textures, styles and colours.

Building a raised deck

1

2

3

4

5

6

1 Test assemble the deck. Then, starting at the house, lay out the site with string, driving stakes where posts will be located. Use a tape measure and the principle of triangulation (see 'Building resources guide') to ensure the layout is square. Take time to make accurate measurements.

2 Mark the wall plate's position by measuring down from the door threshold. Locate the finished deck surface 20–25 mm beneath the sill, so that rainwater won't flow into the house. The upper dotted line represents the top of the decking; the lower one the top of the wall plate.

3 Use a spirit level to make markings because the house or sill may be out of level. Attach the wall plate by drilling holes into the masonry and insert 100–150 mm expansion bolts. Make sure there is a washer under each bolt head before tightening with a socket or spanner.

4 Dig post holes at stake points, sink and plumb posts, and pour concrete around them. Build a form around the posts to raise the footing; this keeps grass and other vegetation away from the bases of the posts. Bevel the tops of footings to shed water.

5 To determine the correct level of the tops of the posts for cutting, use a straightedge and spirit level, with the straightedge resting on the top of the wall plate. Mark the post. Use a combination square to continue the lines around all four faces of each post.

6 Cut the posts to the correct size with a circular saw. If you want the bearers to finish flush with the posts, you will need to set the edge joists into the posts. The face marked here with an 'X' will be notched to accept half of the edge joist (see step 9).

7

8

9

10

11

12

7 Measure down the posts the height of the joists and mark them to give the position of the top of the bearer. Bolt bearers to each side of the posts. We bolted through both posts and both bearers. Use washers and check that the bolts are tightly fixed.

8 Space joist hangers along the wall plate and secure them to it. Nail joists to the wall plate and bearers. We skew-nailed joists to the bearer tops. If you use hangers, the joists will be flush with the bearers and the bearers should be level with the wall plate.

9 Use double joists at edges and ends for extra strength. We notched the posts to carry the outer joists and skew-nailed the inner ones between wall plate and posts, and between pairs of posts. Alternatively, you can extend the bearer past the posts, rest the joists on it, then nail it to the post.

10 Install stairs before attaching decking boards. To calculate the size of the goings and risers, see pages 132–3.

11 Lay out one of the stair strings with a square. Cut out the string. Be sure to subtract the thickness of a tread from the

bottom riser, so that steps will come out equal in height. Uneven risers will cause someone to stumble and may cause accidents.

12 Assemble the staircase by nailing spacer boards at the top and bottom of the strings. Nail treads to all but the top step; wait until you've installed the decking before nailing the final tread. You'll need to pour a concrete footing for the base of the stairway or bolt it to a precast pad so that it doesn't move.

13 Drill holes, then use bolts to fasten the top stair spacer to

13

14

16

15

Pool surround

Decking can provide the perfect way to allow easy access to any swimming pool, especially an above-ground pool. This above-ground pool was installed on a steeply-sloping site where it would have been difficult and expensive to build an in-ground pool. The stepped deck allowed the pool to be integrated into the site and provided the space to build several comfortable areas for relaxing and informal entertaining.

A deck is also the perfect place to install a spa, perhaps with built-in benches and a screen to give privacy. The principles of building decks are always the same.

For additional decking ideas to use with above-ground pools, see pages 186–90.

the edge joist. You can also attach stairs with metal stairway hangers, or use coach screws to attach the stringers to the ends of joists.

14 Install decking boards, starting at the house to ensure a snug fit under the sill (see page 138). Lay decking boards with the bowed side up. Hold spacers between boards, and then drive two nails into each joist. Trim the ends.

15 We nailed a Western red cedar board around the perimeter joists, bored holes through it and the joists, and then fastened the railing balusters to it with bolts.

16 To make the rail more comfortable to use, round rail edges with a router or buy routed timber. Drill holes and then drive coach screws through the balusters into the rail.

BELOW: A deck is the most practical way to surround an above-ground pool.

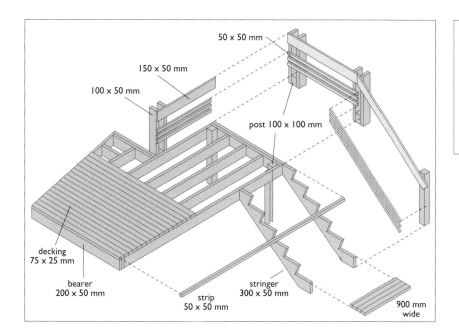

50 × 50 mm

150 × 50 mm

100 × 50 mm

post 100 × 100 mm

decking
75 × 25 mm

bearer
200 × 50 mm

strip
50 × 50 mm

stringer
300 × 50 mm

900 mm
wide

Deck out a slope

Decks are the ideal solution for those 'wasted' spots in your garden. The well-designed deck, below, turns a steep bank into a handsome niche, and at the same time provides a passage from the paved patio to the level below. The distinctive railing is used to unify the deck and the stairway leading to the lower level.

The frame consists of a number of 200 × 50 mm bearers resting on the patio at one end and on two 100 × 100 mm posts at the other end. To prevent movement, the ends resting on the patio are screwed to galvanised angle brackets that have been attached to the masonry with expansion bolts.

The decking is of 75 × 25 mm treated pine, finished along the edge with a 50 × 50 mm pine strip.

ABOVE: Construction details for the deck and stairs.

LEFT: A combination of deck and stairs is used here to connect two levels of the garden. The whole is unified by the distinctive railing.

Decking styles

Decking boards can be laid in a number of different styles. Choose one that suits the shape of your deck and gives it the character you want it to have. But be sure when planning your deck to design a suitable framing pattern to support it.

1. Trim the ends of decking boards at 45° angles and install them diagonally to the house wall instead of parallel to it. Use a table saw to make the angled cuts easier and more accurate, or you can construct a jig for your portable power saw.
2. Some decking patterns require different framing plans. In this example, butting boards at a diagonal calls for the installation of a double header from corner to corner of the deck.
3. For a herringbone pattern, double the joists and space them 600 mm apart. Cut the board ends at 45° angles and install them in alternating directions.
4. Grid-pattern decking requires spacers nailed between joists. Additional framing increases the weight and cost of a deck, so be sure to plan a sub-structure that can carry the load.
5. A parquet effect can be created using the same framing plan as for grid-pattern decking.
6. For a really strong (but expensive) deck, skew-nail 100 x 50 mm boards set on edge. To calculate the number of boards you'll need, take the width of the deck in millimetres and divide by the thickness of one board plus one space.

ABOVE RIGHT: A standard longitudinal decking style, accentuating the width of the deck.

RIGHT: These six decking board styles represent some of the more popular patterns:
  1 Boards set diagonally
  2 Boards butting together on the diagonal
  3 Boards set in the popular herringbone pattern
  4 Boards set in grid pattern
  5 Boards set in parquet pattern
  6 Boards set on edge

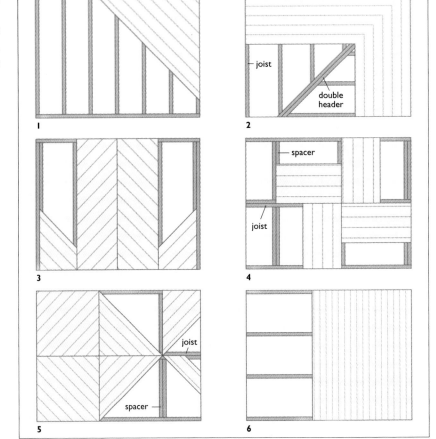

Railing styles

The choice of railing style for your deck may be influenced by the design of your house and any specific needs – such as privacy or protection from the wind. For example, glass panes between metal railings give wind protection and allow you to preserve a view. However, timber is still the most popular material, and a range of timber railing styles is presented on the following pages.

ABOVE: A simple railing design links all areas of this garden. As well as being functional it's very unobtrusive.

LEFT: A lattice railing continues the theme established by the large screen at the end of the deck.

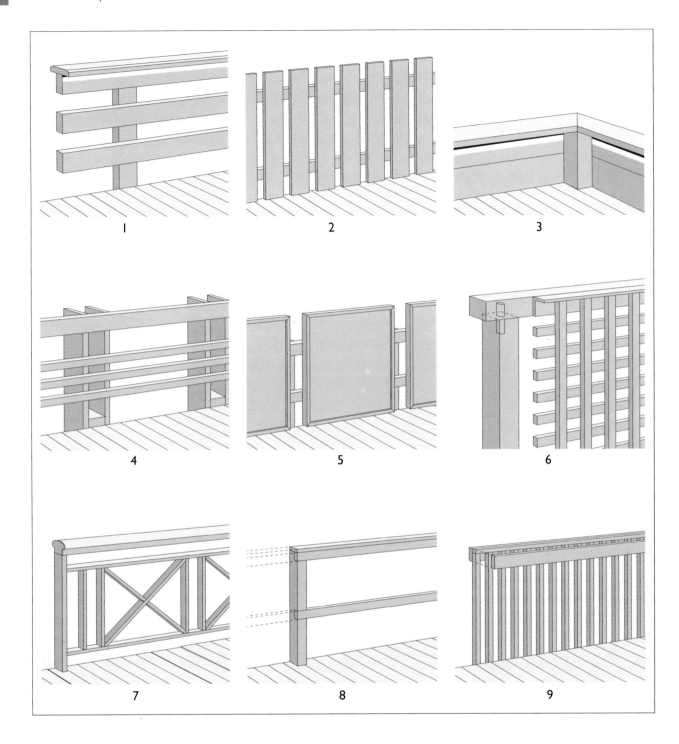

1 Horizontal railings can be made from three boards 100 x 50 mm or 150 x 50 mm capped with a handrail 150 x 50 mm. Bolt the verticals and rails together; nail the handrail on after chamfering its edges.

2 For a screen that ensures privacy but lets in cooling breezes, space 200 x 25 mm timbers 50 mm apart. Nail all boards to one side of the rails, or alternate them on opposite sides for design interest.

3 On low decks, build a low, solid railing of horizontal 200 x 50 mm timbers capped with 150 x 50 mm boards. Keep the solid railing less than about 600 mm high, or wind will play havoc with it.

4 If the decking posts are not long enough to reach railing height, extend them. Bolt a 150 x 50 mm board to each side. Then nail 50 x 50 and 150 x 50 rail materials to the extensions.

5 Exterior-grade plywood makes a good contemporary railing. Frame 900-mm-square panels with

50 x 25 mm battens. Space the panels 100 mm apart. Alternatively, you can use laminated or wired glass, or trellis.

6 Trellis can be used to provide a decorative screen at the edge of the deck. Fix it to a framework of 100 x 100 mm timbers. Also see pages 114–7 for further instructions on using lattice.

7 Use cross-braced panels to close the gap between handrail and deck. Make the panels from 100 x 25 mm timbers. The handrail can be made from a 100 x 100 mm timber that is routed to shape.

8 Create a rustic look by using rough sawn timber in a classic post-and-rail style. Notch the post first and then attach the railings with screws. Use 100 x 100 mm posts and 100 x 38 mm railings.

9 Use 38 mm thick slats sandwiched between more substantial 100 x 38 mm timbers to achieve a railing or screen that provides privacy and shelter from winds. Vary the height to suit your garden.

ABOVE: Frame your favourite view in trellis with a combined rail and screen.

LEFT: One side of this deck uses a high railing of vertical slats to echo the garden screens. A useful low bench separates the deck from the garden below.

Timber steps

Outdoor steps can be much the same as an open flight of stairs indoors, except that you should employ designs that avoid trapping moisture or exposing the end grain of the timber.

Timbers suitable for outdoor steps are durable hardwoods and preservative-treated pine, the latter being cheapest. Consult your timber supplier for details of suitable species and availability.

Steps have several important parts (see diagram, below):

- Stringers, which are the sides of the steps that provide support for the treads.
- Treads, which are the actual walking platforms that span between two stringers.
- Going, which is the overall horizontal distance covered by a flight of steps. Also can refer to the depth of each tread.
- Rise, which is the vertical distance between the upper surfaces of the treads. This term may be interchanged with 'riser' to indicate the height of each evenly-spaced step. Traditionally, however, a riser is a vertical board that links the treads of a closed flight of stairs.
- Fixings, which attach stringers to the surface of the lower floor and the upper floor. These may be brackets, battens, bolts or nails.

Measuring up

Unfortunately, there is no such thing as a flight of steps that fits every location; each needs to be designed to suit the particular situation. However, there are several basic rules that you should follow to ensure success.

1 All risers should be of equal height. This includes the first riser from the ground and the last riser on to the upper level.

2 Step treads should be a minimum clear width of 250 mm.

3 Riser height should be between 150 and 180 mm. However, if elderly or disabled people will use the steps frequently, it would be wise to reduce the riser height to about 145 mm.

4 In a correctly designed flight of steps, the riser height and clear tread width (or going) are linked. One guideline requires that the clear tread width plus twice the rise should be not less than 585 mm or more than 630 mm. Another quotes a range of 585 mm (minimum) to 700 mm (maximum). Stay within these limits.

ABOVE: This broad set of stairs has a regular fall – the result of an acceptable balance between the tread and riser dimensions. Its well-constructed railing is another generous feature.

RIGHT: These are the common terms used in building steps. Tread widths should be carefully calculated to ensure good design.

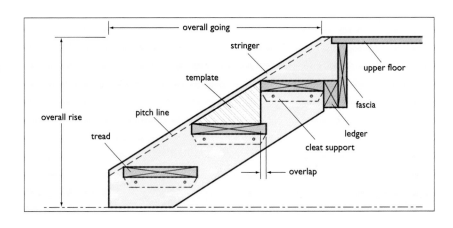

Tools and materials

You will need:

- saws
- hammer
- measuring tape
- pencil
- sliding bevel gauge
- spanner
- plane or sander
- drill and bits
- chisel
- 400 x 200 mm scrap plywood/hardboard/particle board, for template
- 300 x 50 mm PAR (planed all round) straight-grained hardwood or treated pine – lengths to suit design of steps. You will need sufficient for stringers and additional lengths of, say, 900 mm for each tread
- coach screws
- expansion bolts
- galvanised lost-head nails, bolts, nuts and washers
- wood primer
- paint, stain or other finish

Building the stairs

Step 1

Measure overall rise or the height of the steps. This is the vertical distance from the top platform (e.g. decking surface) to the existing patio or pathway.

Step 2

Divide this figure by a number between 150 and 180 to give you the total number of risers required. For example, if the overall height is 640 mm, it will divide neatly into four equal risers of 160 mm.

Step 3

Calculate clear tread width. For instance, using the figures above and following the guide given in paragraph 4 in Measuring up, the acceptable clear tread width would be a minimum of 265 mm. If the maximum recommended overlap of 25 mm is added, the design would call for a total minimum tread width of 290 mm.

Step 4

To calculate pitch, make a full-size template from thick cardboard,

LEFT: A simple set of stairs – two treads with only one riser – which can be easily built. The treads have been bolted to solid stringers.

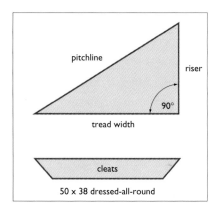

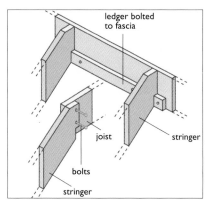

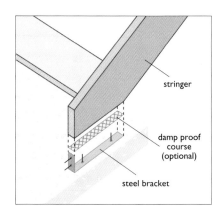

then from plywood, particle board or hardboard (see diagram).

Step 5

To calculate stringer length, multiply the pitch length by the number of risers to give the overall length of the pitch line.

Step 6

Cut two stringers of the appropriate length.

Step 7

Mark out the stringers using the template. Allow a 50 mm margin at the top edge of both stringers.

Also mark the upper line, which indicates the top vertical line of the stringer, allowing for full tread width, including overlap for the last (top) tread. With the outline of the stringer marked, also locate and mark a portion of the cut-out for the ledger, as well as the necessary cut-away to fit the angle bracket at the foot of the steps.

Step 8

Cut out stringers as marked. Spot prime or otherwise seal all the exposed end grain of the timber.

Step 9

Cut cleats to pattern. Fasten in position using two galvanised bolts, nuts and washers for each.

Step 10

Position the stringers and mark where each foot meets the base. Fix galvanised angle brackets in place by means of expansion bolts.

Step 11

Cut the ledger to length, allowing about 150 mm to project at each side of the stringers.

Step 12

Fix the ledger in place on the fascia or trimmer board, or to the edge of the deck using three galvanised bolts, nuts and washers or coach screws (see diagram, above).

Step 13

Fix the stringers to the angle brackets at the foot and skew-nail them to the ledger, make sure they are parallel, vertical, and spaced for the treads (see diagram, above).

Step 14

Cut the treads to length.

Step 15

Prime or seal the end grain of each tread and the upper edges of cleats.

Step 16

Fix the treads in place, nailing through the stringer into their ends and through pre-drilled holes into the cleats. Hammer three 100 mm galvanised lost-head nails into each end of the treads and through the treads into the cleats.

Step 17

Sand or plane off all sharp edges, then apply the required finish.

ABOVE LEFT: Make a template to the actual size from thick cardboard, then use it to cut an identical one from plywood, particle board or hardboard.

ABOVE CENTRE: Bolt the ledger to the fascia or trimmer board, using galvanised bolts, nuts and washers, or coach screws.

ABOVE RIGHT: Fix stringers to angle brackets at the foot. A damp course can be used, if required, between the concrete and stringers.

Steps – an alternative approach

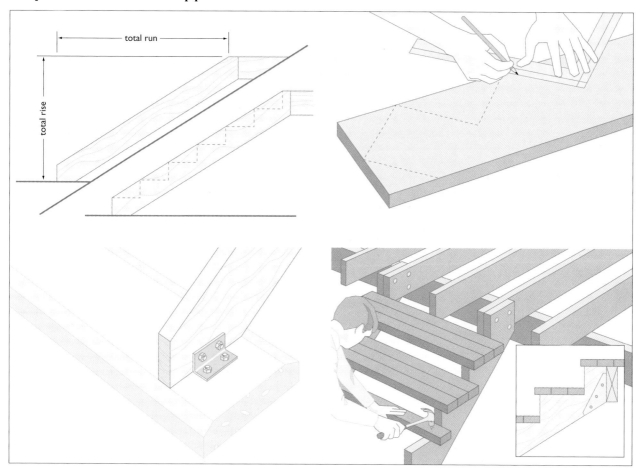

ABOVE: To make these stairs, use hardwood for the stringers and the treads. As in the previous project, calculate the timber needed and make up a plywood template (or use a steel square) to mark the checkouts for the treads. The bases of the stringer need to be cut level and bolted to metal brackets.

Bolt the top of the stairs to the deck or secure with metal anchors; use galvanised nails to fasten the treads.

RIGHT: This L-shaped set of stairs is well-finished in durable materials. Note the checkouts for the treads in the long stringers.

Pergolas and Shelters

Outdoor living areas can be greatly enhanced by the addition of a pergola or shelter, allowing enjoyment even through the hottest months. Sun and light can be controlled, and valuable privacy can be gained.

Pergolas add a definite style to courtyards, patios and decks. They can use materials and design features that complement the house and provide a link with the garden. Climbers, vines and small trees are often introduced to complete the effect gained by a pergola. Similarly, pergolas lend themselves to lighting, giving you the opportunity to use your outdoor area in the evenings as well. It's interesting how just erecting a pergola over an existing deck will give that deck a different, more comfortable 'room-like' feeling.

Another structure to consider is an arbour, which can include a garden seat and so provide a romantic sanctuary in a quiet corner of your garden. Arbours, clad in trellis, are perfect for climbing plants, which can be encouraged to grow over, around and through the structure.

A shadehouse can be included in your garden plans to provide a valuable buffer between house and outdoors, a pretty patch of greenery next to a pool and a perfect connecting 'room' from one outdoor living area to the next.

Using much the same techniques as for a pergola, a carport can be built to give protection to your car and double as a useful covered entertaining area. In many smaller gardens, an attractive combination of carport, covered walkway and patio/pergola can multiply the available outdoor living areas.

This vine-covered pergola produces a gentle, dappled light on the deck and combines with the lattice screen to give a sense of privacy. Lighting and potted plants complete the feeling of being in a shaded outdoor room – a sought-after addition for any house.

Pergolas

Trees provide shade, but they take time to grow, and a tree large enough to give you a useful area of shade may be too large to fit comfortably into your garden plans. A pergola may be the answer: clad with climbing and scrambling plants, it gives the same cool shade as a tree, or you can cover it with closely-spaced battens to provide instant shade. Shadecloth and canvas are possibilities, too; it all depends on the style of your house and garden, and your personal preferences.

We usually think of a pergola as being attached to the house to extend the living area – but it need not be. It can be freestanding, positioned to shade a path or create a secluded spot for a seat.

ABOVE: These trellis-like pergola supports are an attractive feature on their own. Here the clever use of wire mesh allows vines to add greenery to the pergola.

RIGHT: A well-designed pergola can be used to enhance the appearance of your house and add individual style. Note the possibilities introduced by the perimeter bench on the deck.

ABOVE: A banksian rose provides a colourful crown for this simple, open-style pergola. The foliage ensures this will be a cool, shady spot even in the hottest weather.

LEFT: This stylishly roofed pergola is a real asset for a garden. Offering all-weather protection for outdoor dining, it has been designed to take full advantage of the late afternoon sun.

Building a pergola

You can add a pergola to an existing deck or patio, or plan it as part of a new outdoor living area. It is important to provide adequate footings for the posts, but the framing need not be as strong as for a deck, as pergola roofing materials are usually light in weight. Of course, the framing must be sturdy enough to withstand strong winds and resist collapsing under the weight of climbing plants and, occasionally, snow.

Choosing materials

A pergola can be built from treated pine or a hardwood such as oak. When deciding on a timber, consider costs as well as the aesthetic effect you want to achieve. Consider the style of the posts, beams and rafters you require – and whether a particular surface finish is needed to match the house. As well as timber, you need concrete, post brackets and fixings to secure the beams and rafters, if used.

In choosing a roofing material, first assess how much shade you'll need. A pergola on the south or west side of the house may require full protection from the sun, while one on the north may be better left open to the weather. You may also choose to use a material that will shelter you from the rain. Remember, however, not to use anything that will prevent light or ventilation from reaching indoors. See page 158 for a selection of popular roofing materials.

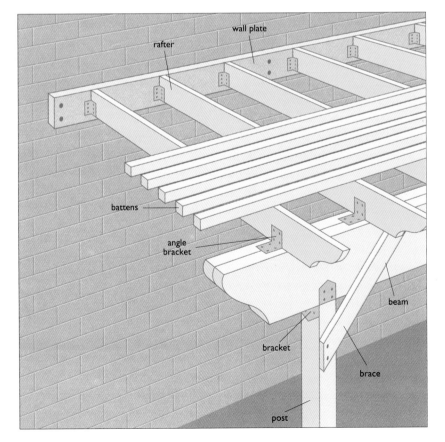

ABOVE: An uncomplicated pergola adorned with roses which will, in time, cover it completely.

LEFT: Anatomy of a pergola.

An attached pergola has a solid wall plate (at least 150 x 50 mm) attached to the house, and a beam (joist or header) on the other side. The beam rests on posts (usually 100 x 100 mm). Fastened to the wall plate and resting on the beam are rafters. Diagonal braces can be used to strengthen the post/beam connection. Shade battens are nailed to the rafters.

A freestanding pergola has posts both sides and two beams, instead of a beam and wall plate.

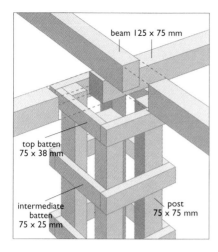

beam 125 × 75 mm

top batten
75 × 38 mm

intermediate
batten
75 × 25 mm

post
75 × 75 mm

Ready-made pergolas

Although building your own pergola will allow you to tailor the design to meet your requirements exactly, many garden centres and large DIY stores sell pergola kits, which come with all the necessary posts, beams, brackets and fixings. These are modular in design, allowing two or more to be joined together to form quite complex structures, either attached to the house or freestanding.

Attaching a pergola to the house

A pergola is attached to the house by means of a wall plate. To attach a wall plate to a brick or stone wall, use 100 mm expansion bolts, drilling their holes with a masonry bit and electric hammer drill. If your house is weatherboarded, attach the wall plate to the wall studs (through the board), using 75 mm galvanised coach screws, having first drilled pilot holes.

The height of the wall plate will determine the height of the pergola. You can make it any height, but to ensure adequate headroom, make it a similar height to the ceilings inside your house. Make sure the wall plate is level along its length.

Pergola posts

Most pergolas have plain posts that suit the relaxed garden atmosphere, but there are many ways to dress them up. For a more formal setting, choose columns to reflect that, or be innovative and make your pergola posts a design feature.

If you want 'columns' rather than mere posts, make them from three 150 x 50 mm lengths of timber. Cut down the length of two of them, removing 50 mm from each of the outer corners. Fix the cut timbers to each side of the uncut one to form an octagonal column. Shape the ends of the beams with a jigsaw.

Pergola posts can be structures in their own right. Construct a post with four verticals (75 x 75 mm) joined by horizontal battens (75 x 38 mm at top and bottom with 75 x 25 mm battens in between) at 500-mm centres to form trellis-like posts that can support climbing plants (see diagram, above).

FAR LEFT: Small horizontal battens attached to the four posts combine to create a tiered effect. Note that the beam is supported by the top battens rather than by the four posts.

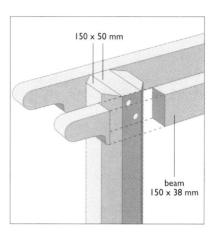

150 × 50 mm

beam
150 × 38 mm

ABOVE: An octagonal column can be made from three 150 x 50 mm timbers cut to shape.

ABOVE LEFT: This 'trellis' pergola support is attractive and functional, enabling you to bring climbing plants and vines into the pergola.

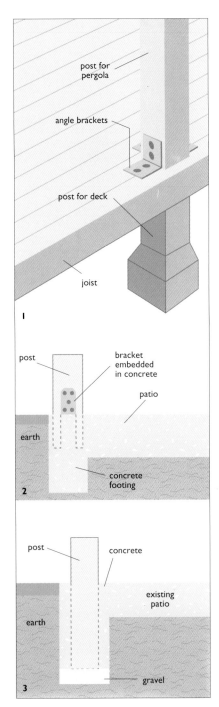

I

post for pergola

angle brackets

post for deck

joist

post — bracket embedded in concrete

patio

earth

concrete footing

2

post — concrete

existing patio

earth

gravel

3

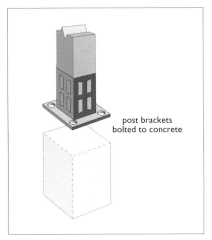

post brackets bolted to concrete

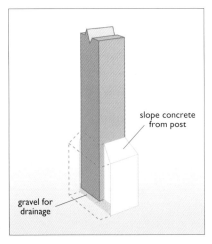

slope concrete from post

gravel for drainage

Fixing the posts

When adding a pergola to a timber deck, locate the posts above the deck supports. Use posts about 100 mm longer than the plan calls for, then trim their tops. Secure the new posts with angle brackets or post brackets.

Posts should not rest on a concrete patio that has no footings underneath, as the concrete could crack. If building a new patio, pour a concrete footing along with the patio and embed post brackets in it (see diagram 2, left). If you are adding a pergola to an existing patio, position the posts just outside the paving to avoid having to break into the concrete. Dig post holes about 230 mm wide and 300 mm deep in the required places, put gravel in for drainage and set the posts in concrete (see diagram 3, left).

ABOVE: A traditional pergola construction: rafters on beams with the occasional batten to support a vine. The beams are cut into the posts, bolted and tapered at the ends.

ABOVE FAR LEFT: Three different methods of fixing posts for a pergola.

ABOVE TOP LEFT: Pergola posts need firm foundations, such as this concrete and bracket method.

ABOVE LEFT: When setting posts into the ground ensure they have a gravel base and that the concrete 'collar' around the posts displaces any surface water.

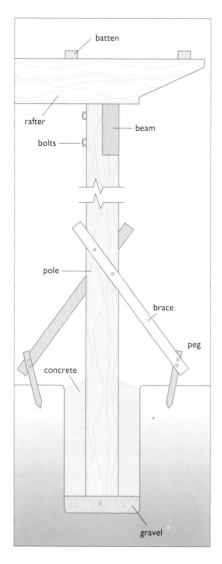

batten

rafter

beam

bolts

pole

brace

peg

concrete

gravel

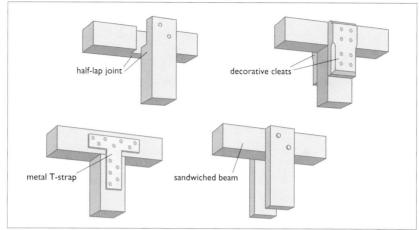

half-lap joint

decorative cleats

metal T-strap

sandwiched beam

Erecting the pergola

The basis for most pergolas is the 100 x 100 mm post set firmly into the ground. Place the posts so that they do not block access to doorways or an attractive outlook.

To improve the appearance of our pergola (see pages 154–5), we constructed beams by placing a strip of plywood between two 300 x 50 mm lengths of timber to create a section that was the same thickness as the 100 mm post. The plywood was nailed to one length of timber first and then the beam nailed together from both sides. For a lighter pergola, use a single 150 x 50 mm beam. For rafters, choose 150 x 50 mm timber. Battens can be of 50 x 50 mm or 38 x 38 mm timber.

ABOVE: Four different methods of attaching beams to pergola posts.

BELOW: This stylish pergola is attached to the house using four posts supported by brackets in concrete footings at the edge of the patio. Rambling pink roses soften the hard edges.

ABOVE: After you have positioned the pergola posts with the cutouts facing outwards, brace them and then pour the concrete. Ensure the concrete is tamped well with a rod to remove any air bubbles, and leave it to cure for at least ten days before adding the roof framing.

RIGHT: This efficient and attractive method of fitting the pergola beams and posts allows a flush finish at the top. The tapered ends provide a classic touch.

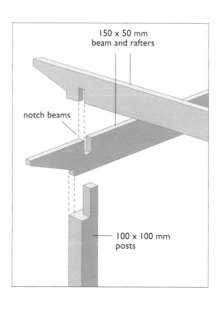

150 x 50 mm beam and rafters

notch beams

100 x 100 mm posts

ABOVE: A simple pergola, elegantly finished, graces a tiled patio. Notice the fluted posts and their mouldings. The rafters are high and unclad, allowing in plenty of light – while grape ivy (*Cissus rhombifolia*) dresses the front.

1

2

6

7

1 Determine the post placement. Erect the posts (100 x 100 mm) and, if needed, a wall plate. Transfer a level line from the plate to the posts, or from post to post. Mark cut lines, allowing for rafter and beam thicknesses.

2 Cut the posts to the proper height. Make two passes with a circular saw and remove the waste. Don't use a chain saw: standing on a ladder, you won't have enough leverage to operate it safely.

3 Nail a metal post cap to the top of each post. Alternatively, you can bolt the beams to the sides of the posts, or secure them with galvanised steel nail plates

to both sides of the beams and the posts.

4 Construct the beams as described on page 153 or use a 150 x 50 mm timber for a less massive effect. For design interest we shaped the ends of the beam and rafters with a jigsaw.

5 Set the beam into the post caps or fix it to the posts. If necessary, use a level to check that it is horizontal. Check for square, too. Then drive nails through caps or nail plates into the beam.

6 Post caps alone won't handle the stress placed upon post-and-beam connections. Cut

3

4

5

8

9

10

diagonal 75 x 25 mm braces and nail them to one or (for stronger support) both sides of the post and beam.

7 Attach galvanised angle brackets to the beam and (if applicable) the wall plate. For 150 x 50 mm timbers, space the angle brackets 400–600 mm apart, depending on the weight of roofing materials to be supported.

8 Cut the rafters to length and shape their ends with a jigsaw, if desired. Install the rafters level or, to slope them away from the house, measure and cut notches at each end of the rafters, as shown above.

9 Nail through the angle brackets into the rafters. The brackets will be adequate structurally if you are using rigid roofing material. If not, brace between rafters with short lengths of 150 x 50 mm timber.

10 Cut 50 x 50 mm battens to length and nail them to the rafters at 100 mm centres, using one as a spacer between battens. For some other roofing possibilities see page 158.

RIGHT: Stylish columns give a grand feel to this extended pergola. Thin posts accentuate the structure's height, while matching battens support a shadecloth covering.

A freestanding porch

A freestanding porch bears its own weight, although you will need to stabilise it against the wall of your house. The alternating long and short battens in the porch pictured below give an unusual fringed effect to the structure and allow greater interplay of light and shadow. A more regular effect could be achieved by using battens of one length, if that would suit the style of your house, and a formal look is achieved by shaping the ends of the beams and rafters. This example is made of cedar, but you could easily use treated pine.

Building the porch

The height and span of the porch will be determined by your entrance; if the span is more than four metres, you will need heavier timbers than specified. In this porch, the cross-beams are 1800 mm long and attached to the soffit at the eaves. The posts are located no more than half this distance (i.e. 900 mm) out from the fascia board. With a two-storey house, the beams could attach to the wall.

1 Dig footing holes and pour two concrete footings (300 x 300 x 300 mm), inserting post brackets in each to hold the 100-mm-square posts. Check that the brackets are in line. Allow all footings to cure for one week.

BELOW: Pergolas make ideal porch covers. This unusual shade has alternating long and short battens for decorative effect.

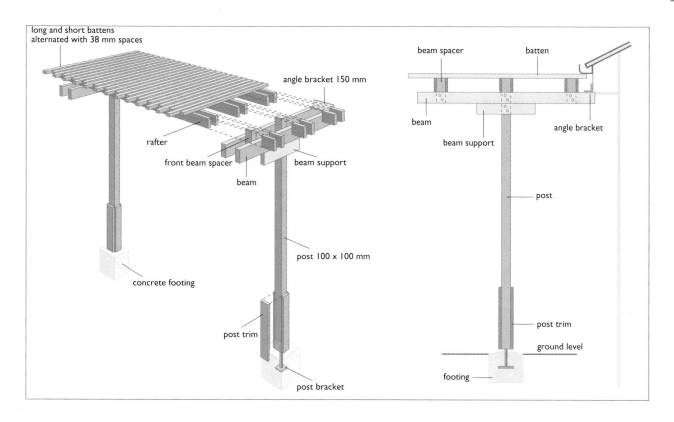

long and short battens alternated with 38 mm spaces

rafter

front beam spacer

beam

angle bracket 150 mm

beam support

post 100 x 100 mm

concrete footing

post trim

post bracket

beam spacer

batten

beam

beam support

angle bracket

post

post trim

ground level

footing

ABOVE: A pergola with T-shaped supports can be a useful alternative if attaching a wall plate to the house is impracticable. A small pergola can be supported on two posts. Attaching it to the house with metal brackets will add extra stability.

2 Bolt each pair of beams to the posts, 150 mm down from the top, using two 200 x 10 mm bolts at each junction. Nail 250 x 100 x 50 mm blocks (beam spacers) between the pairs of beam timbers, 200 mm in from each end, flush at the bottom and rising 150 mm above the upper surface. Nail each pair of 600-mm-long beam supports to the posts beneath the beams, using 60-mm galvanised nails.

3 Stand the two post structures in their brackets and drill and bolt them in place.

4 Use galvanised angle brackets to fix one end of each beam to the soffit board or wall of the house.

5 Nail a 150 x 38 mm rafter to each side of the tops of the posts, as well as to each side of the spacer blocks protruding between the beams. Nail three rafter spacers, evenly placed along the span, between each of the pairs of rafters.

6 Use 50-mm nails to fix the battens across the tops of the rafters, with 38-mm spaces between them. Alternate the long battens with the short ones.

7 To conceal the post brackets, chisel out the bottoms of the post trims so that they will fit over the metal, and use 100-mm nails to fix the trims to each face at the bottom of the posts. Paint with preservative.

Materials			
Component	Material	Length/size (mm)	Quantity
Post	100 x 100	2700	2
Beam	100 x 38	1800	4
Beam spacer	100 x 50	250	4
Beam supports	100 x 38	600	4
Post trim	100 x 50	600	8
Rafters	150 x 38	3600	6
Rafter spacers	100 x 50	150	9
Battens (long)	38 x 38	1800	24
Battens (short)	38 x 38	1650	24

Other: two 150-mm galvanised angle brackets; two post brackets; four 200 x 10 mm galvanised bolts; 100-mm, 60-mm and 50-mm galvanised lost-head nails.

Roofing materials

When you design your pergola, give some thought to whether you want to roof it and, if so, the type of roofing material. Do you want protection from the rain or only partial shade cover? Would you prefer to add a green touch and grow a leafy vine across the top? Some useful materials are described below.

BELOW: A grape vine covers this pergola and provides the perfect atmosphere for outdoor dining on a summer's day.

Some roofing options

In the last few years, the availability of polycarbonate sheeting (which includes UV protection in clear finishes) has widened the choice of transparent and translucent roofing materials – so this may be worth considering in preference to other, more traditional materials.

Shade battens

Nail battens (usually 38 x 38 mm) to the rafters, using one batten as a spacer. Use wider or narrower bat-

tens and space them according to the amount of shade required or for a decorative effect. Alternatively, you can use long and short battens to create a fringed look.

Trellis

Crossed wooden slats will produce a trellis effect across the top of a pergola, providing good support for climbing plants. The strips can be left to weather, or can be painted or stained.

Reed or bamboo

These inexpensive materials have a limited lifespan. Prolong their use by rolling them up and storing them inside during winter.

Shadecloth

Fabric mesh coverings filter strong sunlight, and they let air and moisture through. Shadecloth is a good alternative to the traditional canvas and makes an ideal covering for a pergola. It is light, maintenance-free and comes in a range of densities (from light shade to extra heavy). It is normally available in green, although other colours may be available from some suppliers.

Canvas

Heavy cotton duck provides some protection against rain, but it is essential that it be stretched taut so that it won't sag and allow water to collect on it.

LEFT: Shadecloth is available in a range of weights for different shading requirements. Here it protects a border garden full of ferns.

Polycarbonate sheeting

New advances in the manufacture of polycarbonate sheeting (made from polymers) offer an attractive roofing alternative. Stronger than glass or acrylic of equal weight, polycarbonate sheeting is flexible, light, highly resistant to UV degradation and able to screen out nearly all the sun's harmful ultraviolet rays. A range of tints is available, which will help reduce glare.

Fibreglass

Corrugated GRP panels are easy to cut and fix with screws. Slope the canopy so that water will run off.

Climbing plants

Grape vines, other climbing plants and deciduous creepers continue to be popular coverings for pergolas. They give shelter from the sun in summer, yet allow the winter sunlight to penetrate.

BELOW: Roof slats are spaced closely to block at least 50 per cent of the sun's rays. Ideally, they should run north–south so that plants are not subjected to strips of full sun all day.

Shadehouses

Pergolas have become popular and attractive additions to today's gardens, but to be of any practical use, they really do need to be covered with foliage; otherwise it can become too hot in summer to sit under them. One disadvantage of this is that plants need to be pruned regularly to keep them neat and tidy, and also out of the eaves and guttering. You can get around this task by turning your existing or planned pergola into a shadehouse, creating a sheltered space ideal for family living and a huge range of beautiful plants.

ABOVE: A sheltered garden retreat makes a lush and private outdoor living space. The luxurious canopy of creepers over the rustic pergola provides coolness and creates a tranquil shadehouse for hot summer days.

RIGHT: An airy, elegant garden house – the perfect spot for peace and contemplation.

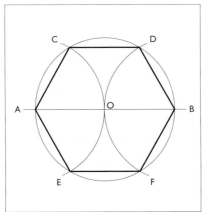

LEFT: A simple way to design an hexagonal gazebo.

1 Draw a straight line AB across the given circle to pass through the centre, point O.

2 Using points A and B as centres, scribe an arc to pass through the centre (point O) to meet the circumference at points CE and DF.

3 Draw sides to meet at points obtained on the circumference.

FAR LEFT: All shade-loving plants thrive in the bright, sheltered conditions of shadehouses. Here, beds of soil allow some plants to be grown in the ground.

your shadehouse with shadecloth. It will help to keep insects out and further reduce the intensity of the sun and wind.

Gazebos

A gazebo is usually a simple, hexagonal structure, often built without walls or a solid roof. It can be used as a support for climbing plants or roofed and partially walled to provide a sheltered, shady spot for sitting and enjoying the garden.

As well as a closely slatted roof, a shadehouse usually has slatted walls, which makes it both shady and sheltered from winds. However, if your site is already sheltered from cold winds, you could get away with just a roof and perhaps a western wall. If desired, you can line the walls and roof of

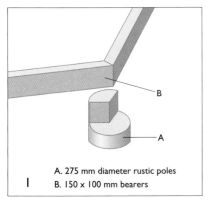

A. 275 mm diameter rustic poles
B. 150 x 100 mm bearers
1

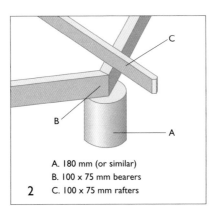

A. 180 mm (or similar)
B. 100 x 75 mm bearers
2 C. 100 x 75 mm rafters

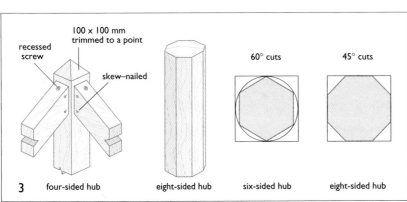

recessed screw
100 x 100 mm trimmed to a point
skew–nailed
60° cuts
45° cuts
3 four-sided hub   eight-sided hub   six-sided hub   eight-sided hub

1 Fixing beams to the top of the poles. Once the upright posts have set in concrete, mark them for height (using a water level) and trim accordingly. Use framing anchors to fasten bearers on to posts.

2 Attaching hip rafters. These are angled at 60° to the corners and notched to provide a level surface for nailing. Use battens to support the roofing material, such as shingles or polycarbonate sheeting.

3 Joining rafters to the hub. Depending on your choice of roof covering, the hub may project above the top of the rafters or be trimmed flush.

RIGHT: This rotunda complements the formal water lily pool in the foreground.

BELOW RIGHT: This gazebo makes an impressive summerhouse – complete with high-pitched shingle roof and lattice walls – and provides welcome shade for poolside living.

Pergola styles at a glance

Pergolas are simple structures that greatly enhance outdoor living. They can provide shade and protection from weather if clad with slatted battens, fabrics or foliage, or support waterproof sheeting such as polycarbonate.

To make a pergola, you construct a horizontal criss-cross timber framework and support it on columns or posts. There are many possible variations and methods of construction On the following pages, we illustrate eight different methods for combining the basic components of pergolas: posts, joists, rafters, shade battens and shade fabrics. Our examples illustrate the basic sizes and spacing of the timber required for structural purposes, but you can vary the dimensions and the number of components depending on how sturdy or light you want the structure to be. Study our pictures and diagrams to construct a pergola that appeals to you.

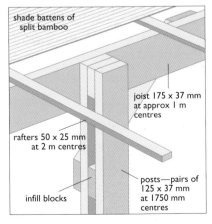

ABOVE AND RIGHT: A structure can be effective using just a few basic components. Here the horizontals projecting from the house are extensions of the interior's ceiling beams. Although they do not support additional layers of timber rafters, battens or shading fabrics, the well-established variegated ivy creates a shady extension to the home's living areas. The thickness of the timber gives the structure a simple but sturdy appearance.

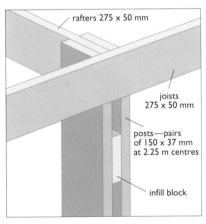

rafters 275 x 50 mm

joists 275 x 50 mm

posts—pairs of 150 x 37 mm at 2.25 m centres

infill block

TOP RIGHT AND RIGHT: This fairly lightweight structure creates a lovely halfway point between the inside environment and the open garden. Paving and planting also help to link the pergola with the garden. The post bracket set into concrete is the most permanent and satisfactory way of standing posts.

shade battens of split bamboo

joist 175 x 37 mm at approx 1 m centres

rafters 50 x 25 mm at 2 m centres

posts—pairs of 125 x 37 mm at 1750 mm centres

infill blocks

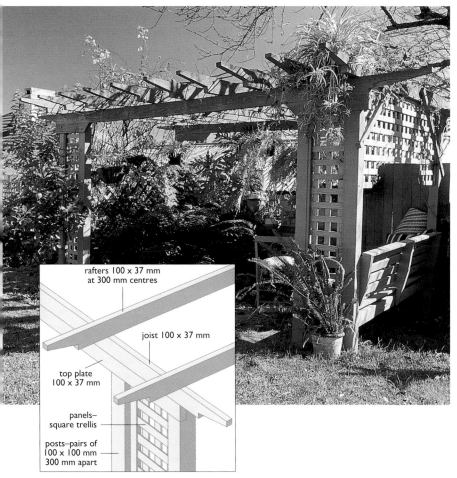

LEFT AND INSET: Your pergola could take the form of a completely freestanding structure like this. By building pairs of columns at the corners, 300 mm apart, and using trellis panels as an infill, you gradually enclose the structure. Be careful not to block it off from the rest of the garden. By screening substantial areas of the walls, the structure will become a gazebo or shadehouse.

rafters 100 x 37 mm at 300 mm centres

joist 100 x 37 mm

top plate 100 x 37 mm

panels— square trellis

posts—pairs of 100 x 100 mm 300 mm apart

BELOW LEFT AND BELOW: Don't be afraid to take in whole sides of your house with your new pergola, especially if your outdoor entertaining area faces the western sun. Allow the structure to follow the lines of the house. All a corner requires is another post to support it. Decide if you want the shade battens to continue over the entire structure or only specific sections of it.

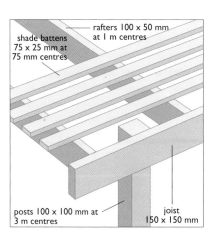

rafters 100 x 50 mm at 1 m centres

shade battens 75 x 25 mm at 75 mm centres

posts 100 x 100 mm at 3 m centres

joist 150 x 150 mm

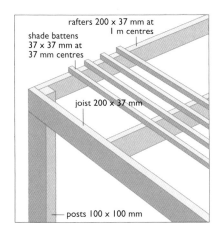

rafters 200 x 37 mm at
1 m centres

shade battens
37 x 37 mm at
37 mm centres

joist 200 x 37 mm

posts 100 x 100 mm

ABOVE AND RIGHT: Often it is possible for the pergola to follow the pitch of your roof. Here, because the roof's rake is gradual, the added structure can continue without interfering with head heights. Extend the pergola to avoid a tacked-on appearance. Shade battens partially enclose the framework. Rafters and joists are set into the post to give a flush outer surface.

LEFT AND BELOW: Here a more complicated design features paired joists and post plates, as well as two different types of shade battens. The posts in this case are extensions of those that support the deck flooring. By using extra timber for trims, trellis screens and bracing, you will achieve a more substantial appearance. Notice the broken sunlight (indicated by the shadows on the decking) that filters through the shade battens.

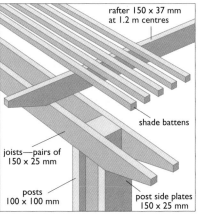

rafter 150 x 37 mm
at 1.2 m centres

shade battens

joists—pairs of
150 x 25 mm

posts
100 x 100 mm

post side plates
150 x 25 mm

RIGHT AND INSET: Integrate your plans for a new pergola with other structures in your garden. You will add interest to your garden and create a place that is fun to pass through. Beneath the pergola here, the lawn is interrupted by paving slabs from which you step up to a deck that is open to the sky. The upward tapering of the pergola rafters is the traditional way to add finish to the structure.

shadecloth

battens 75 × 37 mm
at 1 m centres

rafters 175 × 37 mm
at 1 m centres

joist 200 × 37 mm
at 3.5 m centres

posts 100 × 100 mm
at 3.5 m centres

BELOW AND BELOW RIGHT: Take your pergola from the corner of your house if you want to. The best way to handle the structural problem in this situation is to build a hip rafter into the design and allow it to slope down to the corner post. All other rafters can then butt up to it. Shade battens need only cover the width required to protect the windows and doors from sunlight.

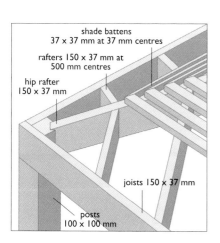

shade battens
37 × 37 mm at 37 mm centres

rafters 150 × 37 mm at
500 mm centres

hip rafter
150 × 37 mm

joists 150 × 37 mm

posts
100 × 100 mm

Creating a walkway

Interest can be added to a long pathway by building a pergola over it. The longer the structure, the more impact it will have, adding variety to the garden by providing a shadow pattern and a support for climbing plants. Or it can be covered to provide some degree of protection from the elements.

Refer to the basic pergola and free-standing porch construction described on pages 152–7, adapting it to suit the shape and style of walkway you want. Be sure to make it high enough that drooping stems of climbing plants will not touch the walker, and wide enough for two people to pass comfortably (about two metres is a good width). If you want to connect rafters and beams with housing joints, see 'Post and rail joinery techniques' in the 'Building resource guide'.

Rustic poles make an unusual and very effective walkway. Set the posts at least 200 mm into the ground and three metres apart.

Make the walkway two metres wide, and drill and bolt the top rafters in place at 600-mm intervals. Saw 400-mm lengths of pole to 45° and skew-nail them in place on each side of the post tops so that they form braces for the beams. Try to retain the rustic effect by not using metal brackets or housings. Add climbing plants (see pages 121–5).

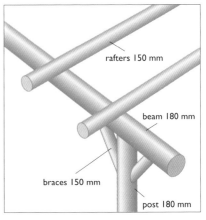

rafters 150 mm

beam 180 mm

braces 150 mm

post 180 mm

TOP: Logs have been used to construct this rustic-effect walkway. They would look well in any informal setting.

ABOVE: With a log walkway, braces are used to hold the structure rigid, as metal brackets or housings cut in the logs would ruin the rustic effect.

LEFT: This wisteria-covered walkway connects two sections of the house and creates a useful border for the courtyard.

Garden seat arbour

This garden seat will make a pretty focal point for your garden, as well as a destination for a stroll and a place to sit while viewing the results of your gardening efforts. The trelliswork sides can be used to support climbing plants.

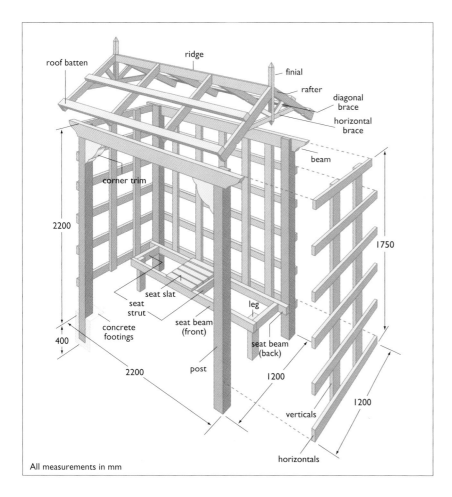

roof batten
ridge
finial
rafter
diagonal brace
horizontal brace
beam
corner trim
2200
1750
seat slat
seat strut
leg
concrete footings
seat beam (front)
400
seat beam (back)
2200
post
1200
verticals
1200
horizontals

All measurements in mm

LEFT: Construction details for an arbour with a bench seat. See page 152 for information on erecting posts and pouring concrete footings.

Building the arbour

1

2

1   Peg out the site using the dimensions on our drawing as a guide. Dig all the holes approximately 400 mm deep, depending on the degree of site slope.

2   Make two U-shapes for front and back, using the posts and two beams. Shape ends of the beams and cut out the top of the posts so the beams sit flush. Drill and bolt joints.

3

4

5

6

7

8

Materials			
Component	Treated pine	Length/size (mm)	Quantity
Post	100 x 100 mm	2600	4
Beam	150 x 50 mm	2400	2
Rafter	100 x 50 mm	1800	8
Ridge	100 x 50 mm	2300	1
Finial	50 x 50 mm	1200	2
Diagonal brace	38 x 38 mm	400	4
Horizontal brace	75 x 38 mm	850	2
Roof batten	75 x 25 mm	2300	4
Seat beam (front)	75 x 38 mm	2010	1
Seat beam (back)	75 x 38 mm	2200	1
Seat strut	75 x 38 mm	312	3
Leg	75 x 75 mm	420	2
Seat slat	75 x 25 mm	2100	5
Back horizontals	75 x 19 mm	2200	5
Side horizontals	75 x 19 mm	1200	12
Verticals	75 x 19 mm	1750	9

Other: four bags pre-mixed concrete; eight 100-mm bolts with washers and nuts for frame corners; galvanised 40-mm clouts for verticals and horizontals; 75-mm lost-head nails for roof frame; eight 100-mm coach screws for seat.

3 Nail a temporary brace 500 mm up from the bottom of the posts to keep the two frames square. Add a 365 mm grid of hardwood verticals and horizontals to the back.

4 Check that all the diagonal measurements are the same to ensure that the structure is square. Nail a temporary diagonal brace across one corner.

5 Stand posts in holes. Use a spirit level to check they are vertical and the beams are horizontal. Prop posts in place.

6 Make sure that the two frames are at the same height before filling the holes with concrete and leaving for 48 hours.

7 Make the two gables to a 30° pitch, cutting a half-lap joint at

9

10

11

12

13

14

the intersection of finial and horizontal brace.

8 Cut out birds' mouth notches in the rafters, where they will sit on the beams. Skew-nail all the joints and then undercoat as you proceed.

9 For total accuracy, stack the gables and rafters together to mark on them the position of the roof battens.

10 Now make up the two sides of the roof by nailing the battens to the two central rafters. Check diagonals are square.

11 Nail one side of the roof to the two gables, then position the ridge and, then, nail on the second side.

12 You will need help to lift the roof structure into place. Set

15

16

birds' mouths over each beam and skew-nail rafters to beams.

13 Make up panels of side verticals and horizontals and then nail them to the corner posts.

14 Make up the seat platform with its five seat slats according to the drawing.

15 Use coach screws to attach the back beam of the seat to the posts and the legs to the front of the seat.

16 Drill and jigsaw post trims and screw in place. Paint or stain the structure – or just sit back and relax!

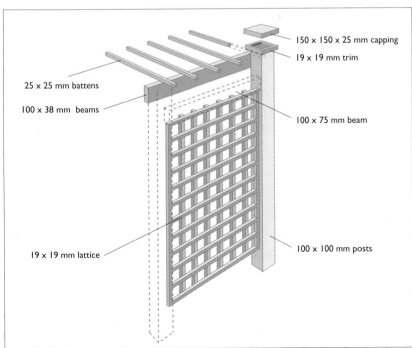

150 x 150 x 25 mm capping

19 x 19 mm trim

25 x 25 mm battens

100 x 38 mm beams

100 x 75 mm beam

19 x 19 mm lattice

100 x 100 mm posts

ABOVE AND LEFT: This unusual arbour is positioned at the edge of a paved outdoor living area. Horizontal lattice bands achieve a window effect on one side. Note the additional capping to finish off the posts.

Simple arbour

A simple arbour can be built in a few hours, even if you are relatively new to woodworking. Covered with a climbing rose, it will make a beautiful focal point in your garden, or add interest to a gate.

BELOW RIGHT: Lattice walls provide privacy and an attractive contrast in this arbour, romantically set among *Clematis montana* 'Rubens' and *Alyssum*.

BELOW:

1 Erect two posts (see page 152). Fix two short lengths of 150 x 50 mm timber to each post. Check to be sure these cross-beams are centred on the posts and square with them before tightening the fixing screws.

2 If desired, use a jigsaw or a router to shape a decorative motif at the ends of the two longer beams. Drive at least two nails through these into the ends of each cross-beam.

3 Cut 50 x 50 mm battens to length and drive one nail through each into each of the longer beams. To minimise measuring, use spacer blocks when fixing the battens.

Use an arbour to mark the entrance to your garden, position one to highlight the transition from one area to another, or simply place one next to a garden path. Wherever you build an arbour, you add charm and character to your garden, and gain a feature that will become even more attractive over the years. Clad with a scented climber, it will provide a delightfully perfumed oasis for contemplation.

1

2

3

RIGHT: A nicely fashioned arbour –
which would be a feature in any
garden – gives a touch of class
to a gateway. The scalloped brace
supports are in keeping with
other features in this quality
construction.

BELOW: Only simple woodworking
techniques are needed to make
this comfortable and attractive
arbour with seat. Paint or varnish
the finished structure so it blends
in with your garden, or leave
it to weather.

Trellis arches

Trellis arches, whether square, curved or angled, are useful garden structures. Once covered with flowering climbing plants, they form attractive dividers between one area of the garden and another.

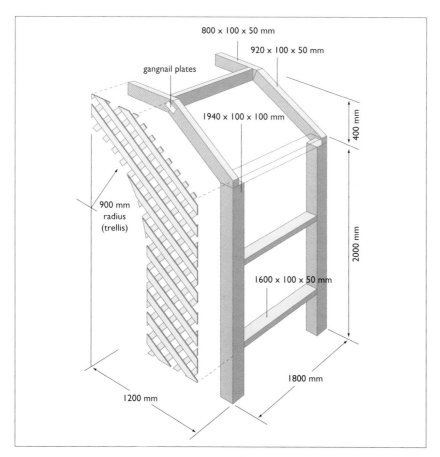

800 × 100 × 50 mm

920 × 100 × 50 mm

gangnail plates

1940 × 100 × 100 mm

400 mm

900 mm radius (trellis)

2000 mm

1600 × 100 × 50 mm

1800 mm

1200 mm

LEFT: An angled trellis is an easier structure to make than the curved variety. Face it in lattice (shaped to fit with a curved inner edge) and produce a stylish effect.

RIGHT: A dark timber finish will give your garden arch a solid appearance. To achieve the 45° splays on the roof shape, reinforce the joints with gangnail plates. Once you have a rigid framework, cut curved shapes for the sides from prefabricated lattice sheets.

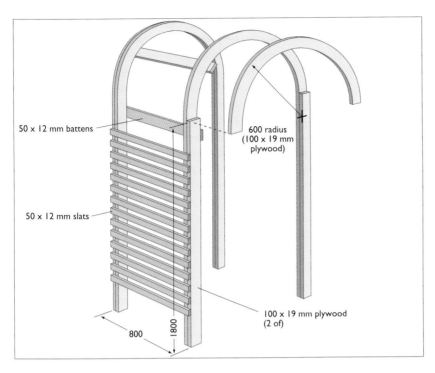

50 x 12 mm battens

50 x 12 mm slats

600 radius
(100 x 19 mm
plywood)

100 x 19 mm plywood
(2 of)

800

1800

LEFT AND BELOW: There's nothing like a real arch complete with climbing roses to add romance to the outdoors. Make the uprights and curved shapes in two layers of 19-mm-thick exterior plywood. By staggering the joints and jigsawing the segments to your chosen radius, you can make a strong curved timber piece. Use 800-mm-long, 50 x 12 mm battens with 35-mm spaces to enclose the structure and support the weight of your climbing plants.

Carports

BELOW: Consider allowing your carport structure to extend into an adjoining fence. The secret is continuity of both materials and colour. Masonry piers echo the structure and detailing of the house, and the use of identical roof tiles makes the carport seem anything but a recent addition.

The carport is often looked upon as the poor relation of the garage, often being designed purely for function. However, it can act in much the same way as a pergola: as a structure that makes a visual link between the garden and house. It is important to remember that a carport should be built in scale with the house, and in a complementary style and materials.

The construction techniques for a simple carport are very similar to those used for building a pergola, and on the following pages, we show you how a basic flat-roofed carport can be constructed.

Framing a basic carport

Putting together the posts and superstructure of a basic flat-roofed carport is no more difficult than many of the outdoor living projects we have featured previously. This carport measures 5000 x 3000 mm.

1 Use stakes and stringlines to mark out the site. Use a square to check corners and a spirit level if the site is flat enough to enable you to set the posts at the same height.

2 Dig the holes to 400 mm, and use stakes and scrap timber as formwork to keep the concrete footings square. The posts are at 2.5-m centres along the sides of this carport.

3 Fill the holes with concrete, mixed to a workable consistency.

4 When the concrete has partially dried, set 100 mm post brackets in place.

5 Stand posts when the concrete is set. Use timber braces and the spirit level to check that they are vertical in both directions. Mark and cut the posts at the same finished height, using a spirit level and stringline to make sure that they are level.

6 The top plates should measure 250 x 50 mm in section; you will have to cut the tops of the posts to accommodate them. Note that at the corners, the top plates run around two sides of the posts; the inner 50 x 50 mm section will be all that remains. The side posts have only half of their section cut away.

Two additional posts stand alongside the two front corner posts of this carport to support the garage door, but for the most basic carport, these posts would not be necessary.

7 Use 50-mm steel joist hangers in order to fix the secondary roofing timbers to the inner faces of the top plates, at approximately 1-m centres.

8 Bolt the top plates in place, using mitred joints at the corners.

9 Position the central longitudinal rafter first.

10 Add transverse rafters at 1-m centres. Fix them with joist hangers at the top plates and skew-nail at the central rafter.

Tip

- To open the doors on both sides of the car, you will need a width of between 2800 and 3200 mm; the average length of a carport is 5000 mm. Check with your local council to see if you need planning permission.

RIGHT: A carport doesn't have to be completely without walls. Use trellis to provide an airy enclosure, and paint it to complement other structures.

Pools and Ponds

Many home owners find great delight in having a water feature in their garden. If the relaxing sound of running water is your particular interest, a cascade might be the answer. Surprisingly, not a lot of space is required, and with some imagination the result will be very pleasing.

A pond also takes up little space and can provide a wonderful display of aquatic plants. Choose a sheltered garden area with filtered light, add a little landscaping (perhaps with rocks) and some specialised planting, and you can create an individual garden feature.

There are various pond styles to choose from, ranging from the raised, formal pool, perhaps with a central fountain, to the natural-looking pond that will attract wildlife and appear as though it has always been a part of the landscape. Prefabricated fibreglass ponds are available in a variety of shapes and sizes, allowing quick construction, but for greater flexibility you can use a PVC or butyl rubber liner that can be tailored to your exact needs.

Finally, if space is not too limited, a swimming pool may be a consideration. Whether you choose an in-ground or an above-ground pool, modern designs include smaller and more decorative shapes, allowing them to be integrated into the overall garden landscape with ease. On the following pages, we show many ways of designing your pool area to fit in with your deck, entertaining area or surrounding garden.

A pond borders the slate patio providing tranquillity and a sense of space. In this case, the use of water heightens the colours and the mystery of the densely planted, multi-layered garden. From the patio, the pond presents a focal point of constant interest, shimmering with movement and reflected light.

ABOVE: Steel fixing for a pool prior to the concrete pour. This is a specialised skill and critical to the success of your pool.

BELOW: A large sandstone pool surround like this creates a gracious and inviting poolside area in this leafy garden.

Pools

With pools, you have two choices: an above-ground pool is an alternative to the major undertaking of excavating an in-ground pool. Both types are examined on the following pages.

In-ground pools

An in-ground pool is a large undertaking; your plans need to include (at the least) provision of access for the excavator and materials, and a budget for 'extras' such as paths, poolside paving and landscaping. Allow for extra costs if excavation of rock is required or if your site has poor access. Not that this should deter you, for, if well designed, an in-ground pool can become the focal point of your outdoor living area.

Running costs

The initial filling of the pool will lead to excess water charges if your supply is metered, but this is a one-off cost. It is more important to consider ongoing costs, which include the price of chlorine and other chemicals, electricity to run the filter and fuel to heat the water (although the cost of the last can be reduced with solar heating).

Locating the pool

A spot that stays sunny for the greatest part of the day over the longest period of the year is best. Shelter from wind is also important, but nearby trees may be troublesome when they shed their leaves. A site near the house will simplify routing power and water supplies.

Landscaping the pool

A pool needs an attractive setting if it's to be a pleasant place to spend time. Trees and shrubs will provide privacy, shelter and shade, and dense plantings can hide fences or unattractive outlooks.

Wise selection starts with knowing your plants. Before you plant

LEFT: This interestingly shaped pool enjoys a warm, sunny aspect. The cluster of terracotta pots adds some floral interest.

RIGHT: A striking trellis facade creates a design highpoint in this small garden. The structure doubles as a shadehouse.

anything, it's important to know its ultimate height and spread. Excessive size can create unwanted shade, while overhanging branches will drop litter into the pool.

If you want to minimise pool cleaning chores, keep plants at least two metres from the water's edge. If you like the look of overhanging plants, choose only those with big leaves – they're easier to pick out than hundreds of little ones. Most evergreen trees shed leaves, bark, flowers or fruit year-round, and even if they are planted well away from the pool, the wind will carry some of this into the water. Deciduous trees can be a better choice near a pool, as they tend to drop all their leaves over a few weeks in autumn, and these are easily collected if the pool has a well-fitting cover or fine netting is stretched over it.

Although a pool squeezed into a small garden doesn't leave much space for landscaping, you can overcome this by gardening in pots. Terracotta planters could match the colour of brickwork and allow a variety of shrubs and climbers to grow large enough to soften walls without taking up much space.

Keep paved areas around the pool from looking bare and uninviting by arranging clusters of pretty potted flowers. Tubbed trees would work well, too.

BELOW: A small area elegantly designed. Terracotta tubs complement the brickwork; shrubs, bamboo and climbers soften the walls.

BELOW LEFT: Trellis screens create a private dining nook in this poolside area.

ABOVE: The lush plantings surrounding the L-shaped pool add
charm to this garden corner.

RIGHT: The unusual shape of
the swimming pool is highlighted
by the eye-catching foliage around
its edges.

Above-ground pools

Above-ground pools are constructed with steel uprights which can bear the weight of the water. Flexible wall panels conceal the pool structure and accommodate the curved shape essential to this type of pool construction. The vinyl liner is pushed against the sand floor and pool wall by the pressure of the water.

Because of the nature of the structure, the wall height and, therefore, the depth of an above-ground pool, is restricted to approximately 1.25 m.

The advantages

Above-ground pools are particularly suitable for sloping sites, where the cost of an in-ground pool is magnified because of the additional expense of excavation and construction.

An above-ground pool is relatively quick and uncomplicated to erect, and offers many possibilities for inclusion in a garden. It can be partially set into the ground if required. More importantly, it can be about a third of the cost of a comparable in-ground pool. This may allow you the luxury of a large budget for landscaping, decking and furniture – or perhaps a gazebo and a spa.

Landscaping the pool

An additional benefit of these lower costs is that you can afford to spend more on presentation and camouflaging the pool walls. A sloping site presents some advantages because it allows you to bury the pool partially, so that you can have one side where the pool lip finishes close to the ground.

On the lower side of the slope, you can disguise the high pool walls with tall plants. The walls of the pool are not built to withstand the horizontal pressures exerted by the soil and the moisture it contains, nor the opposing forces from the

BELOW LEFT: Combining decking with an in-ground pool is a creative way of landscaping your garden.

BELOW: Here timber is used to enclose the pool sides and highlight the split-level surround.

OPPOSITE: Another above-ground pool to suit a sloping site. Notice how the deck fits neatly under the rigid polymer edge-capping.

LEFT: This above-ground pool features a generous deck area that adds to the overall appeal of the outlook.

BELOW: The combination of decking and brickwork make this poolside an ideal place to relax.

pool's water. Therefore, land drains must be installed in trenches at the base of the walls to be buried and the backfill placed after the pool has been filled with water.

To enhance an above-ground pool on a level site, consider going to the extra expense of partially burying the whole pool and building decking around one side, with steps leading up to it and shade-loving plants beneath.

You can build your decking to follow the curved line of your pool by constructing faceted ends. Joists may have to run in opposite directions in alternate sections, but the end result will be well worthwhile: a continuous deck platform surrounding the pool.

Use decking timber to close in the vertical surfaces around your pool shape. Then you can create entertainment areas on the low side of the pool. If you make a feature of the steps between the upper and lower levels, you'll have a split-level pool surround – much more interesting than a single level. A practical pool surround is one that is constructed of non-slip tongued-and-grooved decking.

Plants for pool surrounds

Planting around pools is always difficult because of the effect chlorine has on the plants and the soil. It is necessary, therefore, to choose the hardiest varieties of plants and, where possible, to raise the flower beds above the level of the pool or to plant in pots and containers.

Cabbage palm (*Cordyline australis*), hibiscus, *Yucca gloriosa* and oleanders all look good in pots, as do juniper and box. Agapanthus planted in large, shallow terracotta pots looks marvellous near a pool. When placing pots around pools, keep them as far as possible from the water. Pots with small necks are a sensible choice, as they will reduce the likelihood of soil spillage if knocked accidentally. As a rule, when planting at the poolside, it is wise to choose plants that have leathery leaves, rather than those that have fleshy leaves. (See listings in the 'Garden resource guide'.)

ABOVE: The terracotta pots and colourful flowerbeds complement this swimming pool perfectly.
It is wise to choose hardy varieties of plants to grow in areas around pools as they can be affected by chlorine or salt.

ABOVE: Cascading shrubs on a terraced slope complement this elegantly landscaped pool area. A sense of spaciousness and quality is evident in the design and workmanship of the paving.

LEFT: Small plants close to the water's edge create an interesting pool border.

Ponds

BELOW: Moss-covered rocks, groundcover and dense planting enhance this pond. To achieve the look of clear water, you will need to install a filter and use algicide in the water. Unfortunately, that means no fish and no water plants.

Water is one of the most desirable features you can add to a garden, not only for its intrinsic appeal, but also because it attracts wildlife and allows you to introduce fish and a range of interesting aquatic plants to your landscape. The surrounding plants will benefit, too: as water evaporates, the immediate area will be cooled, and moisture-loving plants will respond happily and thrive in the slightly higher humidity that is created.

ABOVE: A hidden garden pond, complete with fountain and surrounded by greenery, is a delightful addition to any garden.

RIGHT: Building a pond.

1   Dig out the pond, sloping the sides at a 45° angle.

2   Make sure the rim is level.

3   Lay the liner, secure it in place and fill the pond with water.

4   Place edging around the pond and stock it with plants and fish.

OPPOSITE: Adorned with water-lilies, this rectangular pool attracts a host of wildlife that can easily be viewed from the nearby stone bench.

The right pond in the right place can be exceptionally appealing in any garden, and the wide range of pond types and sizes available allows you to select one to suit your particular situation.

Choosing the site

If you plan to keep fish or grow water-lilies, site your pond where it will receive at least five hours of full sunlight a day. Otherwise, its position should be influenced by the slope and style of your garden. Water will naturally flow to and collect in the lowest part of the garden, so a pond will look most natural there. If that site is unsuitable, however, place the pond where it will be seen to its best advantage. If you want to incorporate a fountain or a cascade, or if you want to filter the water, a conveniently located power point will be needed.

Choosing size and shape

When it comes to ponds, the bigger and deeper the better. Small ponds evaporate quickly and the temperature of the water fluctuates too widely for the comfort of fish and many plants. While areas of shallow water around the edges will allow you to grow interesting marsh plants, make sure that at least two-thirds of the surface area has 600 mm of water below it. This will enable you to grow deep-water plants such as water-lilies, and it will also help protect fish from cats and sunburn.

Two possible pond styles are the natural and the geometric. Both have their place, but, obviously, you should choose the form that best fits its immediate surroundings and the style of your garden.

Building a pond (liner)

Begin by laying out the shape. For an irregular, natural-looking pond, establish the shape with a long piece of rope or garden hose. If you

want a square or rectangular pond, use a stringline stretched taut between stakes. Be realistic about the size of hole you can dig. If you try to create a lake and then can't finish the digging, you'll end up with an undesirable, large, shallow area of water.

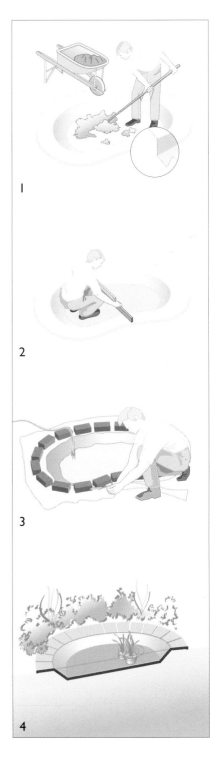

1

2

3

4

A pond liner is the simplest means of containing water. The best liners are made from butyl rubber (or synthetic rubber). They are quite expensive, but are guaranteed for 20 years and may even last 50. Black PVC is cheaper, but punctures easily and after a few years in the sun will have to be replaced. Alternatively, you can buy a ready-made moulded fibreglass liner, although they restrict your choice of shape and size, or you can construct a pond from concrete. Unless it is expertly laid, however, concrete will soon crack and leak.

1 Start the excavation by scraping off the topsoil. This layer of dark soil is valuable; either spread it thinly over the rest of the garden or store it for later use. If you need to dispose of any soil, let it be the subsoil. Dig out the pond, sloping the sides at a 45° angle. If you like, you can incorporate shelves around the edges for plants that like to grow in shallow water. Make provision for an overflow in the event of heavy rain, and do consider where that water will run to.

2 Use a spirit level to make sure that the rim is even all around. Clear the edges and bottom, removing anything that could puncture the liner.

3 Before placing the liner, add a 50–80 mm layer of sand to the excavation. Place the liner in the hole and mould it to the shape of the pond. It is not necessary to smooth out every wrinkle. Secure the edges of the liner with bricks and begin to fill it with water. As the pond fills, it may be necessary to release sections of the secured liner. After filling, leave the pond for a week to settle and allow you to inspect it for leaks.

4 To hide the edge of the liner, dig a trench 150 mm deep right

ABOVE: The formal, geometric shaped pond, carefully finished with sandstone capping, fits in well with the paving and shrubbery.

around the pond. Lay the excess liner in the trench, trimming off any that can't be buried, and fill the trench with soil, sand or cement. Complete the pond by trimming the edge with rocks, bricks, sandstone or timber, making sure the trim hides the trench from view.

Building a brick-lined pond

The finished depth of this pool will be 450 mm, which is the correct depth for growing water-lilies.

The tools and materials you will need are pre-mixed concrete or sand and cement; wheelbarrow and board for mixing concrete; shovel; trowel; spirit level; bricks; coping stones; butyl rubber or PVC pool liner; and a recirculating pump.

1 Choose the site for your pond and dig a hole approximately 600 mm deep and the required shape, allowing an extra 230 mm all round to accommodate the brickwork (see diagram, below).

   If you intend to put fish in your pond, you may want to make the hole a little deeper; make the height of the walls at least 250 mm above the water level so the fish can't jump out.

2 Pour 100 mm of concrete into the hole to form the pond's base.

3 Build the sides of the pond with 230 mm of brickwork. When this is completed, render the inside brickwork with a mortar mix of 1:4 cement and sand.

4 Cut the liner to size, making it the length plus twice the depth of the pond long and the width plus twice the depth wide, allowing ten per cent extra on each. Lay in place, folding the corners.

5 Fold the edges of the liner over the top of the brickwork and weight them down temporarily with bricks. Fill the pond with water. Trim the edges of the liner flush with the outer edges of the bricks and then bed the coping stones on mortar to secure and conceal them.

6 For extra interest, install a small submersible pump with a fountain outlet. This will add zest and sparkle to the water, and provide the pleasant, relaxing sound of running water. These pumps are placed in the pool and connected to a nearby power point. They are quite safe – most rely on a low-voltage supply through a transformer; the cable should be buried in a shallow trench where it is not likely to be disturbed through digging.

Allow time for water plants to establish and stabilise the water before adding fish.

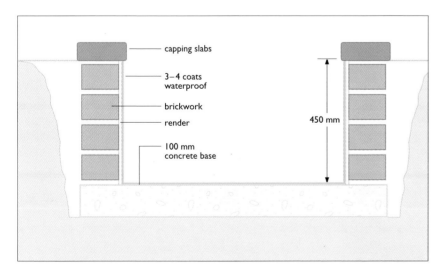

capping slabs

3–4 coats waterproof

brickwork

render

100 mm concrete base

450 mm

LEFT: Construction details for a brick-lined garden pond. The rendered surface applied to the bricks can be waterproofed with a proprietary waterproofing compound or by adding a flexible butyl rubber or PVC liner.

LEFT: Stepping stones across a pond – an unusual feature which adds to this distinctive setting.

BELOW: In this garden, the veranda and the patio are separated by planting; the indirect route between the two makes the small garden feel bigger. The patio is the entire garden; shaded by deciduous trees, it has a pool with water-lilies as its focal point. The floor is made of blocks of timber with hardwood strips for pattern.

RIGHT: This large garden pond, positioned to benefit from the natural water course, also attracts birdlife.

BELOW: A pond in pictures.

1 Dig the pond the desired shape, sloping the sides at a 45° angle.

2 Line the pond, fill, allow to settle for one week, then trim the edges with bricks, rocks or paving slabs.

3 Three months later and the pond is the showpiece of the garden.

A pond in pictures

1

2

3

Bringing the pond to life

You can buy a small range of aquatic plants at major garden centres, or visit a nursery that specialises in them for a much wider choice. The latter will also often sell fish and hardware such as pumps, filters and fountains. It is usually better to grow aquatic plants in containers sunk into the water than to plant them in soil on the bottom. As well as flowering plants that appear above the surface, you should also establish some underwater, oxygenating plants. These release oxygen into the water, which is taken up by the fish.

ABOVE: *Iris laevigata* 'Variegata'. Both flowers and foliage are attractive. The blue-violet blossoms begin to appear in late spring.

BELOW: An impressive, spray-covered orb is an imaginative addition to this secluded pond.

Fish add visual interest and keep the pond free of mosquitoes and other insect pests. They will need shelter from the sun, and while clusters of pots of aquatic plants will provide some, it's a good idea to build additional 'caves' for them from bricks or stone.

Plants for ponds

A lovely aquatic plant is the pickerel (*Pontederia cordata*), which has a vertical shape with its slim stems carrying spear-pointed leaves and blue-purple flower heads. It is a hardy perennial which requires

little attention. Beside this, place a potted water-lily, whose horizontal growth habit will give balance and contrast. There are many different species of water-lilies (*Nymphaea*), which could be chosen. Pondlilies (*Nuphar*), with their globular blooms, are a good alternative for moving water.

Water plantains (*Alisma plantago-aquatica*), with their bright green foliage and pink and white flowers, are suitable for the margins of both formal and wildlife ponds. Species such as *Azolla* add interest, as they will form a mat of soft, leafy foliage, although they should be thinned from time to time. These are small free-floating ferns that propagate readily, and you need only a few plants to quickly cover a pond sur-face. Probably the most unusual floating plant available is the water soldier (*Stratiotes aloides*), the foliage of which resembles the top of a pineapple, and is offset by cream, papery flowers.

Special aquatic planting compost is available for water plants, but good-quality garden soil is just as good. You can feed plants with slow-release fertiliser pellets.

For shallow water or boggy soil

Pictured on this page is a selection of plants that can be grown either in constantly wet soil or in water up to 15 cm deep.

ABOVE LEFT: Pickerel rush (*Pontederia cordata*). Originating from the marshes of North and South America, this plant is grown for its magnificent colourful flowers and distinctive foliage. It flourishes at the margins of a pond in full sunlight and is happiest in 25–30 cm of water.

ABOVE: Marsh marigold (*Caltha palustris*). A native of the far northern hemisphere, this brilliant spring bloomer is best suited to cool, southern gardens. It may grow up to 60 cm tall. There is a double variety as well.

CENTRE LEFT: Reedmace (*Typha* spp). Only for the large pond, rushes can grow to 2 m and spread rapidly. However, where space permits, they look magnificent and provide good shelter for both fish and birds. There are smaller members of this genus as well.

BOTTOM LEFT: Monkey musk (*Mimulus variegatus*). Better in constantly boggy soil than in water, this and other *Mimulus* flower for months during the late spring and summer. Where successful, they'll usually re-seed themselves. Best in frost-free gardens.

For deep water

These plants (see this page and overleaf) require 45–60 cm of water, although some can grow in depths of up to a metre.

Water hazards

Some water plants have the potential to become choking weeds if they are allowed to grow out of control. By using containers for marginal plants, you will prevent them from spreading into each other and make control much easier. Floating plants, too, can be invasive, so think carefully before introducing them.

Growth of algae will soon make a pond in full sun look like a pool of motor oil. Now, while algae is not harmful to plants and fish actually eat it, it is unsightly and obscures your view into the water. It can be controlled chemically, although we don't recommend this when a good balance of water plants will do a similar job for you naturally. Excluding any areas of shallow water around the margins of the pond, you should aim to have one third of the surface area covered with foliage (either floating or held erect) when the plants are fully grown. In addition, grow nine submerged oxygenating plants for every square metre of surface. It is not necessary to spread them evenly over the floor of the pool; simply use that number of plants and position them as you wish.

ABOVE: The yellow-fringed water-lily (*Nymphoides peltata*).

LEFT: These fish are in perfect health due to the natural balance of plants with water.

RIGHT: The symmetrical lily pond, complete with ornamental statue, adds an air of elegance to this garden.

CENTRE RIGHT: Well sited at the base of a rock garden, this lily pond cools and humidifies what would otherwise be a very hot spot. Algae in the water, though not harmful to either fish or plants, looks unsightly in excess. Submerged oxygenating plants will help control its growth.

BELOW: This small raised pond with its water-lilies provides variety in the garden.

BELOW RIGHT: Water-lily (*Nymphaea* spp).

LEFT: An old galvanised wash tub makes an interesting water feature, with the umbrella grass (*Cyperus* spp), white water-lily and red-leafed *Caladium* making a delightful arrangement. However, the *Caladium* is not an aquatic plant and could only be considered an annual when grown like this. Water-lilies, too, would not be a long-term success in such a small container.

Leave them in their pots

It is sensible to grow water plants in pots (plastic will hold up better) or proprietary planting baskets, set on bricks to bring them up to the required height.

The following are but a small selection of the plants you can choose for your pond:

1 Water-lily (*Nymphaea* spp). Water-lilies are probably the most desired of all water plants. There is a vast range of sizes and colours to choose from. All species will grow in large tubs and need plenty of room to spread their leaves.

2 Water fringe (*Nymphoides peltata*). Suitable for growing in deep water, this plant is similar in appearance to a small water-lily and produces masses of floating, heart-shaped leaves. During summer, bright yellow, fringed flowers appear.

3 Dwarf pond lily (*Nuphar minimum*). This pond lily can be grown in a tub or small pond. It has leathery floating leaves and produces small, globular yellow flowers on tall stems.

4 Yellow flag (*Iris pseudacorus*). Yellow flag will grow in moist soil or water up to 30 cm deep. It has tall, narrow leaves and bright yellow blooms.

Water-lilies

Beautiful water-lilies are easier to grow than you might think.

When gardeners seek plants for their newly-built ponds, water-lilies are usually uppermost in their minds. And not surprisingly, for these striking, sweetly scented flowers are

---

Water-loving plants at a glance

These can be grown with roots immersed:
- Asiatic water iris (*Iris laevigata*)
- Sweet galingale (*Cyperus longus*)
- Arrowhead (*Sagittaria sagittifolia*)
- Water fringe (*Nymphoides peltata*)
- Water forget-me-not (*Myosotis palustris*)
- Pondlily (*Nuphar* spp.)
- Water plantain (*Alisma plantago-aquatica*)
- Water-lily (*Nymphaea* spp.)

These can be grown in surrounding soil:
- Goat's beard (*Aruncus dioicus*)
- *Euphorbia palustris*
- *Hosta crispula*
- Siberian iris (*Iris sibirica*)
- Creeping jenny (*Lysimachia nummularia*)
- Yellow musk (*Mimulus luteus*)

among the loveliest of aquatic plants. They produce beautiful blooms that range in size from 5 cm across to 30 cm. All of them need full sun all day to flower well, and all need at least a square metre of water surface per plant. They can be grown in very large tubs, but are more suited to ponds. Moreover, they like still water to flourish, not moving.

Growing water-lilies

In tropical climates, water-lilies flower throughout the year, but in cooler areas flowering is confined to the warmer months. The more exotic tropical types can be grown in northern climes, but only under glass. Cool-climate water-lilies will die back in the autumn and can be left in the pond over winter. If in a shallow pool, the water should be drained off, their crowns protected with straw and the pool covered with plastic sheet to keep off rain. All water-lilies are gross feeders and need rich soil.

Plant enough water-lilies to cover a third of the surface of your pond. The leaves will block sunlight from the water, preventing the growth of algae. It's not wise to include a splashing fountain, as moving water will restrict the plants' growth.

Raise a few goldfish in your lily pond. They'll gobble up any mosquito eggs and other aquatic insect pests, as well as adding an interesting touch of wildlife to the garden.

Step-by-step planting guide

Follow the steps and photographs below to bring the beauty of water-lilies to your pond.

1 Fill a large pot with good-quality soil or special aquatic planting compost. Hollow out a good-sized planting hole.

2 Set the roots into the hole with the crown just above soil level. Plant as quickly as possible.

3 Hold the plant in position and bury its roots with soil. If soil isn't fertile, add fertiliser.

4 Sprinkle a 2-cm layer of fine gravel on top to keep soil in place and prevent fish from disturbing it.

5 Cut the leaves right back to the crown and place the pot on the floor of the pond. Within a few days fresh foliage will appear on the surface.

6 Blooms appear in less than six weeks as a rule. Cool-climate water-lilies come in white, pink, red, yellow and soft apricots; tropical lilies include vivid blues and violets.

1

2

3

4

5

6

Cascades

Water flowing from a cascade will greatly increase the impact of your pond. A sloping garden is well suited to a cascade, but you can have an effective one on a flat plot, too, as long as you keep the scheme low and wide so that it looks natural. Stones can be placed at the edges of each fall for a more attractive appearance and to protect the lining from the constant force of the water. Cascades don't have to look natural, though. Geometric formal pools, built above ground and connected by wide falls, can be striking and ideal for inclusion around entertaining areas.

Selecting the site

Choose the site for your cascade carefully. The water will have to be recirculated continuously, with only occasional topping up to compensate for evaporation. That means an electric pump. Pumps need power to run, but don't let proximity be the overriding consideration. It is better that your cascade looks as if it belongs than to place it in an improbable place that is handy to a power supply. Set water features low down, for that is where water is normally found.

Each level of a stepped cascade should have a vertical drop of at least 150 mm, although a fall of up to a metre can be very effective.

But remember, the higher the lift, the smaller the volume of water a pump can handle. Flexible vinyl tubing can be used to transport water from the bottom to the top of the cascade.

What to get

Two types of pumps are available – submersible and surface – but for most garden installations, submersibles are cheaper, easier to install, quieter and able to move a sufficient volume of water. Submersibles range in price depending on capacity. They must be supplied by an armoured cable buried at least 600 mm below ground level.

ABOVE: This pond, set in low-lying ground and bordered on one side by a rocky outcrop, looks like a natural waterhole – and it's a haven for wildlife.

RIGHT: How a cascade works.

1 Large flat rock as a pouring lip.

2 Siting pump under last fall prevents unwanted cross-currents.

3 Pool liner ends above the water level.

4 Pipe laid underground from pump directly to top pool.

5 Stones.

6 Outlet.

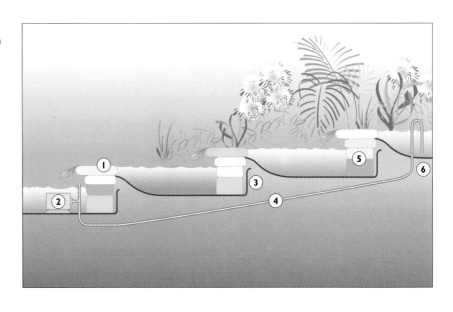

Low-voltage models supplied by transformers are simpler to install and safer, but less powerful. In general, pumps cost little to run.

Prefabricated pools are priced according to size. For a cascade, you'll need several purpose-made elements. Kits including the pump and piping are available.

Cascade mechanics

A submersible pump with a transformer is the recommended choice, but as its name suggests, it must be fully submerged at all times. Choose one of a suitable capacity to lift the desired volume of water to the desired height – the supplier will be able to help you here. Place your pump so that the length of pipe between the upper and lower pools is as short as possible. Avoid placing the pump at the end of the pool opposite the cascade, as this creates currents that cloud and cool the water to the detriment of fish and some plants. If not using prefabricated pools, be sure to lay a sturdy pool liner. Concrete is not recommended, as it cracks easily, leading to leaks.

ABOVE: A fountain adds real sparkle to this garden pond. You can buy a recirculating pump with a fountain attachment that lets you adjust the height of the spray to your liking.

ABOVE LEFT: A cascade of less than 15 cm adds interest and music to a large still pond. The 'stream' bed is flat so only a relatively small volume of water is needed to cover it completely.
A few river stones help create that babbling sound.

ABOVE: Water from the upper pond overflows into the lower pond, where a recirculating pump sends it back through a hose hidden among the rocks. Goldfish and water plants help create a serene and peaceful effect.

RIGHT: Fountains can be the focal point of a water system and add elegance to your garden.

RIGHT: A sloping block can be the perfect place to build a cascade.

BELOW: Stepped cascades can work with a minimum of fall. But the wider each cascade, the greater the volume of water and the larger the size of pump needed. Smaller falls look wider.

Garden Enhancements

Once the core features of your garden are in place, you can look at adding furniture to your relaxation areas. An elegant outdoor setting completes the picture in a courtyard or patio and can add a welcoming touch for coffee or a casual lunch. For many people, their outdoor entertaining area needs to accommodate tables and seating for barbecues.

Whether your needs are substantial or minimal, it's often best to design furniture especially to suit your deck or patio. In some cases, a fixed bench allows for more efficient seating, especially in smaller areas. Cantilevered seats can provide an attractive perimeter to a deck as well as taking advantage of the best positions for sun and shade. In other cases, the seating style may be informal, and an elegant low table will be the perfect match for your benches.

The following pages include plans for a table and bench unit, deck benches and low tables. By selecting appropriate timber and finishes, you can design and build these features to match the style of your pergola, deck or patio.

As well as eating outdoors, you can, of course, cook outdoors. If your entertaining plans include a barbecue, you might find that one especially constructed for your garden is more appealing. Two styles are included in this chapter.

Another delightful idea is to build a seat around your favourite tree. As well as being an attractive addition to a garden, a tree seat can allow you to sit in comfort in the midst of your garden and enjoy its tranquillity.

A cosy, separate seating area can be constructed on the edge of a deck. Besides offering an efficient use of space, the seating effectively screens the view of the garden beyond and incorporates flower boxes – bringing colour and greenery right to where you sit.

Patio setting

Make the most of your outdoor living area with this handsome furniture, pictured below. It has been designed to fit into a narrow space – although it would look great in any garden. The fixed seat may be bolted to a handrail, while the table and bench can be shifted to follow the sun. And you don't need to be a master craftsman to build it. Just choose good-quality timber – we used western red cedar for its rich colour and resilience, but treated pine would do – and follow our simple techniques for joining and recessing screws to achieve a really professional look. Rounding the visible edges is another detail that makes all the difference. If you like, adapt the dimensions to suit your needs, but make sure you read the instructions thoroughly before you begin work.

Making the table

Cut out the top supports, feet, legs and crosspiece to the lengths specified in the materials list, opposite. To give the table a stylish finish, taper the top supports and feet to 60 mm deep at each end, leaving a level section 100 mm wide in the centre on which to butt the leg. Round the edges before assembly.

BELOW: All the ingredients for enjoying outdoor living – a bench, a roomy table and a long fixed seat.

Mortise and tenon joints

These require patience, but will pay dividends, providing tough, tidy and accurate joints. Cut 100 mm tenons at both ends of the two legs by marking out a 100 x 25 mm rectangle in the middle of the end of the timber and sawing with the grain to a depth of 100 mm. You will need to clamp the timber to your workbench to hold it steady. Then saw 25 mm in from the two sides to remove the two blocks of waste timber. To make the corresponding mortises, mark a 100 x 25 mm rectangle on the top and bottom of each of the top supports and feet. Then, using a 20-mm chisel, cut the 25-mm-wide cavities.

For the crosspiece, make the tenons 100 mm long and allow them to protrude 25 mm through

Materials				
Item	Material	Length (mm)	No.	Order
Top supports	100 x 75 western red cedar (WRC)	750	2	1 @ 1.5 m
Feet	100 x 75 mm WRC	600	2	1 @ 1.2 m
Legs	100 x 75 mm WRC	660	2	1 @ 1.4 m
Crosspiece	100 x 75 mm WRC	1400	1	1 @ 1.4 m
Top slats	100 x 50 mm WRC	2000	8	8 @ 2 m
Fixings: 65-mm brass screws; PVA glue; 13-mm dowel.				

the legs. Cut the mortise cavity into the table leg, 500 mm from one end so that the crosspiece is closer to the table top than to the ground. Glue and slot the frame together.

Cut the top slats as specified in the materials list and round the edges. Fix the slats to the frame,

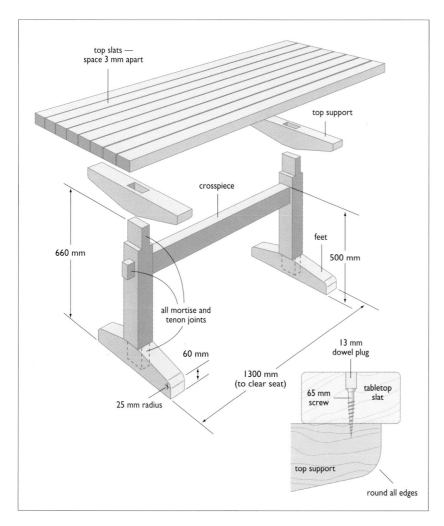

LEFT: Construction details for the table.

RIGHT: Generous-sized timber components make a sturdy and pleasing design.

385 mm from their ends, using 65-mm screws recessed by about a quarter of their length into the slat. Start by drilling a 13-mm-diameter hole in the centre of the slat, then continue with a pilot hole for the screw. Insert the screw and plug the hole with a 13-mm dowel cut roughly to size. Sand it flush with the surface. Space the slats evenly with the aid of a piece of 3-mm hardboard or plywood.

Making the bench

Cut seat supports, legs, feet and crosspiece to the lengths specified in the materials list. Also, see the diagrams on bench construction. Seating is always much more comfortable if it is dished, so saw the top surfaces of the T-supports at a slight angle, dropping 10–15 mm towards the centre. (Note that the mid-support is turned so that the 100-mm surface is uppermost.) Taper the ends of all horizontal pieces as for the table. Round edges before assembly.

Lay supports, legs, feet and crosspiece out in the order in which they'll be fitted in the bench. This will show you where to cut the halving joints on the inner faces. Form the halving joints by making two saw cuts 100 mm apart and half the depth of the timber. Chisel out the waste between the cuts. Repeat for the adjoining section of timber so that you can neatly fit the two pieces together. Assemble and glue all main frame pieces in this way.

Cut seat slats and edgings (as per the materials list) and round the edges. Attach seating slats as for the table, using 65-mm screws and plugging with 13-mm dowels, spacing them 3 mm apart. Screw the

Materials				
Item	Material	Length (mm)	No.	Order
Seat supports	100 x 50 mm western red cedar (WRC)	300	3	1 @ 2.7 m
Feet	100 x 50 mm WRC	350	2	
Legs	100 x 50 mm WRC	380	2	
Crosspiece	100 x 50 mm WRC	1640	1	1 @ 1.7 m
Seat slats	50 x 50 mm WRC	2000	6	6 @ 2 m
Seat edging	75 x 50 mm WRC	2000	2	2 @ 2 m
Fixings: 65-mm brass screws; PVA glue; 13-mm dowel.				

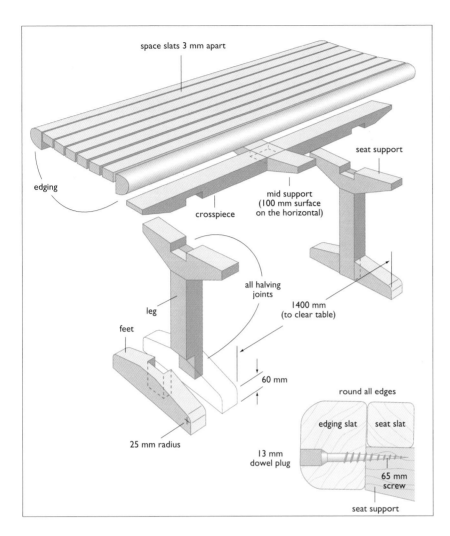

space slats 3 mm apart

edging

crosspiece

mid support
(100 mm surface
on the horizontal)

seat support

all halving
joints

leg

1400 mm
(to clear table)

feet

60 mm

25 mm radius

13 mm
dowel plug

round all edges

edging slat

seat slat

65 mm
screw

seat support

LEFT: Construction details for the bench.

BELOW: Dowel plugs hide screws, and the timbers are rounded for a smooth finish.

edging battens to the ends of the supports, again using 65-mm screws and 13-mm dowel plugs (see the diagram). Shape to a round profile with a power sander.

Making the fixed seat

You can suspend this seat from an existing handrail or build it from the ground up. Either way, the posts will need to be firmly anchored in 300 x 250 mm concrete footings. Unless you use stronger seat slats than those specified in the materials list, the posts should be about 860 mm apart.

Cut timber to the lengths given in the materials list. Angle the seat supports for comfort, dropping 10–15 mm towards the back. Taper one end of the support (as shown in the diagram) for a neat finish. Bolt

Materials				
Item	Material	Length (mm)	No.	Order
Posts	125 x 50 mm hardwood	1100	4	2 @ 2.4 m
Seat supports	100 x 50 mm hardwood	600	4	1 @ 2.4 m
Braces	100 x 50 mm hardwood	460	4	1 @ 2 m
Backrest/ seat slats	50 x 50 mm western red cedar (WRC)	3000	13	13 @ 3 m
Top rail	150 x 50 mm WRC	3000	1	1 @ 3 m
Front rail	100 x 75 mm WRC	3000	1	1 @ 3 m

Fixings: 125-mm bolts; 65-mm and 100-mm brass screws; PVA glue; 13-mm dowel.

the other end of the support to the concreted post. Place the brace in position and bolt the upper end to the seat support; then attach the lower end to the post with a 100-mm screw.

To make the backrest more comfortable, saw the posts at an angle to a depth of about 200 mm from the top, as shown in the diagram. This enables you to recess the backrest slats. Round the edges of seat and backrest slats, and screw in place using 65-mm screws recessed to about a quarter of their length. Plug with 13-mm dowels. Space slats 3 mm apart.

Finally, screw the top rail to the post tops and the front rail to the seat supports, again using 65-mm screws and 13-mm dowel plugs. Sand the rails as shown below.

LEFT: The seat is fixed in concrete and may also be bolted to a handrail.

BELOW: Construction details for the fixed seat.

OPPOSITE: This table and bench unit can be easily moved to your favourite position in the garden. The use of round seat rails gives an informal effect.

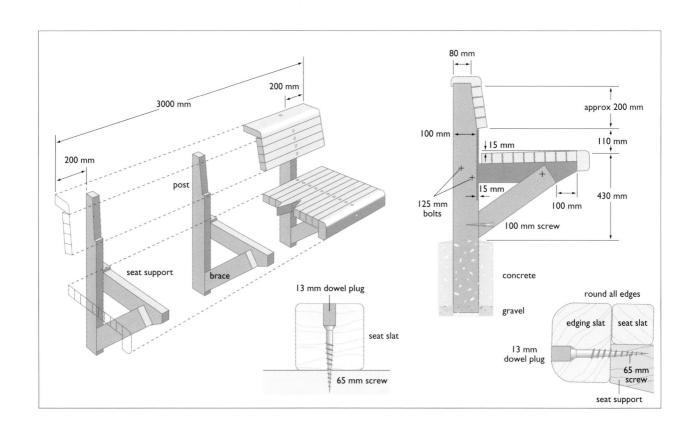

RIGHT: Construction details for the table, end view.

Table and bench unit

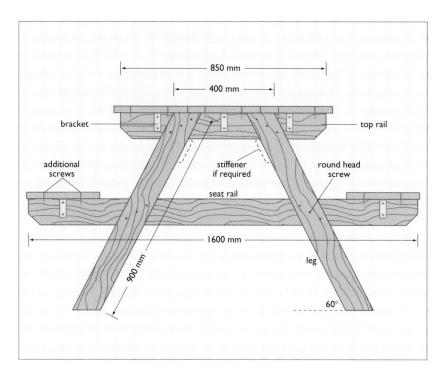

bracket — top rail

850 mm

400 mm

additional screws

stiffener if required

round head screw

seat rail

900 mm

1600 mm

leg

60°

This useful garden table and bench unit can be made from preservative-treated, planed pine. The timber requirements are: six legs (each 1000 x 100 x 38 mm); three top rails (each 900 x 100 x 50 mm); three seat rails (each 1800 x 100 x 50 mm); three top boards (each 2400 x 300 x 38 mm); and two seats (each 2400 x 300 x 38 mm).

Other requirements are: rust-proofed screws for making the frames (75-mm roundheads); 20 heavy-gauge, metal brackets (galvanised steel or brass); 25-mm rust-proofed screws to match; some 75-mm galvanised nails and 50-mm countersunk rust-proofed screws for fixing the slats.

Cut the six legs, top rails and seat rails to length. Lay the first set of legs in position and (with the nails) tack the top rail and seat rail in position. Check that the legs are at 60° to the rails. Drill pilot holes and drive three 75-mm screws into each joint as shown in the diagram. Remove the nails. Use this assembled frame as a template for the other two.

Fix metal brackets to the outer faces of the end frames and both sides of the middle frame. Place them to coincide with the centre of each top or seat board. Cut the seats and top boards to length.

Once the table has been assembled, leave it for a few weeks to allow time for timber shrinkage. Then, using the 25-mm countersunk screws, attach the top and seats to the rails.

Make sure you chamfer the edges and ends of each piece of timber as you assemble this table. Finally, sand and finish the timber to your taste.

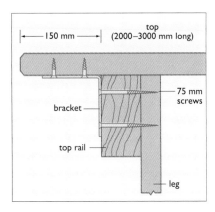

ABOVE: Construction details for the table top, end detail.

RIGHT: Take some aged hardwood planks and a little creativity and you soon have eye-catching outdoor furniture with real rustic charm.

BELOW: A rustic, solid table-and-bench setting provides the perfect accompaniment to this private courtyard. Filtered light, the trellis and a flowering climber complete the mood.

Tree seat

This hexagonal seat will be the perfect spot to relax on a summer afternoon. If the tree is still a sapling, make sure the fully-grown trunk will fit within the 600-mm central opening. If the trunk is, or is likely to become, larger than that, you will need to enlarge the diameter of the seat and make the slats longer.

BELOW: A tree seat is a practical addition to a garden, providing seating in the shade – and offering the perfect setting for reading or just enjoying your garden.

Making a tree seat

1 Establish the position of the bench. Working from the tree, mark out two equilateral triangles with 1575-mm sides to form a star with six points. The correct angle at each corner will be 60°. The opposite pairs of points will be 1850 mm apart; these points are where the front edge of each of the six supports will rest at ground level (marked 'check point' on the diagram).

2 Cut the support components (see materials list). Use a jigsaw to shape curves on the cross-support and rear support (for the seat).

3 Assemble the six support frames. Use 175-mm bolts to attach two cross-supports to each rear and front support. Fix the bottom ends of the front and rear supports together, using 100-mm galvanised coach screws.

4 Dig 400-mm-deep holes at the six points of the marked-out star. Treat the lower portions of the supports with preservative and stand them in the holes so that the check points are at the points of the star. Use lengths of scrap timber to prop up the supports, nailing them as necessary.

5 Lay a length of timber to one side of the tree trunk and check that opposing pairs of support frames are parallel and an equal distance from the trunk. Use a spirit level to check that they are upright and the cross-supports level.

6 Fill the six holes with concrete and allow at least 24 hours before removing the props.

7 Measure between the supports as placed and make any necessary adjustments to the slat lengths. Then cut the slats to size. Trial-fit slats between one back and seat support to another. Use a sliding bevel gauge to determine and mark the appropriate angle, measuring from the centre-line of each frame. Cut with a tenon saw.

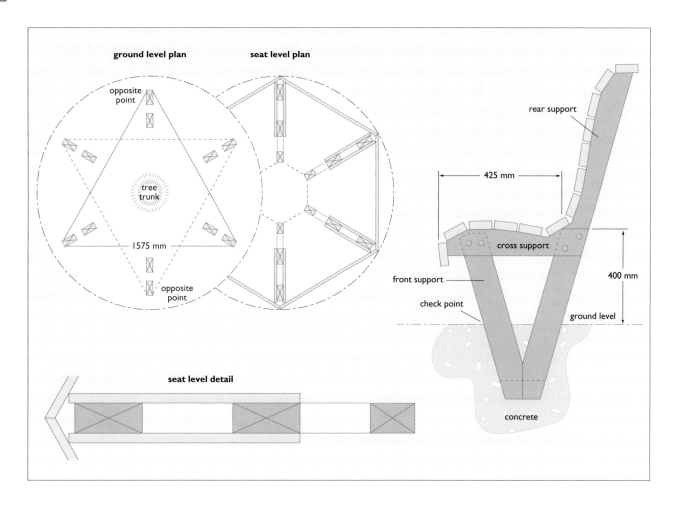

8 Fit the front seat slats and top back slats all around first, cutting the ends to the correct angle as you go. These will brace the whole structure. Now space the remaining slats evenly, as shown in the diagram, bevelling the edges where necessary.

9 Finish the seat with paint or varnish as desired.

Materials			
Component	Treated pine (mm)	Length or size (mm)	No.
Front supports	100 x 50	750	6
Rear supports	100 x 50	1300	6
Cross supports	100 x 50	525	12
Seat slats	50 x 25	1020	12
		1010	6
		1000	6
		950	6
		850	6
		750	6
Back slats	20 x 25	600	48

Other: twenty-four 175 x 10 mm galvanised bolts, nuts and washers; six 100-mm coach screws; 50 mm galvanised lost-head nails; two bags of concrete; preservative; paint or varnish to finish.

ABOVE: Construction details for a tree seat.

This plan is designed to accommodate a tree trunk with a diameter no more than 500 mm. If your tree is bigger, adjust the plan accordingly. The plan is based on two intersecting triangles, with a seat support at each of the six points. When laying out the seat, work from the six check points – these are the points where the front of each support will rest at ground level.

Deck benches

Construct some comfortable benches on your deck and you'll be surprised at how much more often you use it. Place them so that they face an attractive view or allow you to take advantage of a sunny spot. And choose a style to suit your deck: a backless bench will block less of the view from a ground-level deck, but on a raised deck, you can incorporate the back of a bench into the railing. To achieve an integrated look, use the same timber as the railings.

These simple cantilevered seats form a little nook, a perfect spot for conversation or just relaxing alone. They also provide a neat finish to the edge of the deck, dividing it from the open garden area beyond.

Planning the bench

Plan the size of your bench carefully, using the dimensions given overleaf under 'Standard bench dimensions'. The height of the back can be adjusted so that it doesn't block a view, or to provide either privacy or shelter from wind.

Tip

- If you want a clear finish on timber for outdoor structures, use a good-quality marine varnish. Other types of clear lacquer don't handle an exterior environment well, and you will often need to replace them.

An open, slatted construction lets air circulate and discourages water from forming pools.

You can secure benches to the same posts that support the deck or fasten uprights to joists. They can also be fixed to the decking. For safety, be sure to use bolts, not nails, at all critical structural points. However, benches need not be permanently attached to the deck;

freestanding benches built of the same materials as the deck can be moved around for different purposes. Those on high decks should, of course, be butted against a firmly attached railing for safety's sake.

When planning your benches, think about how they could be integrated with other structures. For example, two benches and a table could be built in booth style, or a trellis or pergola could be added above the bench.

Standard bench dimensions

A bench seat should be 400–450 mm wide and 400–450 mm from the ground. About 600 mm of seat width should be allowed for each person. The back, ideally, should be 400–450 mm high. For comfort, cant the bank of the bench at about

BELOW LEFT: Building a deck bench

1 Taper off one corner of two 300 x 25 mm timbers and attach them to both sides of a post, nailing a short 100 x 50 mm piece between them to support the leg assembly. Repeat for other supports. To prevent rust, use hot-dipped galvanised nails for outdoor projects.

2 For the legs, assemble three-sided 100 x 50 mm boxes. Slip these into the back support, and nail them to the cross-braces and deck. Also nail through the 300 x 25 mm pieces into the 100 x 50 mm boxes. Check that everything is plumb, level and square.

3 For comfort, round off the front edges of the 100 x 50 mm seat and back slats with a plane or router. Your timber supplier may be able to do this for you. For seating, use only good-quality timber and seal it well. Careful finishing is important when making benches and other seats, as only a comfortable bench will be a useful addition to your outdoor furniture.

4 Nail back slats to each 300 x 25 mm piece. Nail seat slats to the 100 x 50 mm legs. Countersink nail heads so that they cannot snag clothing. Cap the back with a 150 x 25 or 150 x 50 mm timber to protect cut ends from moisture which could cause rot. If you prefer, screw fix the slats for greater security, but be sure to use brass screws and countersink them below the surface.

Building a deck bench

1

2

3

4

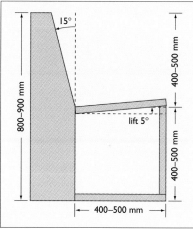

15° and lift the front of the seat by about 5°. This will also stop water forming puddles on the seat.

A comfy corner

This attractive and all-purpose bench is just the thing to make use of a spare corner of a deck or porch. It is simple to construct and its size can be adjusted to suit the space you have. Do, however, keep in mind the standard bench dimensions specified.

ABOVE: Now you can enjoy the sandpit, too! This perimeter bench makes a comfortable place for parents to sit while children play.

LEFT: Bench dimensions, showing ideal proportions and rake.

Use 150-mm timber for the beam if you are spanning more than 1200 mm, and be sure to insert struts of 75 x 25 mm timber at 400-mm centres. For the seating slats, you can also use 75 x 25 mm timber. It's best to leave 5-mm spaces between them to allow water to drain away.

Use a router to round off the edges of the slats, then sandpaper them to remove splinters and rough areas that could catch clothes. Paint or stain the wood as desired.

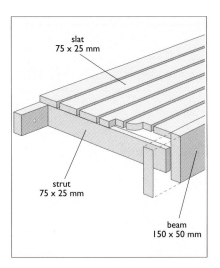

slat
75 x 25 mm

strut
75 x 25 mm

beam
150 x 50 mm

LEFT: Design of bench seat, showing timber specifications.

BELOW: This simple bench is just the way to fill in an awkward corner. Once it's there, you'll be surprised how often you use it.

Mosaic table

Geometric patterns of varnished timber slats give an inlaid appearance to this attractive table. If you want, you can build matching benches. Just use construction techniques similar to those given for the table and see the information on planning your bench.

The table measures approximately 1.2 x 0.9 m and is 425 mm high. It requires 1.8 m of 75 x 75 mm, 8.5 m of 75 x 50 mm and 26 m of 50 x 25 mm planed western red cedar.

Making the table

1   Glue and nail mitred 75 x 50 mm battens (table top sides and ends) to form table top's frame.

ABOVE AND DETAIL: This beautiful table will provide the finishing touch for your patio. It is simple to make – but test-assemble the slats before you start building so you can check that the components are the correct length.

2 Cut four 75 x 75 mm uprights to size to form the table legs. Screw one upright into each corner of the frame, countersinking the screw heads and then plugging the holes.

3 Install the 75 x 50 mm stretcher inside the frame. Strengthen with 75 x 50 mm side and diagonal cross-members, mitring corners where it is necessary.

4 Mitre corners on four 50 x 25 mm (edge slats) to form the outer frame of the table top. Cut the other 50 x 25 mm slats to size and, if desired, stain and varnish them.

5 Assemble the table top, starting with the other 50 x 25 mm slats and working towards the centre. Glue and nail the slats to the base, spacing them about 5 mm apart. Countersink the nail heads and fill the holes. Finally, chamfer and finish as required.

Materials			
Component	Size (mm)	Length (mm)	No.
Legs	75 x 75	400	4
Table top sides	75 x 50	1180	2
Table top ends	75 x 50	890	2
Stretcher	75 x 50	1100	1
Crossmember (side)	75 x 50	385	2
Crossmember (diagonal)	75 x 50	510	4
Slats (side edge)	50 x 25	1200	2
Slats (end edge)	50 x 25	914	2
Slats	50 x 25		

Other: wood plugs; glue; screws; nails; wood putty; stain (if required); varnish.

Tip

- When using glue on outdoor structures, use epoxy resin as it won't break down when it rains. Follow the manufacturer's instructions carefully and don't mix too much together at one time.

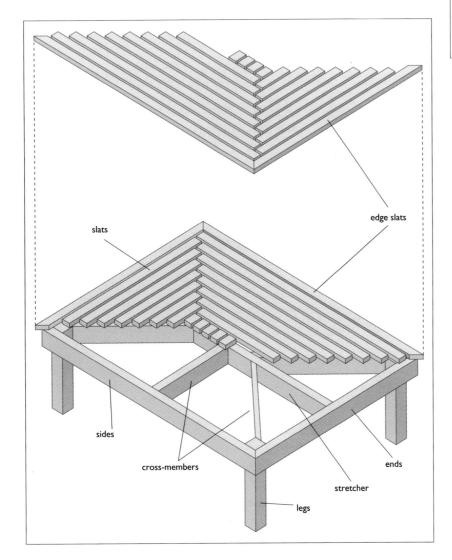

LEFT: Construction details for a geometric table.

The diagonal cross-members support the slats, which are both glued and nailed to the table frame for extra strength.

Simple barbecue

A good barbecue is basic to the enjoyment of outdoor living. It should be located within easy reach of the kitchen and a shady outdoor eating area, but away from foliage that could catch fire.

Building a simple barbecue

You don't need to be an expert to build a simple barbecue; just remember to plan it carefully and to check constantly for horizontal and vertical levels. We used a curved back wall for extra interest, but you can follow the same steps to make a square design.

Planning your barbecue

Choose the bricks carefully. A barbecue is a small structure, so bricks without a lot of contrasting markings will be the most suitable.

Plan the size of the barbecue on paper. This one was planned around a prefabricated hotplate and grate. It comes with its own supporting angle-iron frame. The unit measures 660 x 480 mm, and you will have to allow 215 mm of brickwork outside that. We had to make some of the mortar joints as wide as 15 mm to expand the structure sufficiently to fit the hotplate unit. When laying the bricks, adding a cap of plasticiser to the mix will make the mortar more workable.

Materials

300 quality bricks,
70 common bricks,
fine builders' sand,
cement,
plasticiser,
hotplate,
grate,
angle-iron frame,
four lengths of 25 x 6 mm flat steel, 75 mm long,
rubble and cement for infill

RIGHT: This simple barbecue can be made with a round or square back, whichever style appeals to you.

BELOW: Building a simple barbecue

1   Lay out the area and dig it out to a depth of one brick. Set common bricks into a mortar bed. For the mortar use six parts fine builders' sand and one part Portland cement.

2   Cover the foundation course with mortar and smooth over. Add water, this will make the bonding of the mortar stronger with the next layer of bricks.

3   Cut bricks if your design has a curved back. Lay the bricks on grass or a bed of sand and cut with a bolster chisel and club hammer.

I

2

3

4

5

6

7

8

9

4   Using good quality bricks, set out the first course as shown above, filling wedge-shaped joints with mortar. Scrape joints off flush with bricks.

5   Check the level as you proceed. It is important to keep the courses level right from the beginning.

6   Continue upwards until there are seven courses, laying bricks over joints. Avoid running joints, as they will result in a weaker structure and are liable to collapse.

7   Fill the centre with rubble or common bricks. Finish with concrete to make the fire platform. Use a mix of four parts combined aggregate (ballast) and one part Portland cement.

10

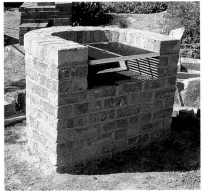

11

8   Smooth the platform. Lay two courses of double thickness brickwork around the edge of the platform, checking regularly that the iron frame will fit.

9   Ensure that the bricks on the inside of the curve of these two courses are neatly cut as they will be visible behind the fire.

10   Lay mortar for a third course. At this point set lengths of flat steel (75 x 6 mm) into the mortar. These will eventually take the barbecue frame.

11   Finish with a row of header bricks to trim and strengthen the structure. Your barbecue is now ready to enjoy.

Complete barbecue setting

This well-designed barbecue setting includes a handy plate rack, large storage cupboard and generous worktop. These features will make barbecuing easier, especially when entertaining.

The barbecue is built from bricks, with a concrete footing and steel bars for the grid. Don't cut the bars until after you've built the barbecue – so you can be sure they'll fit. The cupboard has a timber frame and doors, while the worktop is tiled for ease of use and cleaning. You can use 12-mm exterior-grade plywood for the top instead of cement sheet.

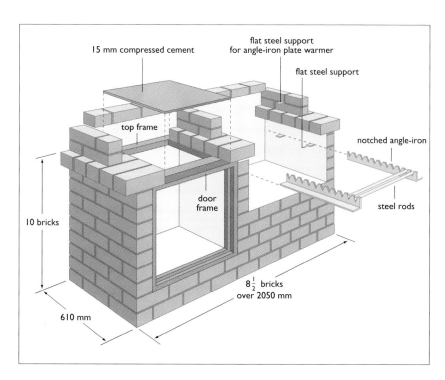

ABOVE LEFT: An attractive addition to the garden, this barbecue setting is big enough for any party of family or friends. It is also easy to use, with the built-in storage cupboard and tiled worktop.

LEFT: Construction details for the complete barbecue setting. You'll need some bricklaying ability and basic carpentry, as well as tiling skills to build this unit.

Materials

250 exterior bricks
40 common bricks
two bags of mortar
one roll of 90-mm-wide mesh
    reinforcement
three wall ties
six 100-mm lengths of 25-mm
    flat steel
two 590-mm lengths and a 960-
    mm length of 38-mm angle
    iron
six 25-mm M8 bolts, nuts and
    washers
nine 12-mm mild steel bars,
    approx. 960 mm long
3 m of 50 x 25 mm western red
    cedar
3 m of 25 x 25 mm western red
    cedar
600 x 900 mm sheet of 15-mm
    compressed cement or 12-mm
    exterior-grade plywood
7.5 m of cedar t&g boards
two door knobs
four 100-mm T-hinges
one square metre of tiles

Building the barbecue

1

2

6

7

1   Use pegs and string to peg out
    the site to 2200 x 760 mm and
    dig the area free of grass.
    Check that the site is level and
    dig out or fill if necessary.

2   Prepare ready-mixed mortar,
    or mix one part cement, one
    part lime and six parts sand. As
    an alternative to the lime, add
    one cap of plasticiser to make it
    easier to work.

3   Lay the first course in a mortar
    bed and tap to achieve a level.
    Use one row of bricks around
    the outline and one for the
    partition between fire and
    cupboard.

4   Run a strip of wire reinforce-
    ment mesh under the next
    course. Check for level. The
    wire reinforcement is an impor-
    tant part of the structure as it
    bonds the structure into
    a single block of masonry.

5   Stagger the courses so that
    each brick bridges a joint.
    Where necessary, cut bricks
    (on grass or sand) with a wide
    bolster chisel and a club
    hammer.

6   Use wall ties at the junction
    points every third course to
    help bond the structure
    together. Lay only two courses

for the front wall of the cupboard and five for the front of
the fireplace.

7   As you go, build up the corners
    to a couple of courses so that
    you can use the corner bricks
    to keep the courses straight.
    Run a level line between the
    corners, using spare bricks to
    hold it in place.

8   Add another strip of wire
    reinforcement mesh above the
    mortar on top of the seventh
    course of bricks. Lay an eighth
    course of bricks, then another
    mortar course on top. Smooth
    the mortar.

3

4

5

8

9

10

9 Set four 100 mm long, flat-steel supports on top of the eighth course. Place them across the wall so that they project inwards. They will support the notched angle-iron for the grill.

10 On the tenth course place bricks cross-wise across the end walls and partition to form projections. Include wall ties above the partition's projecting course.

11 Lay two or more courses of bricks in normal staggered bond along the back and part way along the end walls and partition. Include two flat steel plate-warmer supports

11

12

between the courses (see diagram). Add one more brick course along the back.

12 Fill in the bottom of the cupboard and fireplace with bricks

and mortar. Drill and bolt the angle-iron plate rack to the flat steel supports. Position the notched angle-iron and bars. You have now completed the basic structure.

Building the cupboard and worktop

Let the brickwork sit until the mortar is completely dry. Then you can begin work on the cupboard and worktop. Make the door frame by fitting together a 50 x 25 mm frame and then nailing 25 x 25 mm battens along the inner edges as a door stop. Cut the 25 x 25 mm battens so that their ends overlap (see the picture for Step 3).

To finish, add the extra lining board across the front of the tiles, above the door.

1   Sit the door frame in place to check that it will sit square within the brick opening.

2   Check that the top horizontal sits perfectly level, otherwise the worktop will slope.

3   Nail the frame together and then drill, plug and screw it in place. Check for square.

4   Make two doors using tongued-and-grooved boards with diagonal back braces. Ensure they fit.

5   Butt-joint 50 x 50 mm timbers to make the frame for the worktop. Place it in position to check the fit and then nail home.

6   Drill holes into the brickwork and screw the frame in place so that it rests on the door frame. Check for level as you go.

7   Cut the cement sheeting to fit the top frame and screw it in

place. Plan the number of tiles that will fit across the worktop. Cut the tiles to fit.

8   Start tiling at the front, laying tiles on a 10 mm bed of mortar against a flat edge. Wet the tiles to help the bonding process.

9   Cut tiles to fit against the back and sides. Use a straightedge, spirit level and a block or mallet to tap the tile surface flat.

10 Use mortar as grouting and to finish the edges. Clean the tiles thoroughly before the mortar dries on them. Your complete barbecue setting is now ready for action!

4

5

6

10

RIGHT: This deck, supported
by brick piers, uses a clever
innovation. One pier is extended
to incorporate a brick barbecue,
avoiding any intrusion into the
deck space.

Gardens for Special Purposes

Gardens are an intrinsic expression of personal taste and can provide the keen gardener with inspiration as well as purpose and fulfilment. For most people, plants represent the unifying and softening element in their design, and balance paths, paving and timber work.

Many factors apart from taste determine the type of garden you create and the plants that you choose. Your garden's micro-climate, soil and natural features will play a large part in determining what you can do. This chapter deals with ideas for special garden requirements, dictated by climate, soil and position. On the following pages you will find useful ideas for gardens in areas of low rainfall, by the sea and in the shade.

In many cases we inherit established gardens and adapt them to our own purposes. It's a good idea to spend time looking at what has flourished, even in a neglected garden. Thriving survivors can give you the clearest indication of what will work in your own garden plan, and an overgrown garden may yield a delight of established, self-seeding flowers.

On the following pages are suggestions and ideas for a wide range of garden styles and purposes: from colour themed and scented to oriental, low maintenance and container displays. In addition, a range of popular and useful gardens is featured – as well as encouragement to create a special area for children.

A path wanders through a delightfully carefree cottage garden, giving glimpses of colour and shaded nooks. The crab apples (*Malus floribunda*) are in full blossom and create a stunning counterpoint to the variety of greens, blue-greens and blues in the garden. The effect of spontaneous and uncontrived abundance disguises much careful planning behind the long-term growth of this garden.

Container gardening

With the ever-increasing array of containers from all over the world to choose from and a dazzling range of plants to fill them, it is hardly surprising that maintaining a mobile garden has become perhaps the most popular gardening activity. Millions of pots, window boxes and hanging baskets are planted up twice or even three times a year and as many again feature permanent planting. The benefits are plain to see. A trip to the local garden centre and ten minutes work can result in an instant eye catcher. There is no digging or weeding involved, although you do need to make a commitment to regular watering. It's no good expecting natural rainfall to provide for their needs, as even drought resistant succulents will benefit from a good soaking from a can or hose pipe.

BELOW: This dramatic bank of colour illustrates the impact a blend of foliage and flower can give in late summer and autumn. But nothing can outshine the glowing yellow, dark-centred daisies of *Rudbeckia* 'Sonora'.

Year-round containers

Almost anything can be grown in a container, from vegetables to size-able trees, so it is an opportunity missed to plan and plant for just ephemeral, seasonal colour and leave your pots lying empty through autumn and winter. Even hanging baskets can be a success in the winter if sited in a warm alcove, away from icy winds.

Planting in layers can work wonders in the winter and spring. Imagine bulbs growing up through a carpet of heather, backed by choice evergreens such as dwarf conifers and red-budded skimmia, giving a three-tier line up. By topping up with seasonal colour as it becomes available (primroses in March for example), the container never flags.

For summer, there are plenty of hyperactive performers that will bloom unceasingly until the first frosts. Busy lizzies, fibrous-rooted begonias and petunias are all great value for money and for permanent features, hostas, Japanese maples and dwarf ornamental grasses will give years of pleasure.

ABOVE: This window box looks a picture from outside the house, as well as from indoors. These delightful spring miniatures include pansies, white double daisies and dainty *Narcissus* 'Hawera'.

RIGHT: Bold foliage plants grown in large pots lend an exotic flavour to a paved courtyard.

Scented gardens

Smell, perhaps more than any other of the senses, has the power to conjure up images and moments from our past; that intoxicating perfume from angels' trumpets cutting through the balmy Mediterranean night air, or walking through a 'wall' of fruity, mock orange scent in a childhood back garden. Many gardeners will now only plant a rose or honeysuckle if it has a respectable perfume. There are plenty of plants with heady and sometimes unique perfumes. Trees, shrubs, climbers, annuals, bulbs and of course herbs can all play a part in creating a landscape overflowing with a potpourri of fragrances.

BELOW: Two arches have been joined to form a rustic centrepiece in this cottage-style garden. Rambling 'Albertine' roses ooze scent and are complemented by carpets of lavender and cotton lavender.

Planning for scent

Of course, there's no point in planting a dozen different scented plants, one for each month of the year, if, for example, in January the witch hazel is so far away from the house that it can neither be seen or smelt without a major expedition. However, in a pot by the house wall, it can be easily enjoyed and the spicy scent will drift indoors through an open window on sunny days. Other rewarding locations to savour perfume are alongside seats and around doorways. It's worth remembering that scent is heavier than air and will drift downhill and linger when trapped in hollows or against walls and fences.

Pungent foliage

Scented leaves have a major part to play. Some plants like lavender and choisya are blessed with scented leaves and flowers, but in order to release the essential oils contained in foliage it is necessary to squeeze or brush against them. It makes sense, therefore, to plant scented-leaved pelargoniums, lemon verbena and pineapple sage, for example, alongside a well-trafficked path where they will be disturbed as you pass. Alternatively, grow them together in a roomy pot alongside a seat where you can reach out and run your fingers through their leaves, or pick a few to float in a drink.

Plants for perfume

Acacia dealbata

Witch hazel

Lilies

Honeysuckle

Jasmine

Daphne lilac

Tobacco plants

Chocolate cosmos

Narcissus Jonquilla

Roses

ABOVE: A wicker basket can be crammed with pots of old-fashioned pinks and edged with lobelia. Use hay to disguise and steady the pots and position the basket on a table or beside a seat.

RIGHT: *Acacia dealbata* makes a lovely open-branched tree for a warm, sheltered spot where the scent of its fluffy flowers will fill the air in winter and spring.

Low maintenance gardens

The work-free garden is as impossible a dream as the house which never needs cleaning. The essence of a garden is that it is alive; its quiet rhythms of growth, burgeoning and decay are those of nature itself. Although gardening is good therapy, none of us wants to be a slave to our garden. It makes sense not to design any more work into it than we have time to do.

ABOVE: *Geranium ibericum* – a lush groundcover for sun or semi-shade.

BELOW: A wide range of plants, such as these heathers, can be planted through a weed-suppressing plastic membrane which is then disguised with a mulch of gravel.

Planning an easy-care garden

What are your expectations of what a garden should be? If your heart is set on lavish and constant displays of flowers, or if you shudder at the thought of a leaf out of place, you'll be spending a lot more time gardening than someone who is content with a mainly green garden, adorned with such flowers as and when their easy-care plants choose to produce them.

Garden work comes under two headings: the care that plants need to grow well, and what we might call garden housework – raking leaves, weeding and mowing the lawn. With forethought and planning you can reduce both of these chores to a minimum.

Infant gardens often need more attention – it's only as they begin to establish themselves that even the most carefully thought out 'low-maintenance' gardens earn their title.

Selecting easy-care plants

What is an easy-care plant, the kind sensible gardeners make the backbone of their plantings? Ideally, it should flourish with no more attention than you think it is worth. If it flourishes but bores you stiff, then don't grow it; but don't fall into the common gardener's mistake of equating rarity and difficulty with beauty. Remember that a plant that grows easily in another part of the country may not do well in yours, if your climate and soil are not to its liking.

Before you decide to grow any plant, find out whether it will flourish in your climate and soil. Ask if it needs regular watering or fertiliser, or spraying against common pests and diseases. Does it have to be pruned in order to look presentable, or to flower or fruit well? Is it likely to outgrow its allotted position, so that it will need constant cutting back? Misjudging the final size of plants is one of the commonest sources of unwanted work. Will it take over the garden? (Bamboo is the classic example.)

Does it make a mess, shedding leaves, bark or fruit where they'll be a nuisance? The importance you place on this depends to an extent on where you plan to plant – a rain of leaves can be allowed to fall among the shrubs where they'll make a mulch; you probably won't be so happy sweeping them off the patio. An edging of low ground-cover like *Pachysandra terminalis* is ideal to trap them.

ABOVE: Daffodils look superb naturalised in long grass especially when planted around silver birches or trees that blossom in the spring. Delay mowing until at least six weeks after the flowers have faded.

Keeping the weeds at bay

Of the general 'housework' jobs, weeding should not become too much of a burden if you get rid of the perennial nasties before you plant. After that mulching and dense planting should keep further invasions at bay.

However, perhaps the most effective way to control weeds is to spread a woven layer of black polythene that allows water through but is too fine to let weeds penetrate. Any planting is tucked in through cross-shaped slits made in the membrane. To conceal the membrane, a thick layer of chipped bark can be spread on top. Alternatively, pea gravel or chippings make a more attractive mulch.

Having a lawn

Lawn mowing, and its attendant trimming of the edges, is most people's pet hate. You could eliminate lawns altogether, and pave and gravel the places where you want to walk. Or you could lay the garden out as a woodland with much of it floored in leaves or bark, making extensive use of groundcovers. However, if children are to play and tumble, there's still no better surface than grass.

It's easy to get obsessive about the perfect lawn: keep it a simple shape with no difficult-to-get-at odd corners or wriggly curves; and don't clutter it with little beds to trim around. Don't put grass where it's too steep to mow comfortably; banks are best planted with shrubs or groundcovers.

Watch the junction of grass and groundcovers carefully; they'll invariably try to invade one another's space. Where you want grass sweeping right up to your plantings, make the plants knee-high shrubs, set densely together. Then you can tuck the mower under their outside branches, and mow under their overhang; and the added benefit is you won't have a visible edge to trim.

There are some excellent, hard-wearing dwarf strains of ryegrass available for seeding a lawn. However, although the finer,

OPPOSITE: The evergreen plants that create a shady canopy in this garden do not require much pruning, weeding or watering.

ABOVE: A massed planting of gazanias and *Lampranthus* need little in the way of care for a long season of beauty.

LEFT: Bluebells (*Hyacinthoides hispanicus*).

slower-growing grasses are more trouble to establish, you have to mow them only half as often.

Gardening in the city

This wonderfully casual garden (above) is about as close to the work-free garden as it's possible to get. Only five minutes from the city, it isn't large, but it could be three times the size without being any more demanding.

Originally there was a walnut tree, which the owner liked and kept, as well as an above-ground pool and some lawn, both of which were removed.

Now there is a crazy-paved patio that draws the eye (and the feet) to a hammock that is suspended tantalisingly in the dappled shade beneath the tree canopy. The ground is covered in a thick mulch of leaves and an assortment of groundcovers with some daffodils and bluebells added to make a bright splash of colour in the spring. The garden housework, apart from planting, is merely spreading some fertiliser when it rains and pulling out the odd weed that dares to show its head.

Colour theming

You may start out in gardening with an almost overwhelming desire to fill your plot with a blaze of mixed colours for as many months of the year as you possibly can. But as your tastes get more sophisticated, you begin to realise that restricting the rainbow to two, three or even a single colour can produce more impact.

BELOW: Red and white are colours that are guaranteed to cause a stir when combined together. A two-tone flower, such as this *Dianthus* 'Strawberry Parfait' is a clever starting point. Build up the picture with fibrous-rooted begonias and grey-leaved dusty miller for a long-showing season.

Choosing plants

If it's almost instant results you are after then look no further than bedding plants. Not only are they likely to be in flower when you plant them, they will also grow to a predictable size and shape and have often been selected for a particularly strong, soft or unusual colour.

Best of all, they usually flower for several months after planting. However, successful colour scheming need not rely exclusively or even partly on the likes of petunias and red salvias. Perhaps the most satisfactory schemes of all are ones that blend together hardy and half-hardy varieties. Indeed, some of the

most widely admired and visited gardens do just that. Even if they appear at first to be on a rather grand scale, there will always be an underlying plant association achieved with just a handful of varieties that we can copy at home.

Popular colour themes

One of the most striking themes of all is the red border. It relies on foliage and flowers for impact. Scarlet dahlias and red hot *Crocosmia* 'Lucifer' for example, are

ABOVE: Trellis painted a rich blue coordinates with blue containers filled with a fiery selection of leaves and flowers.

RIGHT: A blend of reds, pinks and white soften the levels of this terraced border. Using a few colours – linked with strong evergreens, such as the shaped box trees – merges the planting into a pleasing slope.

given added potency with a backdrop of purple-leaved cannas and cordylines. At the other end of the spectrum, pastel pinks and blues will give a much more soft and subtle feel, especially when blended with grey and white foliage plants. A yellow and white border or even a single container will always look sharp and refreshing, whereas white on its own may be cool and chic in sunlight, but can look dull and lifeless under leaden skies. Pots, trellis, paving and even garden furniture can all be chosen or painted to complement your theme.

LEFT: You can select spring bulbs and bedding in specific colours, rather than in a random mixture. It is worth the effort, as in this eye-catching blend of yellow lily-flowered 'Westpoint' tulips and forget-me-nots edged with *Aubrieta*.

Japanese gardens

The saying that 'less is more' is vital to the Japanese philosophy of garden making. In fact, one of its most famous gardens, the dry landscape at Ryoan-Ji consists of merely fifteen stones and a bed of gravel. It is debatable whether a truly authentic Japanese garden can ever be created outside its own shores. Western tastes for a rich variety of plants and a landscape crammed full with contrasting features tend to dominate our thinking. There are, however, plenty of ideas that can be successfully recreated, as we can see here.

Defining your space

One of the most convenient aspects of working in an oriental style is that the tiniest of spaces can be utilised. Enclosed courtyards are ideal, but even a narrow side passage or tiny front garden can be transformed with a subtle blend of plants, paving, screens and ornaments. Disguising the boundaries is a fundamental principle and inci-

BELOW: In keeping with a fundamental Japanese gardening principle, this small plot is edged with apple blossom trees, which will in time blur the boundaries between the garden and street beyond.

dentally, one that could apply to many a suburban garden that is not blessed with panoramic views to the sea or out to open countryside. Dense planting of evergreens in conjunction with split cane or reed panels will focus the eye (and the mind) on the garden within.

Selecting the props

Stone lanterns are perhaps the most familiar and one of the most easily obtained eye-catchers you can use. Squat, snow-viewing lanterns with their overhanging roof lines and taller pedestal lanterns like light-houses would have originally housed oil lamps that gave off an atmospheric glow. Water driven

RIGHT: A tall tower lantern backed by a split cane screen dominates this tiny oriental garden with its subtle blend of water, evergreens, rocks, pebbles and gravel.

BELOW: Protecting the entrance, and, no doubt, the Japanese-style garden beyond is a stone buddha.

deer scarers will also add an authentic flavour and contribute both movement and sound as the pivoting bamboo tube releases its reservoir of water and falls back on a sounding stone.

Japanese-style plants

Fatsia japonica
Mahonia japonica
Evergreen azaleas
Japanese maples
Bamboos
Dwarf pines
Nandina domestica
Sagina glabra 'Aurea'

OPPOSITE: A buddha sits on a thin plinth of stone beneath the canopy of a pot-grown Japanese maple, in a composition that would fit into the tiniest of gardens.

RIGHT: For a classic twosome, let a purple cut-leaved Japanese maple, such as this *Acer palmatum* 'Dissectum Atropurpureum', spill over on to the fresh, cool foliage of a variegated hosta.

BELOW: Muted plant colours, combined with rocks are classic oriental features and water is never far away.

Water-wise gardens

Keeping a garden adequately watered can be expensive if you're on a water meter – as well as a chore. With temperatures set to rise, gardeners need to plan ahead and plant to beat the heat. That way, you can enjoy the garden rather than worry about it, and go on holiday without fear of losing expensive plants.

BELOW: Add brightness with orange Californian poppies and annual daisies.

A truly water-efficient garden begins long before planting, and continues throughout the life of the garden. But even when established, there's plenty to be done. Follow our step-by-step guide, to help you choose plants that are adapted to drought conditions, and create a garden that uses less water.

Getting to know your garden

Stroll through your garden to get a feel for it. Ask yourself these questions for clues to achieve the same beauty with less water.

- Where are the hot, dry spots?
- Which areas are cool and moist?
- Which parts are within easy reach of the hose?
- What sort of soil do I have? Feel it: is it gritty (sandy), smooth (clay) or a combination (loam)? Is it different in different areas of the garden?
- What happens when it rains? Go out with an umbrella: how much rain actually sinks into the soil? How much runs off the surface? What path does it take?

Forming a strategy

With this information, formulate an appropriate design strategy for your garden, as follows:

- Group the toughest plants in hot, inaccessible spots where the soil is most sandy.
- Place plants with extra water needs – such as leafy vegetables and pots – close to the house and within easy reach of the hose.

ABOVE: Colourful hardy annuals make a great show in summer when planted as a meadow. Here lupins are used to make a pool of blue.

- Use trees or a climber-clad pergola close to the house to create a micro-climate for thirsty or delicate specimens, such as ferns and hostas.
- Plant hedges as windbreaks against strong, drying winds.
- Choose a garden style which suits local conditions. Many woodland plants like rhododendrons and camellias are unsuitable for drier climates.

Improving your soil

Well-conditioned soil is the key to good gardening in every climate and location. Water-efficient soil draws water in and holds it like a sponge. Every type of soil, no matter how poor, can be improved. Try some of these ideas.

- Increase the humus in the soil by adding large quantities of decomposed organic matter – garden compost, composted bark and well-rotted manure for example.
- Mulch to encourage worms – the soil-improver's best friend.
- Give areas with the thirstiest plants your greatest attention.

- Build two, or even three compost heaps and use it to regularly top up garden beds and borders.

Choosing the plants

One of the golden rules of gardening is to always be guided by local experience. Plants must match the local conditions and thrive through good times and bad. Listed below are some more tips to help you find plants which give maximum pleasure for minimum water and fuss.

- Ask a qualified horticulturist at your local garden centre for advice and recommendations.
- Notice plants in your garden that do well without effort and buy more! Or increase them by division, cuttings or seed.
- Take a walk around the neighbourhood and look at the uncared-for gardens. Try to identify the plants which look good in spite of the lack of attention.
- In established gardens, replace struggling plants with drought-resistant ones.

Planting technique

It's not just what you plant, timing and technique are important, too.

- Plant at a time to suit your conditions. In the autumn, the soil is still warm and moist and plants will then be established before summer's onset.
- Remember that small plants will establish more rapidly than larger specimens.
- Before planting, turn and loosen the soil, fork compost into the base and backfill. Then fill the hole with water and wait for it to drain away.
- Soak newly planted trees and shrubs deeply until established.

Mulching for water conservation

Mulch immediately after planting and elsewhere after heavy rain has thoroughly wet the ground.

- Aim for a constant 'carpet' of mulch 5–10 cm deep.
- Keep the mulch a handspan away from trunks to avoid the risk of rotting.
- Organic mulch (such as straw, leaf-mould, bark chippings and cocoa shell) improves the soil as it breaks down.
- Non-organic mulch (such as gravel and pebbles) needs topping up less frequently.
- A living mulch (such as ivy) will compete for moisture but is a good choice beneath drought-resistant trees or shrubs.

Maintaining water wisdom

A low-water garden means you can relax, but just a little – there are still things to do.

- Water new plants regularly, especially larger trees and shrubs. A deep soaking once a week is by far the best way.
- Remove weeds as they appear.
- In established gardens, gradually reduce the frequency of watering.
- Keep an eye out for any signs of thirst, including limp leaves and drooping flowers.
- Consider an irrigation system if you have plants which need regular watering or a large number of potted plants.

BELOW LEFT: Observe rainwater flow in your garden and shape the landscape to direct water to plant roots. Dig channels across slopes to move water where it is needed.

1 On a steep slope, a V-shaped planting pocket slows run-off and draws water to the roots.

2 On gentle slopes, form a bank on the low side of the plant and extend 'arms' either side.

3 The lower the rainfall, the bigger the 'arms' should be.

BELOW: An old mower box makes a novel container for drought-resistant house leeks (*Sempervivums*) and can be easily attached to a fence panel.

Tips

Here are some good habits for water-thrifty gardeners, which can reduce water consumption and result in long-term gains for the garden.

- Rinse the car on the lawn – it will enjoy the soak. Fork the area afterwards to avoid soil compacting.
- Set up water butts to collect run-off water from roofs. Include a bypass junction that will fill a second butt when the first one is full.
- Reuse water from baths, washing, cleaning vegetables and cooking. Suds-free water can be used on garden beds and pots.
- Check the soil before you water, by digging down to at least 10 cm. You may find it is already moist.
- Weed and mulch constantly.

TOP: Everyday marguerites stand up to dry conditions well and make a great show massed.

LEFT: Shy on water but not on charm, this natural-looking garden relies more on foliage and textures (which give a soft and gentle look) than flowers and greenery. Muted grasses such as blue fescue (*Festuca glauca*) and carex drift in between the pool, clearings and shaded patio.

Shady gardens

Shady spots are often garden trouble-spots, but with thoughtful plant selection and reasonable soil, such problem areas can become delightful shady gardens. In nature, there are thousands of plants that have adapted to life in the shade. Your job is to select those that will tolerate both your soil conditions and the density of shade. The denser the shade, the fewer plants that will grow there.

BELOW: Shady gardens need not be lacking in variety and colour if you choose your plants with care. Hostas and astilbes are attractive in both leaf and flower, whereas the bronze leaves of *Rodgersia* contrast beautifully with variegated bamboo.

In deep, permanent, full shade (like the area under a group of pines or other thick, evergreen trees), light levels are low throughout the year and only dark-leaved foliage plants are possible. But with increasing

BELOW: Spotted laurel (*Aucuba*) is fully hardy and will cast light into the shadiest spots, even under trees where little else will flourish.

OPPOSITE BOTTOM: A damp, shady hollow is the perfect spot to show off a range of hardy ferns. Choose varieties that contrast with each other in both leaf shape and texture. The undivided leaves of the hart's tongue fern should be included in every garden. It will even colonise crevices in walls.

OPPOSITE TOP: Fuchsias, busy lizzies and begonias, all shown here, are three of the easiest shade-flowering plants to grow. All bloom throughout the summer and make attractive additions to your garden whether in hanging baskets, pots or beds.

brightness, a bigger choice of plants becomes available, including some with spectacular flowers.

Deep-rooted trees like oaks provide just the right amount of shade for acid-loving woodland plants such as rhododendrons and camellias, especially if lower branches are lifted to let in more light and air. However, they must not be allowed to dry out in the summer.

Another potential problem for would-be shade gardeners is the cause of the shade itself. If it's cast by established trees and shrubs, the roots of these plants will form a thick mat just beneath the surface. Thus, it may be necessary to plant young shade-lovers in a layer of compost placed on the surface, but be sure not to build this layer up more than 15 cm above the soil.

Tips

- Yellow-leaved spotted laurel and variegated groundcovering *Euonymus* will cast light into areas of shade.
- Spectacular foliage plants such as *Hosta, Rodgersia* and *Rheum* will thrive in the shade cast by walls and fences.
- Explore any native woodlands in your area to see which plants grow well in shade.

RIGHT: In this shaded corner, ivy is used both as a climber and groundcover. Its small leaves make an interesting contrast to the big tree-fern fronds.

BELOW: A stone birdbath brings a focal point to the dark-leaved foliage in this shady corner and should hopefully attract some birds.

Seaside gardens

Garden-making by the sea poses its own special problems. To begin with, you have to strike a balance between openness to the sea view and providing shelter from the sea wind, which isn't always a gentle zephyr. With salt picked up from the sea spray, the wind can cut any plant that gets in its way as effectively as a pair of pruning shears.

ABOVE: The rugged outline of pines contrasts effectively with grey-leaved sea buckthorn (*Hippothae rhamnoides*) and together they form an excellent wind filter.

the house itself provides shelter for tender plants

windbreak, building up from low shrubs to trees, deflects the wind up & over

a solid fence provides little shelter— the wind bounces over the top and comes down just as hard on the other side

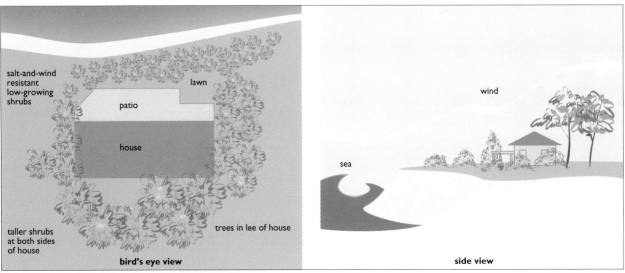

salt-and-wind resistant low-growing shrubs

lawn

patio

house

taller shrubs at both sides of house

trees in lee of house

bird's eye view

wind

sea

side view

It takes a dense mass of growth to deflect the sea wind and protect plants that are not native to the seaside. If your site is blessed with shelterbelts of tough pines, hawthorns, tamarisk and griselinia, these can form the basis of your new design. Within their embrace, resilient shrubs like fuchsias, hydrangeas and hebes can flourish. However, the soil is likely to be poor stuff – sandy, thirsty and hungry for compost.

Maintaining a seaside garden

Despite problems of exposure and damaging, salt-laden winds, seaside gardens do have distinct advantages over those inland. Light intensity is often higher with more sunshine hours, which allows the successful cultivation of sun-lovers like gaza-nias and argyranthemums. Not only will these plants grow to extra-large proportions in the free-draining soil, lack of frost may mean they carry on flowering all year round, unlike in colder areas where they have to be over-wintered indoors.

As on sloping sites, new plants need to be established quickly. This requires extra care, but the initial investment will pay dividends. Famous coastal gardens like Inverewe in Scotland have been created on what were previously barren peninsulas by the judicious use of windbreak plants. Other good tips are to use green plastic netting to make temporary wind filters, to enrich the soil with organic matter, to retain moisture and plant young, healthy plants that will put out new roots and establish more rapidly than outsized specimens prone to wind damage and drying out.

TOP: These diagrams show the dynamics of wind in a seaside garden. Careful planting will help create effective windbreaks and protected areas.

The house itself affords some shelter, and even if you keep the seaward side of the garden open and low, trees to landward will help give shelter for salt-sensitive plants.

LEFT: Fast-growing and with a protracted flowering period, pink *Lavateria* 'Rosea' and *Hebe* 'Midsummer Beauty' make a handsome pairing for seaside gardens.

BELOW: The gazania thrives by the seaside, adding its intense colour.

Bird-attracting gardens

Birds will come, even to city gardens, if they aren't driven away by predatory birds, cats or pesticides. If you provide the sort of environment they like, some birds will decide to take up residence. This means planting trees and shrubs for them to roost in, allowing mulch and litter to stay on the ground where worms and insects can be found, and choosing plants which provide the birds with food.

Choosing the right plants

Resist the temptation to trim and train your trees and shrubs too neatly, as many birds are shy and secretive and prefer dense undergrowth. Thick ivy, for example, provides wonderful nest sites. Leave seeds to ripen on herbaceous perennials and shrubs, as these will provide a natural food source for birds such as finches. You don't have to confine yourself to native plants, just don't leave them out altogether, especially berrying types such as rowan, elder and hawthorn.

BELOW RIGHT: Although heavily disguised in a variegated holly tree, this bird-feeder is easily spotted by this hungry bluetit.

BELOW: Careful planting can attract birds into the garden, such as this goldfinch feasting on a teasel (*Dipsacus*) flowerhead.

Providing home comforts

Think twice about removing hollow trees, or even hollow branches, unless they are unsafe. Many birds use them as nesting places and will happily take up residence.

If you like you can provide birdbaths, nest boxes and feeding tables; but don't feed your birds so generously that they become dependent on you.

ABOVE: A splendid nest box attractive enough to adorn any garden tree. Position it high, out of the reach of cats.

ABOVE RIGHT: By featuring both a bird table and birdbath, this garden will be very welcoming.

RIGHT: A fieldfare grabs a snack of hawthorn berries.

Tip
- Lawns are usually broken up with island beds, but you can use ornaments such as bird-baths or statuary.

Cottage gardens

There are no strict rules to follow in designing a cottage garden, but a few generalisations can be made. Planting is usually dense, especially around the perimeter of the garden. Banks of tallish shrubs provide privacy and shelter from all sides except across the front. The front garden is a showcase of flowers that are meant to be seen from the street. The house is usually festooned with climbers and framed with shrubs or small trees on either side. Grassed areas are kept small to make room for an abundance of annuals, perennials, bulbs, shrubs and even fruit and vegetables mixed in.

BELOW: Not for the obsessively tidy-minded, this slightly unkempt, cottage-style garden has a wild charm, thanks to the free use of perennials and the absence of a formal layout. Plants shown here include yellow *Coreopsis*, *Nepeta* (right front) and blue *Salvia*. Dwarf thyme invades the spaces between stepping stones while grey-leafed *Stachys* provides foliage contrast.

If you'd love a cottage garden but think it wouldn't fit in with modern outdoor living, bear in mind that traditional cottage gardens often disguised an assortment of sheds. Disguise your outdoor living and utility areas with hedges, low walls and thick shrubbery. Use stone, wrought iron and picket fencing; incorporate curving pathways and climber-covered archways. You don't have to live in an old house to have a cottage garden. The style is timeless and makes as delightful a setting for a new home as it did for those built in the last century.

When paving, mix your materials together in as random a way as you have the planting, using 'antiqued' or salvaged products.

Choosing plants for cottage gardens

This list of old favourites is the best place to start.

- Forget-me-not
- Sweet pea
- Ornamental quince
- Daffodil
- Wallflower
- Snapdragon
- Sweet william
- Rose
- Red valerian
- Honeysuckle
- Granny's bonnet
- Arum lily
- Catmint
- Foxglove
- Winter jasmine
- Sunflower
- Violet
- Love-in-a-mist
- Primrose
- Fuchsia
- Pelargonium
- Campanula
- Lavender
- Shasta daisy
- Canterbury bells
- Michaelmas daisy
- Heartsease
- Gypsophila
- Snowdrop
- Hollyhock

ABOVE: Foxglove, veronica and delphinium line the picket fence and part of the brick-paved pathway leading to this picturesque house. The white picket fence, stone birdbath and rose-covered trellis are traditional cottage garden features.

RIGHT: *Lunaria*, violets, bluebells, *Aquilegia* and *Viburnum* flank the pathway of this perfect cottage garden.

LEFT: Interwoven honeysuckle, roses and orange-peel clematis, give the right feeling of informality on the approach to this cottage door, as well as continuity of colour that extends from June to September.

RIGHT: An abundance of stunning flowers provides tonal harmonies and gives height to the garden.

Annual flower gardens

Nothing gives such intensity of colour in such a short space of time as annuals. Most popular of all are the bedding plants typified by begonias, petunias and busy lizzies, which are bedded out in early summer, but hardy annuals that are sown directly into beds and borders give wonderful displays too for the price of a few packets of seed.

BELOW: Sunflowers and *Cosmos* add height and character among the more widely grown busy lizzies and help to build up an impressive bank of colour.

Most annuals need an open, sunny spot and well-drained soil to succeed, however, monkey musk, busy lizzies and begonias will all put up a respectable show in shade. Decide on whether you want a jostling mass of colours or a more refined palette, restricted to two or three colours or even just one. Break up this outpouring of bloom with the coloured leaves of dusty miller and purple-leaved *Canna*.

LEFT: Sometimes the most dramatic use of annuals is achieved with the fewest plants. Here, variegated mallow (*Abutilon pictum* 'Thompsonii') rises above a carpet of red-flowered, dark-leaved, fibrous-rooted begonias forming a brilliant contrast.

BELOW: This dramatic garden uses careful planting to provide a strong visual effect. A 'river' of feverfew (*Chrysanthemum parthenium*) flows between and behind 'hills' of taller snapdragon, iris and other spring flowers. For maximum effect, keep your 'river' to one colour and be sure to plant densely to achieve complete cover.

Herb gardens

Herbs can be grown in terracotta pots, wicker baskets, or in clumps in the flower beds; anywhere in fact where the soil is reasonable and the position sunny. They look their best, though, in a formal setting: a traditional herb garden divided into small beds with narrow paths between them. The paths can be made of stone, brick or pavers, or you could use gravel and small edging tiles.

Planning herbs

Remembering that one uses a lot of some herbs and very little of others, decide which you wish to grow, then plot your garden on paper. Plan for taller plants to go in the centre if the garden is open, or at the back if it's enclosed, and have smaller herbs in the other beds.

Tarragon and mint are favourites with many people, but they're both greedy and prolific so it might be better to devote a separate bed to them elsewhere in the garden, or you could push tiles or other stiff materials into the ground to keep them within bounds.

Choose a sunny spot for your herb garden, and prepare the ground well. Herbs will grow in poor soil, but the more fertile and well drained it is, the healthier your herbs will be. Mix the topsoil with compost or organic material, then all your herbs will need is a light

ABOVE: A seat surrounded by gravel makes a good anchor for a collection of herbs in pots. As you relax, you can run your fingers through the likes of ginger mint, basil and oregano.

LEFT: A classically shaped urn makes an eye-catching centrepiece in this formal herb garden, with the sandstone flagging adding an elegant pathway.

ABOVE: Adjacent to the patio, a pattern of small rectangular beds backed by a picket fence gives a pleasant, cottage feeling, and is filled with a variety of herbs. Many herbs can be a bit nondescript in their off-seasons; an ornament like the birdbath here can make a welcome focal point.

ABOVE LEFT: If you have sufficient space, an enclosed herb and flower garden like this would be a wonderful place to sit and take pleasure in the sights and scents. Petunias, marigolds and nasturtiums mingle happily with sage, thyme, oregano, lemon balm and mint. Yarrow and *Artemisia* provide extra colour and fragrance along the rustic split-rail fence.

dressing of lime in autumn, a complete fertiliser in spring, and an occasional weeding at other times.

Intensely aromatic herbs such as marjoram, thyme and lemon balm will release their fragrance when bruised, so let them spill on to narrow pathways in and around the herb garden. Herbs will grow beautifully in the sunny centre of your lawn, and topsoil mixed with compost or manure should be fine for growing, but you do need to ensure good drainage. The easiest way to do this for heavy soils is to raise the beds. Otherwise, remove about 15 cm or so of topsoil, spread a layer of small rubble, then replace the prepared soil, water it and leave it to settle for a week or so.

Herbs for all soil types

For dry soil with good drainage:
- Marjoram
- Oregano
- Rosemary
- Sage
- Summer savoury
- Winter savoury
- Thyme

For moderately moist soil:
- Basil
- Bay
- Bergamot
- Borage
- Burnet

- Chervil
- Coriander
- Chives
- Dill
- Garlic
- Lemon balm
- Parsley
- Tarragon

For wet soil:
- Apple mint
- Mint
- Spearmint
- Pennyroyal
- Peppermint
- Sorrel

Tips
- Statuary looks wonderful as a formal herb garden centrepiece, but you could also plant a bay tree or rosemary in a large pot.

Kitchen gardens

A well-tended kitchen garden has a beauty of its own. If you enjoy growing vegetables and herbs, make them a special feature of your garden. There's no need to grow all the plants in rigid rows, though they are easier to tend that way. Instead you can cut beds from the lawn and plant flowers, and make a vegetable border, with shrubs or a climber-clad fence as a background. You could consider a pattern of raised beds and paving to continue the architectural lines of the house and patio. A decorative approach would be to plant the beds with a variety of flowers, perhaps annuals, to contrast with the green colours of the vegetables and herbs.

And why not let edible plants take their place in the rest of the garden? A sheltered, sunny pergola could be covered with grapes, a fence can support a thornless blackberry, and an arch red- and white-flowered 'Painted Lady' runner beans. Remember that most fruit trees are as beautiful in spring as are their ornamental cousins; herbs can lend subtle tones of green as well as scent to a planting of flowers.

ABOVE: A network of smart brick paths makes it possible to maintain a kitchen garden without treading on the soil. Flowers add a decorative element as well as attract insect pollinators.

RIGHT: This small vegetable garden uses radiating lines, curves and paving to echo the design of the patio. A border of flowers provides a colourful highlight.

RIGHT: Runner beans are worth growing for their flowers alone and when mixed with the yellow creeper, *Tropaeolum peregrinum*, on an arch or pergola, you have an association that is both decorative and productive.

BELOW: Edible plants can take their place as ornamentals too. Here parsley and the red-stemmed silver beet ('Ruby Chard') contribute to a red-and-green colour scheme with primulas and an azalea.

Children's gardens

Children vary in their needs and temperaments as much as adults do, and their desires change with alarming speed as they grow up. So think carefully before investing in any of the playground-style equipment that you see in the shops; however well made and designed, it has a limited life.

Very young children need a secure place to play in, preferably fenced in and close to, and visible from, the house. Give it a soft surface - a thick (at least 10 cm) mulch of bark chips will provide a soft landing. It doesn't take much for a fall on to hard ground, let alone paving, to cause serious injury. Plan the area with an eye to the future. When it is no longer needed as a playground, can it become a vegetable garden, a herb patch, an extension to the patio or a place for a teenager to pull apart a motorbike?

Wheeled toys such as tricycles and scooters need a hard surface. Certainly, a child can go round and round on a patio, but the fun soon palls. Could you create a mini-grand prix circuit with paths right around the garden? Would linking the patio, lawn and vegetable garden with paths help in the running of the garden in any case? Would such a system of paths help tie the whole design together? A cycle track could also provide the venue for head to head races with radio-controlled cars.

On hot, sunny days, youngsters like nothing better than to splash about in a shallow paddling pool. For this, an area of grass is essential. Neither is there a good substitute for grass when it comes to practising footballing skills, though a strip of artificial grass can reduce the wear and tear on cricket wickets.

ABOVE: A tricycle can turn on a 1.2 m circle or stay on a 60 cm path, but more generous space is desirable. For several trikes and go-carts – or mini-bikes – you need a space of at least 4 by 5 m just for children to ride around without constant collisions.

LEFT: A sandpit is twice as exciting when you can make sand castles, then drop anchor or sail out to sea.

A basketball net and back board can often be fitted above a garage door. On a more cerebral note, outdoor chess and draughts boards are getting increasingly popular and can be enjoyed by the whole family. Garden lighting will extend the playing time well into the evening.

RIGHT: Teddy bears' picnics are a perennial favourite and a flat-paved area provides the perfect base for improvised tables and chairs made from upturned flower pots dressed with napkins.

LEFT: Start children off with easy to grow salad crops and flowers. These non-hearting lettuce make a quick growing edging that can be picked over for summer salads. Blue-flowered *Ageratum* flowers unceasingly throughout summer.

RIGHT: A chess or draughts board is easy to lay out using bricks or block pavers of contrasting colours, laid at right angles to each other. In this example, the draughts are hooked with wooden snooker cues.

BELOW RIGHT: A curving cycle track is one of the most exciting features a garden can offer to young, budding cyclists. Make sure it is wide enough for bikes with stabilisers and forms a complete circuit.

BELOW: This impressive rocket is made from empty plastic lemonade bottles with flaps cut out for bedding plants. White *Alyssum* forms the 'smoke' at the base.

Reference Section

In your garden work – whether it be concerned with specific building projects or developing the planting – it is reassuring to receive good advice on the best way to proceed. This may take the form of recommendations for particularly suitable plants, useful construction methods or even basic skills, such as concreting or selecting appropriate timber.

This reference section includes useful resource guides for gardening and building, as well as a detailed glossary of technical terms. The 'Garden resource guide' offers listings of suitable plants for a wide range of climatic conditions and garden needs – from plants that like poor drainage to those that suit a dry climate. In addition, advice on planting hedges, lawns, trees and groundcovers is provided.

Useful basic skills and important information on construction procedures are included in the 'Building resource guide'. These range from joinery methods, through advice on laying brick pavers, mixing concrete, ordering timber and fixing posts at ground level, to time-saving skills such as how to use a water level.

The aim is to help you make the best possible decisions in the course of creating your ideal garden – and to do this effectively, leaving you plenty of time to sit back and enjoy the fruits of your labour.

This garden bed uses different layers to present a range of shrubs and flowers. Yellow highlights predominate and harmonise with the various blues and the white rose. Notice how the extension of the bed to meet the vine-clad pergola continues the use of different heights and provides depth to the backyard.

Garden resource guide

Know your soil

The most important piece of information you need about your garden is the soil type, as this will determine the plants you can grow. You need to check its structure and pH value (whether it is acid or alkaline) at several points around the garden, as the soil may vary.

A simple squeeze test will allow you to determine a soil's texture. Take about a tablespoon of dry topsoil and gradually add water until it can be squashed into a ball. Work the soil between your finger and thumb to gauge its 'feel'. A gritty soil will contain a lot of sand and tend to fall apart; smooth, slippery soil contains a lot of silt; sticky, mouldable soil contains a lot of clay; an ideal loam will have a good balance of sand and clay – it will feel slightly sticky when wet, and soft when dry.

Sandy soils are easy to work, but drain quickly, losing moisture and nutrients, and causing plants to suffer. To improve their moisture-retention capabilities, dig in plenty of organic matter in the form of well-rotted manure, leaf-mould or garden compost. Adding a mulch to beds will also help retain moisture, although it may still be necessary to water during the summer. Since any plant foods you add will also leach out quickly, choose a slow-release fertiliser, such as bone meal.

Clay soils are heavy and hard to work. When dry, they are impossible to dig; when wet their structure is easily damaged just by walking on them. They do not drain at all well. To prevent damage when digging, stand on a plank to spread your weight. Dig in grit and plenty of organic matter to open up the soil.

All soils contain nutrients that help plants to grow, but the level of acidity or alkalinity (the pH value) can prevent some nutrients from being available to some plants. The pH values for most soils fall between 4 (acidic) and 8 (alkaline). A neutral soil will have a pH of about 6.5, and most plants will grow well in this condition. However, some plants prefer particularly acidic or alkaline conditions. If you know the soil's pH, you can avoid plants that will not thrive in it.

Most garden centres sell simple kits for testing a soil's pH, and one of these is a valuable tool. Normally, they work by mixing a sample of the soil with barium sulphate, distilled water and a special indicator liquid. These are shaken in a test tube and the resulting colour of the liquid compared with a chart to determine whether the soil is acidic, alkaline or neutral.

It is possible to alter a soil's pH value, but this is likely to be expensive and should only be considered in extreme conditions.

- To increase alkalinity by 1 pH, add 300 g of ground limestone per square metre about six months before planting.
- To increase acidity by 1 pH, add either 70 g of sulphate of ammonia or 25 g of ground sulphur per square metre about two months before planting.

If you do alter a soil's pH, check it every two years, as it may gradually revert to its original condition.

Note that digging peat into the soil will increase its acidity. Indeed, it is possible to create peat beds (probably raised) within gardens where the soil is predominantly alkaline, thus allowing acid-loving plants to be grown.

Groundcovers

Groundcovers don't have to be low growing. Any densely-leaved plant that covers the soil can be called a groundcover, and that includes shrubs, perennials and some ferns.

ABOVE: Mixed-colour groundcover of *Tiarella* (foam flower), yellow-leafed ivy and dark *Viola labradorica*.

Because groundcovers grow so densely, they help crowd out weeds and, by excluding light from the soil's surface, they prevent germinating weed seeds from growing. The soils will stay moist longer because it is shaded from full sun and sheltered from winds.

Groundcovers are also ideal for planting on slopes, as they add colour and prevent erosion. When you choose a groundcover plant for a slope, select one with a strong root system that will hold the soil in place, such as ivy, violets and *Lamium*. Very low-growing plants such as thyme, *Ajuga*, *Sedum* and *Aubrieta* work well when planted between stepping stones in a path or in crevices of retaining walls.

Getting started

Plant out in spring and keep the plants moist until well established. On slopes, apply water as fine mist until plants have completely covered the soil. Old-fashioned clothes pegs are ideal for pinning down any type of ground-hugging cover and prevent it from being washed away. Feed groundcovers with a sprinkling of complete plant food in early spring.

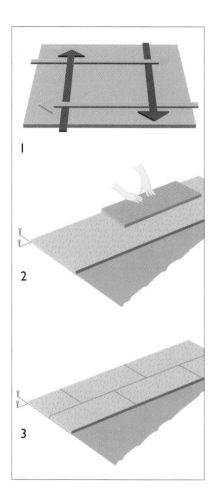

ABOVE: Creating a lawn.

1 Divide seed into four equal lots. Broadcast one lot in each direction.

2 Gently tamp down turfs as you lay them, adding or removing soil from beneath to level.

3 Lay turfs like bricks (in a stretcher bond pattern). If it's necessary to walk on newly laid turfs, use a plank.

RIGHT: Time the period it takes to apply 6–10 mm of water by placing several tins at random around a sprinkler.

Lawns

A lush, healthy, deep-green lawn is not part of the low-maintenance garden, so if you're hoping to minimise maintenance, don't plan a large lawn.

Planning your lawn

Thorough site preparation is all important to a good result. But, before you start digging and hoeing, you have first to decide the boundaries of your new lawn, and to do that you should know something about the needs of grass, and consider the design.

A sunny location

All grasses love sun. The more the better, with an average of half a day all year around being the minimum needed for healthy, thick growth. If you have mature trees, consider the shade they will cast, remembering that in winter the sun is lower in the southern sky. Areas that stay densely shaded for long periods are better given over to shade-loving shrubs and groundcovers.

If you have just planted young trees (or plan to), don't forget that, in time, they too will cast shade. Grass grows quite well under trees with light foliage, which cast dappled shade, as long as you provide it with extra food and water to replace what the tree's roots will take up.

Shape and size

To decide on the shape of your lawn, lay out a garden hose or long piece of rope in the desired shape.

As a rule, long sweeping curves look better than straight lines. If you want to include a bed within the lawn, keep its size in proportion with the size of the lawn and be sure to leave ample space to get a mower right around the bed.

Preparing the site

When you have decided on the shape and size of your lawn, you can begin to prepare the site. Some experts say you should begin up to three months before planting.

First, remove all rubbish and rubble. Now dig out any unwanted trees and shrubs, roots and all.

Next, kill off all other vegetation by spraying with a herbicide.

After the weeds have had their first spraying, you can begin to grade the site.

The next step is to decide whether or not you need sub-surface drainage. Lawn grasses cannot live in soil that remains waterlogged after rain or irrigation, but boggy soil can be made suitable by the installation of sub-surface drains.

Adding the grass

While you are in the process of preparing the site, you should give some thought to how you want to start your lawn. Sowing seed is the cheapest method by far, but it does have a number of drawbacks. For a start, you have to ensure that the soil remains evenly moist at all times until germination is complete. This can take up to 21 days, and during windy or warm weather it

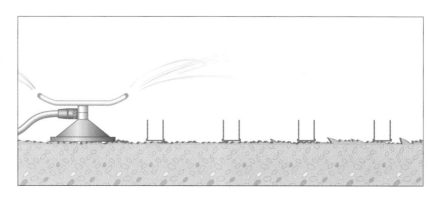

Some lawn grasses				
Type of grass	Suitable climate	Available as	Advantages	Disadvantages
Couch	Subtropical, temperate	Turf, sprigs, runners	Soft, comfortable, quality fine-leaved appearance.	Can wear thin in high traffic areas, runners are very invasive of garden beds if not controlled, needs frequent mowing, goes brown after frost.
Kikuyu	Subtropical, temperate	Turf, runners	Hard-wearing, inexpensive as turf, soft, good around pools as it resists chlorinated water.	Runners are invasive, fast growth necessitates frequent mowing, needs a lot of water and fertiliser, browns off after frost.
Buffalo	Subtropical, temperate	Turf, runners	Very hard-wearing, takes . more shade than most other grasses, takes light frosts, needs less mowing.	Expensive, prickly and rough, fairly coarse looking.
Saltene	Subtropical, temperate	Turf, runners	Handsome fine leaves, soft, takes brackish water.	Looks unattractive through coldish winters.
Kentucky bluegrass/ ryegrass blends	Cool	Turf, seed	Stays green through cold winters, hard-wearing, attractive blue-green colour.	Demands a lot of feeding and watering in summer and very frequent mowing.
Bent	Cool	Turf, seed	Very luxurious-looking, very soft and comfortable, stays green through cold winters.	Not hard-wearing, needs frequent de-thatching and a lot of summer water, easily invaded by weeds.
Bahia grass	Tropical, subtropical	Runners, seed	Hard-wearing, fast-growing, takes some shade in the tropics, relatively inexpensive.	Rather coarse-looking, needs a lot of dry-season water.
Zoysia	Tropical	Turf, runners, plugs	Very attractive, luxurious-looking lawn.	Slow-growing, easily invaded by weeds and expensive.

may be necessary to water more than once a day. Water must be applied as a fine mist, otherwise you may wash the seeds out of the soil.

If the seeds dry out, germination may be patchy and you will have to resow, then keep the resown seeds moist. Newly germinated grass is tender and must not be subjected to foot traffic for several months after sowing. Finally, a seeded lawn won't look established for about a year.

Turf is the most expensive way to establish a lawn, but for the extra cost you get an instant lawn that can be used in just a few weeks. The turf itself is grown on a farm and harvested by being cut into long strips (usually about 2 m long by 70 cm wide). The strips are rolled up and promptly delivered to the customer where they are simply rolled out again. Turf costs vary widely from place to place, so be sure to get a quote from a turf supplier before deciding whether or not to consider its use.

When to establish a new lawn

Grass seed should be sown in the autumn or the spring, when it is neither so hot that the soil quickly dries out, nor so cold that the seeds won't germinate. In summer, the seedlings will struggle in the dry, hot conditions. Turf can be laid at any time, although it will do less well during the winter and summer.

Watering

All lawn grasses grow best in moist, well-watered soil but, since some soils stay moist longer than others, it's not easy to generalise on how often to water. During the hottest weather in summer, a daily watering will be needed, whereas during the winter months, no watering at all may be necessary, except in prolonged dry periods.

As a rule of thumb, apply 6 to 10 mm of water over the entire lawn area every time you irrigate. To find out how long that takes, place five or six tins or jars around the lawn,

some near the sprinkler, others distant from it. Turn up the pressure, then time the period it takes for the desired amount of water to accumulate in the containers.

Cutting

In spring, when lawns are starting into active growth, they can be cut quite short, but as summer approaches raise the height of the mower by a few notches. The extra length of the grass looks lusher but, most importantly, helps keep the soil beneath shaded and cool, thus conserving moisture. Don't lower the height of the mower again until the following spring, as it's important that grass has a considerable leaf length as it goes into winter.

Feeding

Like most other plants, grass extracts its nutrients from the soil, and once these are used up, malnutrition sets in, unless you help out with a ration of lawn food. How often you'll have to help out, though, isn't cut and dried. Naturally-rich, top-quality soils may only need an annual spring feed, whereas sandy soil can demand fertiliser every six weeks during the growing season.

As a rule of thumb, most lawn food manufacturers recommend a full dose of fertiliser in both the autumn and the spring, with two half-rate dressings in between. Always follow the instructions for application times.

Always water the lawn both before and after feeding; better still, apply lawn food during steady rain.

Hedges

Hedges offer privacy, and their impenetrable branches provide secure nesting sites for numerous small birds. Although they do require regular maintenance, with the labour-saving tools now avail-

able, trimming a hedge two or three times a year is not such an arduous task, particularly when you consider the extra beauty, privacy, wildlife and value a hedge can bring to your home. Some hedges don't need to be clipped at all. At its simplest, a hedge can be a row of closely-spaced shrubs forming an effective and attractive informal barrier that never needs shearing.

Preparing the site

For a healthy and vigorous hedge, plant in a trench rather than in individual holes. By digging a trench, a greater volume of soil is dug, aerated and improved (with well-rotted manure or compost and fertilisers), and this will lead to faster, more even growth.

If you plan to grow a single-row hedge, the trench should be at least 45 cm wide (preferably 60 cm) and 30–45 cm deep. For a double row,

LEFT AND BELOW LEFT: **Planting and maintenance.**

1 Erect a sturdy fence between two rows of staggered shrubs to keep animals in or out. As the hedge grows, it will obscure the fence from view.

2 Shear hedges to shape whenever their growth exceeds 15 cm in length. Give them a final tidy up in the autumn.

3 When pruning broadleaf evergreen shrubs, shear them into the shape desired and remove about one third of growth.

4 The distance between shrubs in a hedge depends on the desired height. Space plants 45–60 cm apart for a 1.8 m hedge, 40 cm apart for a 1 m hedge, 30 cm apart for a 60 cm hedge and 15 cm apart for a 30 cm hedge.

5 String line stretched between two posts provides guide for hedge tops. Plumb bob on T-frame for sharp vertical lines.

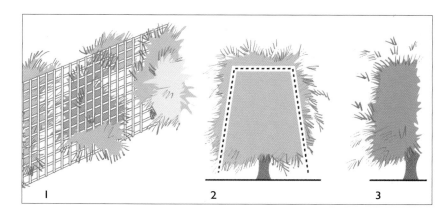

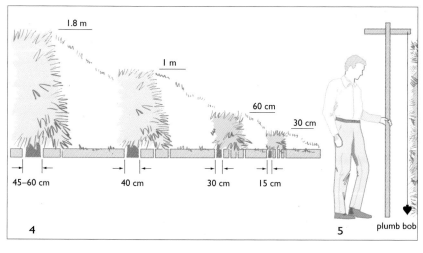

make the width 75 cm. Double rows take up more room, but produce a more impenetrable hedge; to keep animals in or out, erect a chainlink fence between the rows – it will be obscured as the hedge grows.

Choose young, small plants; they are easier to train and much less expensive. But be sure you know their ultimate height and width. Don't plant a hedge that will grow into your neighbour's garden or out over a public footpath.

Training a hedge

Formal hedges should be clipped lightly two or three times a year. Don't wait until the shrubs have grown up before pruning, as your hedge will never be dense and leafy to the ground. Shape the top narrower than the base, otherwise sunlight will not reach the lowest branches and they will die. Lightly shear the growing hedge whenever new stems exceed 15 cm in length.

Informal hedges may also need pruning, when young, to form a dense, twiggy base. However, as they grow, the removal of straggly shoots is usually all that is needed.

Trees

Trees can be bought in containers, balled (dug with a ball of damp soil around roots then wrapped in hessian or plastic) or bare-root in winter in the case of deciduous varieties.

Container-grown or balled trees get off to a faster start, because fewer roots are disturbed in planting. But container-grown trees that are root bound – those with roots running around the perimeter – should be avoided. Balled trees need to have plastic wrapping removed; hessian can be left intact.

When to plant

Planting time depends on the site and the kind of tree you select. Container-grown trees can go in any time, bare-rooted in winter only. Balled evergreens can be planted in late spring (April/May)

or early autumn (September/October). Shaded sites warm up later in spring, but the shade can reduce dehydration of roots and leaves during and after planting.

Digging and planting in autumn instead of spring carries advantages. The warm soil and cool air stimulate root growth. However, the new tree then faces the winter with a limited root system for support.

Heeling-in

Trees can't survive long out of the ground. If planting is delayed for a few days, keep roots and top moist in a spot away from wind and sun. Cover the roots with damp peat, wet leaves or moist newspapers.

If replanting is going to be delayed by weeks, choose a shaded place and dig a sloping trench large enough to accommodate the roots. Place the roots in the trench with the trunk leaning against the sloping side. Cover the roots with loose soil and keep moist. Evergreens should be heeled-in upright and placed close together if there is more than one. Remove the heeled-in tree from its temporary home and plant permanently as soon as possible.

Soil structure

Although trees vary in their tolerance of different soil conditions, most do best in well-drained soils. To test drainage, dig a hole at least 30 cm deep and fill it with water. The next day, fill it again, and if the water is absorbed within 12 hours, the drainage is adequate.

If water remains in the hole for more than 12 hours, the soil probably has a clay consistency. Mix the soil with sand or organic matter. Drainage can be improved even more by digging the hole where you'll plant the tree at least 30 cm deeper than required and filling in the extra space with stone, crushed rock or gravel. Do not add fertiliser to soil replaced in the hole, and do not add too much peat or sand to soils that pass the drainage test.

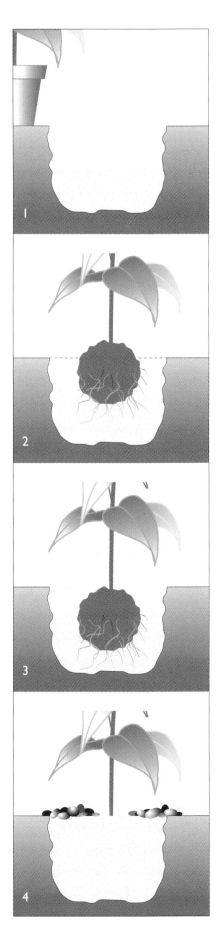

ABOVE: The autumnal colours of the white nerines, conifers and broadleaf trees provide a perfect backdrop for this garden feature.

RIGHT: Fertilising trees. Make holes 15–20 cm deep and 50 cm apart around the trunk in rings out as far as the drip line. These holes will ensure fertiliser reaches the roots and will bring air to the lower levels.

OPPOSITE: Planting a small tree

1 Dig a hole at least twice as wide and deep as the pot and half refill with crumbly soil.

2 Place the tree in the hole and check that it is at the same level as in its pot. If too high or low, adjust the soil below it as necessary.

3 After removing tree from pot, loosen the roots, place them on a mound in the hole and spread them down and out.

4 Fill the hole and tamp down

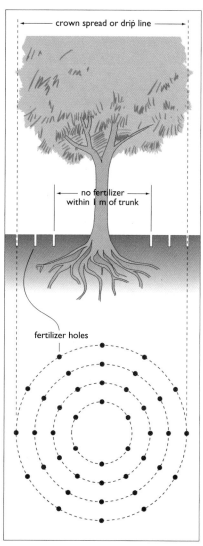

crown spread or drip line

no fertilizer within 1 m of trunk

fertilizer holes

Planting the tree

Although everyone wants a fast-growing tree, remember that medium- to slow-growing trees often live longer and are less vulnerable to insects, diseases and storm damage. You can stimulate tree growth by digging a big hole, the bigger the better. The poorer the soil, the bigger the hole should be. Break up clods and use the same soil around the tree roots or ball.

Dig the hole at least 30 cm deeper than the height of the ball and twice as wide as the root span. If planting on or near the lawn, spread a plastic sheet over the grass and pile the soil on to it. Loosen several centimetres of soil at the bottom of the hole to facilitate drainage.

For bare-rooted trees, build a loose mound of soil at least 15 cm high for the roots to rest on. Make sure the hole is wide enough for the roots to spread out naturally, and deep enough so that the tree, when planted, is at the same height that it was before being dug up (you'll see a soil stain on the trunk, which should be at, or slightly below, the surrounding soil level). Press the soil firmly around the roots until the hole is about three-quarters full. Tread down the soil carefully and lightly to make sure there are no air pockets. Add a bucket or two of water. The tree will settle slightly.

After the water has been absorbed, add more soil to fill the hole, but do not tread it down. Leave a shallow depression around the trunk to catch water. Continue to water the tree well; it may take 25–50 litres.

The process is a little faster with a tree balled in hessian. Set the ball in a hole at least 30 cm wider and 15 cm deeper than the size of the rootball. Cut the binding around the trunk, but leave the hessian intact. It will rot away. This does not apply to plastic balling, which must be cut away.

If the tree has been growing in a container, remove it with tin snips and cut off any outer roots that circle the soil mass. Fill the hole and water as for bare-rooted trees.

Watering

Water your tree every two weeks (weekly during hot, dry weather) for the first year or two. Allow the soil to dry at the surface before you water again. The amount of water needed is the amount the soil can absorb. When water no longer soaks in rapidly, stop watering.

A soaker hose puts a lot of water where it is needed without washing away soil, while a water lance attached to your garden hose puts moisture directly into the root zone, avoiding loss by evaporation. Withhold water when the leaves of deciduous trees drop.

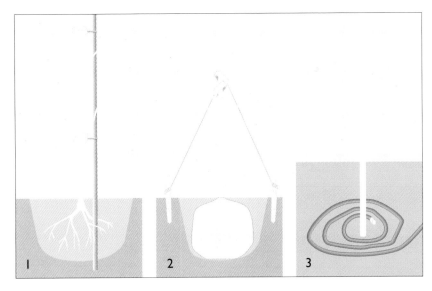

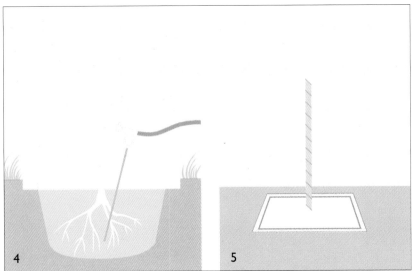

LEFT: Planting a large tree

1 Bare-root trees need a hole that lets roots spread out naturally. Build a conical mound for roots to rest on, and hammer in a stout stake before positioning tree.

2 Balled-and-hessianed trees can be placed in hole and soil packed under and around rootball. Tree may be supported by guy wires threaded through old hose.

3 After soil has been stamped firmly in hole, leaving a slight depression, arrange a soaker hose to put water where it's needed without losing moisture.

4 Another way to conserve water is to shoot moisture directly to the root zone by use of a water lance. Mulch will reduce loss of moisture in summer.

5 Cover a young trunk with tree-wrapping paper, hessian or aluminium foil to stop pest damage and sunburn. A lawn barrier around the tree prevents lawn-mower damage.

Mulching

Reduce summer moisture loss even more with a layer of mulch 5–8 cm deep. Use bark chips, well-rotted manure, peat moss or garden compost. Keep the mulch clear of the tree's bark to reduce potential damage from insects or decay.

Staking

Staking and tying prevents a newly planted tree from being blown over in strong winds before its roots have become established. Doing this also gives the roots an opportunity to become established. Attach one or more stakes to the tree with wire run through pieces of old garden hose so that it won't cut into the trunk. The stakes should be stout and treated with preservative. Keep the tree staked and taut until thoroughly established. This may take up to three years.

Support a balled or container-grown tree with guy wires. Drive two or three short, sturdy stakes into the ground at equal distances around the tree and run hose-protected wires from the trunk to each stake. Place guy wires high enough so that leverage from the top does not loosen them.

Moving trees and shrubs

Because trees and shrubs can grow quite large and will be in the ground for many years, when you plant

Sun-loving plants

Plants can often be at their most useful and attractive when grouped together, you can form them into virtually any shapes or patterns you like. With careful plant selection, you can have masses of different flowers out at the same time, or a continuous succession of blooms over the year.

Annual flowers will give you months of colour, but when the flowers have faded, the plants will have to be pulled out and replaced. Similarly, perennials can flower for months and, where the climate suits them, don't need to be replaced. They usually die back to the ground for a time each year (commonly in winter, but some species are summer dormant) before a new growth cycle commences. Warm-climate perennials are usually grown as annuals where winters are severe.

Small shrubs are the easiest plants to care for, and the most permanent for a flower garden. They usually need only an annual pruning to remain compact and floriferous, although some, such as the daisy bush, are best started anew every three or four years. Always try to create pleasing colour combinations and remember that large drifts of individual colours generally look better than lots of different colours in small areas.

Annuals

California poppy (*Eschscholzia*)
Cosmos
Daisy (*Bellis*)
Pot marigold (*Calendula*)
Straw flower (*Helichrysum*)

Perennials

African lily (*Agapanthus*)
Blanket flower (*Gallardia*)
Chrysanthemum
Fleabane (*Erigeron*)
Gazania
Golden marguerite (*Anthemis*)
Golden rod (*Solidago*)
Indian shoe plant (*Canna*)
Red hot poker (*Kniphofia*)
Snow-in-summer (*Cerastium*)
Tickseed (*Coreopsis*)
Yarrow (*Achillea*)

Small shrubs

Blue mist (*Caryopteris*)
Cinquefoil (*Potentilla*)
Cotoneaster
Heather (*Calluna, Erica*)
Japonica (*Chaenomeles*)
Lavender (*Lavandula*)
Mexican orange blossom
  (*Choisya ternata*)
Rock rose (*Helianthemum*)

them you have to be able to envisage what they will look like when they have matured. This is not always easy. There may be times, as well, when you want to redesign the garden and a shrub or tree may be in the way, although you may want to keep it. In these situations, provided the plant is not too large, you will have to move it.

The best time to move a shrub or tree is in the autumn, after the rain has soaked the ground and the soil is still warm enough to help the roots become re-established. The ground must be moist – if necessary, soak it well the day before so that the roots take up plenty of water.

The younger a shrub or tree, the easier it will be to move. Within the first year, it should be possible to move a shrub or young tree simply by lifting it with a spade. If all goes well, the root ball will remain intact and you can replant it easily.

For more established trees or shrubs, dig a circular trench around the trunk, about 300 mm away from it. Then slice under the root ball to free it. With a helper, tilt the shrub or tree to one side and begin to work a sheet of thick polythene or canvas beneath the root ball. Tilt the trunk the other way and pull the sheet through completely. Wrap the sheet around the roots and secure it to the trunk. This will prevent the root ball from breaking up. Then lift the tree or shrub from the hole.

To make carrying easier, tie a stout pole to the trunk at the point where the sheet is secured and recruit one or more helpers to lift it.

Replant the shrub or tree and keep watered until established. To help the roots become re-established, stake the plant well.

Plants that like moist soil

There are some plants that will thrive in moist soil. Some large specimens will even drain the area for you. Following is a list of perennials, shrubs and trees that like damp places. Note some of the trees are too large for small gardens.

Perennials

Astilbe **x** *arendsii*
Bergamot (*Monarda*)
Bleeding heart (*Dicentra spectabilis*)
Bugbane (*Cimicifuga foetida*)
Bugle (*Ajuga reptans*)
Buttercup (*Ranunculus*)
Christmas rose (*Helleborus niger*)
Dropwort (*Filipendula vulgaris*)
Lady's mantle (*Alchemilla mollis*)
Ligularia
Marsh marigold (*Caltha palustris*)
Meadow rue (*Thalictrum*)
Monkshood (*Aconitum napellus*)
Obedient plant
  (*Physostegia virginiana*)
Pansy, Violet (*Viola*)
Plantain lily (*Hosta*)
Purple loosestrife (*Lythrum salicaria*)
Rodgersia
Spiderwort (*Tradescantia virginiana*)

Shrubs

Alexandrian laurel (*Danae*)
Blue bean (*Decaisnea*)
Desfontainia
Dipelta
Fuchsia

Pachysandra
Pagoda bush (*Enkianthus*)
Stephanandra
Summersweet (*Clethra*)
Willow (*Salix*)

Trees

Alder (*Alnus*)
Hawthorn (*Crataegus*)
Hornbeam (*Carpinus*)
Maple (*Acer*)
Oak (*Quercus robur*)
Ornamental pear (*Pyrus*)
Poplar (*Populus*)
Willow (*Salix*)

Plants that like shady conditions

Annuals and perennials

Barrenwort (*Epimedium*)
Bear's breeches (*Acanthus*)
Brunnera macrophylla
Bugle (*Ajuga reptans*)
Busy lizzie (*Impatiens*)
Christmas rose (*Helleborus niger*)
Ivy (*Hedera*)
Japanese anemone
   (*Anemone japonica*)
Kaffir lily (*Schizostylis coccinea*)

Lady's mantle (*Alchemilla mollis*)
Large-leaved saxifrage
   (*Bergenia cordifolia*)
Leopard's bane
   (*Doronicum plantagineum*)
Lily turf (*Liriope muscari*)
Pansy, Violet (*Viola*)
Pearl everlasting (*Anaphalis*)
Plantain lily (*Hosta*)
Sage (*Salvia*)

Shrubs

Box (*Buxus sempervirens*)
Camellia
Common hydrangea (*Hydrangea macrophylla*)
Honeysuckle (*Lonicera nitida*)
Japanese aralia (*Fatsia japonica*)
Oleaster (*Elaeagnus augustifolia*)
Osmanthus heterophyllus
Rhododendron
Skimmia japonica
Spindle tree (*Euonymus fortunei* var. *radicans*)
Spotted laurel (*Aucuba japonica*)
St John's wort (*Hypericum calycinum*)

Plants for pool surrounds

The most important consideration for plants around pools is that the root system is not extensive or invasive. Many pool owners prefer deciduous trees, as they only have to deal with leaves for about four weeks each year, as opposed to the regular leaf-shedding of evergreens. If salt or wind protection are issues for your poolside planting, see the listing, 'Plants for seaside gardens'.

Flowers for all seasons

The table below is only a general guide, as plants may flower earlier or later depending on local conditions and variations in climate. Discuss your plans at a local nursery to obtain specific advice.

Plants for seaside gardens

These are salt- and wind-resistant plants that will tolerate very harsh conditions. They are suitable for planting as a natural protective barrier for less-tolerant plants.

Perennials

Artemisia
Catmint (*Nepeta*)
Crane's bill (*Geranium*)
Globe thistle (*Echinops*)
Jerusalem sage (*Phlomis*)
Loosestrife (*Lythrum*)
Sea holly (*Eryngium*)
Sea kale (*Crambe maritima*)
Sea lavender (*Limonium*)
Senecio cineraria
Thrift (*Armeria*)

Shrubs

Broom (*Cytisus, Genista*)
Cabbage palm (*Cordyline*)
Common holly (*Ilex aquifolium*)
Daisy bush (*Olearia*)
Escallonia
Firethorn (*Pyracantha*)
Fuchsia
Lavender (*Lavandula*)
Mexican orange blossom
   (*Choisya ternata*)
Pittosporum
Rock rose (*Helianthemum*)
Spiraea
Strawberry tree (*Arbutus unedo*)
Tamarisk (*Tamarix*)
Willow (*Salix*)

Autumn	Winter	Spring	Summer
Autumn crocus (*Colchicum*)	Buttercup (*Ranunculus*)	Barrenwort (*Epimedium*)	Alyssum
Black-eyed susan (*Rudbeckia fulgida*)	Crocus	Bellflower (*Campanula*)	Amaranthus
Busy lizzie (*Impatiens*)	Cyclamen	Candytuft (*Iberis*)	Aster
Carnation, Pink (*Dianthus*)	Daisy (*Bellis*)	Crocus	Begonia
Chrysanthemum	Elephant's ears (*Bergenia*)	Cyclamen	Black-eyed susan (*Rudbeckia fulgida*)
Cosmos	Hellebore (*Helleborus*)	Daffodil (*Narcissus*)	Busy lizzie (*Impatiens*)
Crane's bill (*Geranium*)	*Iris reticulata*	Daisy (*Bellis*)	Columbine (*Aquilegia*)
Dahlia	*Iris unguicularis*	Elephant's ears (*Bergenia*)	Carnation, Pink (*Dianthus*)
Japanese anemone (*Anemone japonica*)	Lily turf (*Liriope*)	Forget-me-not (*Myosotis*)	Dahlia
Marigold (*Tagetes*)	Pansy, Violet (*Viola*)	Gladiolus	Floss flower (*Ageratum*)
Michaelmas daisy (*Aster novi-belgii*)	Primrose (*Primula*)	Honesty (*Lunaria*)	Geranium (*Pelargonium*)
Nasturtium (*Tropaeolum majus*)	Saxifrage (*Saxifraga*)	Hyacinth (*Hyacinthus*)	Globe flower (*Trollius*)
Tobacco plant (*Nicotiana*)	Snowdrop (*Galanthus*)	Iris	Heliotrope (*Heliotropium*)
Petunia	Wallflower (*Erysimum*)	Leopard's bane (*Doronicum*)	Hollyhock (*Alcea*)
Phlox	Winter aconite (*Eranthis*)	Marsh marigold (*Caltha*)	Lobelia
		Pansy, Violet (*Viola*)	Marigold (*Tagetes*)
		Spurge (*Euphorbia*)	Nasturtium (*Tropaeolum majus*)
		Stock (*Matthiola*)	Petunia
		Thrift (*Armeria*)	Phlox
		Tulip (*Tulipa*)	Sage (*Salvia*)
		Wallflower (*Erysimum*)	Snapdragon (*Antirrhinum*)
		Windflower (*Anemone*)	

Trees

Ash (*Fraxinus*)
Grey poplar (*Populus canescens*)
Hawthorn (*Crataegus*)
Holm oak (*Quercus ilex*)
Norway maple (*Acer platanoides*)
Sweet chestnut (*Castanea*)
Whitebeam (*Sorbus aria*)

Plants for dry gardens

Although all plants need water to survive, some tolerate dry conditions better than others.

Perennials

Baby's breath (*Gypsophila paniculata*)
Blanket flower (*Gaillardia aristata*)
Bear's breeches (*Acanthus spinosus*)
Carnation, Pink (*Dianthus*)
Chinese lantern (*Physalis alkekengi* var. *franchetii*)
Cinquefoil (*Potentilla*)
Cupid's dart (*Catananche caerulea*)
Cornflower (*Centaurea cyanus*)
Crane's bill (*Geranium*)
Evening primrose (*Oenothera*)
Forget-me-not (*Myosotis*)
Gayfeather (*Liatris spicata*)
Globe thistle (*Echinops ritro*)
Ice-plant (*Sedum spectabile*)
Iris hybrids
Japanese anemone (*Anemone japonica*)
Lady's mantle (*Alchemilla mollis*)
Large-leaved saxifrage (*Bergenia cordifolia*)
Leopard's bane (*Doronicum plantagineum*)
Lily turf (*Liriope muscari*)
Lungwort (*Pulmonaria*)
Oriental poppy (*Papava orientale*)
Pampas grass (*Cortaderia selloana*)
Pearl everlasting (*Anaphalis triplinervis*)
Perennial sage (*Salvia superba*)
Peruvian lily (*Alstroemeria aurea*)
Plume poppy (*Macleaya*)
Red hot poker (*Kniphofia uvaria*)
Red valerian (*Centranthus ruber*)
Sea holly (*Eryngium*)
Sea lavender (*Limonium latifolium*)
Soapwort (*Saponaria officinalis*)
Spiderwort (*Tradescantia virginiana*)
Spurge (*Euphorbia*)
Yarrow (*Achillea*)

Shrubs and climbers

Bladder senna (*Coluthea*)
Broom (*Genista*)
Butterfly bush (*Buddleja*)
Carpenteria
Climbing hydrangea (*Hydrangea anomala* subsp. *petiolaris*)
Cotton lavender (*Santolina*)
Daisy bush (*Olearia*)
Deutzia
Fabiana
Hazel (*Corylus*)
Heather (*Erica*)
Japanese angelica (*Aralia elata*)
Jerusalem sage (*Phlomis*)
Lavender (*Lavandula*)
Passion flower (*Passiflora*)
Rock rose (*Cistus*)
Rosemary (*Rosmarinus*)
Sea buckthorn (*Hippophae*)
Spanish broom (*Spartium*)
Tamarisk (*Tamarix*)
Tree hollyhock (*Hibiscus*)
Tree lupin (*Lupinus arboreus*)
Virginia creeper (*Parthenocissus*)
Yucca

Shrubs to attract wildlife

Birds, bees and butterflies add an extra dimension to the enjoyment you can get from your garden. These flowering and berry-producing shrubs will encourage them to stay.
Aucuba
Barberry (*Berberis*)
Butterfly bush (*Buddleja*)
California lilac (*Ceanothus*)
Clerodendrum
Common spindle (*Euonymus europaeus*)
Cotoneaster
Daphne
Escallonia
Veronica (*Hebe*)
Japonica (*Chaenomeles*)
Mahonia
Ornamental currant (*Ribes odoratum*)
Prickly heath (*Gaultheria*)
Privet (*Ligustrum*)
Russian sage (*Perovskia*)
Snowberry (*Symphoricarpos*)
St John's wort (*Hypericum*)
Viburnum
Weigela

Plants for rock gardens

Dwarf-growing plants are best suited to the confines of a rockery. Here are some popular choices:

Perennials

Alpine wallflower (*Erysimum*)
Alpine yarrow (*Achillea*)
Astilbe
Bellflower (*Campanula*)
Cat's ear (*Antennaria*)
Creeping jenny (*Lysimachia*)
Cyananthus
Edelweiss (*Leontopodium*)
Gold dust (*Aurinia saxatilis*)
Gentian (*Gentiana*)
House leek (*Sempervivum*)
Lewisia
Mountain aster
Mount Atlas daisy (*Anacyclus*)
New Zealand burr (*Acaena*)
Rock cress (*Arabis*)
Rockery pink (*Dianthus*)
Rockery speedwell (*Veronica*)
Rock jasmine (*Androsace*)
Rock soapwort (*Saponaria*)
Sandwort (*Arenaria*)
Shooting star (*Dodecatheon*)
Stonecrop (*Sedum*)

Shrubs

Heather (*Erica*)
Hebe armstrongii
Japanese maple (*Acer japonicum*)
Mock orange (*Philadelphus microphyllus*)
Rock rose (*Helianthemum*)
Rosemary (*Rosmarinus officinalis*)
Spiraea japonica
St John's wort (*Hypericum polyphyllum*)
Woolly willow (*Salix lanata*)

Conifers

Abies balsamea 'Hudsonia'
Common juniper (*Juniperus communis*)
Dwarf mountain pine (*Pinus mugo*)
Lawson cypress (*Chamaecyparis lawsoniana*)
Picea glauca albertiana
Pseudotsuga menziesii 'Fletcheri'

Building resource guide

Obtaining information

Before undertaking a building project, take the time to acquaint yourself with all the possible alternatives in terms of materials, such as timber, bricks and paving. You can gain much information by visiting builders' merchants, timber yards and DIY stores. Often, their staff will be able to advise you on the best materials for a given job.

Mixing concrete

When mixing concrete by hand, there are three things to remember if you want to achieve a strong mix:

- Use clean aggregate that has sharp edges and is of even size. Crushed material, such as gravel, is ideal. Sand should have fine and coarse particles. Any dirt or vegetation will prevent the mix from binding, weakening the concrete.
- Measure the dry materials (cement and aggregate) carefully and mix them thoroughly. Incomplete mixing will result in some parts having too much aggregate and others too little.
- Add clean water, gradually pouring it into a hollow in the centre of the dry mix. Use only enough to make the mix workable; too much weakens the concrete.

Mortar

When mixing mortar, add lime (one part to one of cement and six parts sand) to make the mix more 'plastic'. Alternatively, add a commercial plasticiser to the mix. For small jobs, it may be more convenient to buy mortar mix in a bag; mix the ingredients well before adding water.

RIGHT: Concreting tools. 1 steel trowel; 2 wooden float; 3 groover; 4 edger.

Laying methods for brick pavers

Foundation material	Method	General comments
Laid dry. 25–50 mm deep sand bed, dampened and compacted. Level with straight board.	Lay tight or with 15-mm gaps filled with soil to encourage grass joints. Tap to level with rubber mallet and length of timber.	Allow 50 normal-size pavers (200 x 100 x 65 mm) per square metre, or calculate according to the dimensions of the pavers chosen.
With dry mortar. 50-mm-deep sand bed mixed with two bags of cement per 10 square metres. Level with straight board.	Lay 5–10 mm apart. Spray with water and leave 24 hours before filling the joints with dry mortar of one part cement to four parts sand. Spray again.	Cut pavers with a bolster and club hammer on a bed of sand. Pavers on sand need a border to maintain stability.
With wet mortar. Layer of sand with 75-mm concrete slab on top. Use 15-mm setting bed of mortar on top of slab to set bricks into.	Wet bricks thoroughly before laying. When using mortar setting bed, push bricks into bed and level with length of heavy timber. Pour and lay about two square metres at a time. Or lay with 15-mm spaces (use scraps of wood to keep them even) and press mortar into the joints with pointed trowel. Wash off with a broom and clean water. For mortar, mix one part cement to three-and-a-half parts sand and half a part of lime.	Brick pavers are the most popular paving material because of their colour and the textured, non-skid patterns they create. They are available in a wide range of shapes, including interlocking varieties that are stable in mortar-free bedding systems.

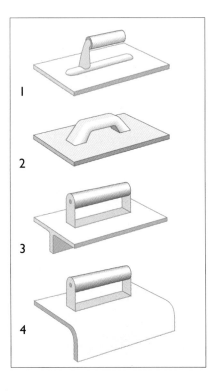

Triangulation

The easiest way to obtain a right angle is to use triangulation. If you have a triangle with sides in a ratio of 3:4:5, the angle between the 3 and the 4 will always be a right angle. Use a tape and any multiples of 3, 4 and 5 (e.g. 300, 400 and 500 mm, or 600 mm, 800 mm and 1 m) to check for square.

Timber

Timber has many uses in the garden, but its durability is of crucial importance to outdoor projects. In its natural state, timber is not impervious to attack from moisture and insects, so it is important to take steps to protect it.

Pine is the most commonly available and cheapest of timbers, but it is also the least durable and must be treated with preservative if it is to survive for long outdoors. Many timber suppliers offer a pressure treating service, which is by far the best method of protecting pine. Alternatively, paint the timber piece with preservative and then stand them on end in a bucket of preservative for a day or two so that the end grain soaks up the fluid.

Timber conditions

Timber is sold in three conditions:

- sawn or rough sawn, which has been brought to a specific (nominal) size by a bandsaw;
- planed, usually planed all round (PAR), but sometimes planed on two sides only;
- milled, which is machined to a specific profile for architraves, window sills, skirting boards, etc.

Timber sizes

Planed timber is sold using the same nominal dimensions as sawn timber, but in fact it will be smaller after planing. For example, if the nominal size is 100 x 50 mm, then once the surfaces have all been machined to a flat, even width and thickness the timber will in fact measure 91 x 41 mm. The chart above shows the approximate differences in measurement for seasoned timber.

Timber is sold in standard lengths, which usually begin at 1.8 m and increase by 300 mm increments to 2.1 m, 2.4 m and so on Short lengths and offcuts may also be available

Saw or nominal size (mm)	Finished size after dressing (mm)
10	6
13	9
16	12
19	15
25	19
31	23
38	30
50	41
75	66
100	91
125	115
150	138
175	160
200	185
225	210
250	231
300	281

Selecting timber

All good timber yards will offer a variety of timber species, and it is important to choose the correct type for the job in hand. If in doubt about which species would best suit your requirements, ask the advice of your supplier.

Pine

Several types of timber are grouped under the heading 'pine'. Normally, you will come across European redwood, also known as deal or Scots pine. Spruce (sometimes known as white deal) comes into this category, too. The nature of the grain makes these woods flex as well as splinter when sawn. The grain has very high contrast and is often quite knotty.

Fir

This timber is also known as British Columbian pine, Oregon pine and Douglas pine. Although prone to splitting, it is stronger than normal pine, is straight-grained and generally knot-free. It is often used for structural work.

Parana pine

Available in large board widths, up to 300 mm, Parana pine is an even-textured wood, often free of knots and shakes, but it may warp or split as it dries.

Cedar

Also known as western red cedar, this wood is quite expensive. However, it is durable in all exterior conditions. Its natural colour makes it even more appealing, and it will weather to a pale grey when left untreated. Its softness can be a disadvantage.

Hardwood

Hardwoods vary widely in strength and weather resistance. Oak and teak, for example are ideal for outdoor jobs, while beech isn't. The denseness of hardwoods makes accurate work easier, but it also blunts tools quicker than working with softwood. They are more expensive, too.

Always buy seasoned timber if possible. Whether kiln or air dried, seasoned timber needs a moisture content of 10–15 per cent, otherwise it may split, warp or bow after it has been fixed in place.

Ordering timber

You will have much less trouble when ordering timber if you are well organised and present the information in a manner that the timber supplier will recognise. First, decide exactly what you need:

- the species, e.g. British Columbian pine;
- the condition, e.g. rough sawn or planed;
- the nominal section size, e.g. 100 x 50 mm;
- the length, e.g. 2.7 m;
- the number of lengths.

You will then be able to prepare an order, such as 100 x 50 mm rough-sawn seasoned British Columbian pine, one of 2.4 m; 225 x 38 mm planed seasoned parana pine, two

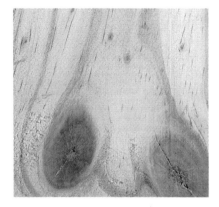

Radiata pine

Pacific maple

Western red cedar

of 2.1 m. Always obtain three quotes for your order before deciding which supplier to use, as prices can vary considerably from one timber yard to the next. Once you have made your choice, always visit the timber yard and select the individual pieces yourself so that you can check them for bowing, large knots and splits. This will be easier if the timber yard is well organised, with the same species of timber stored together.

Tools for outdoor carpentry

There are few tools required for outdoor carpentry that you won't already have in a basic tool kit. However, there are some that will make your work much easier.

- a spirit level about one metre long for use on large structures
- a large steel square with sides about 600 mm long
- an adjustable bevel gauge,

especially for jobs such as sloping the ends of pergola beams
- a steel tape, which should be at least 8 m long
- a sturdy wood chisel approximately 50 mm wide
- a panel saw for cutting structural timbers
- a electric jigsaw for cutting curves and fiddly shapes or bevels

Remember, too, to keep all your cutting tools very sharp.

Post-and-rail joinery techniques

You can attach the rails of a fence to its posts with one of these traditional timber joints.

All of the joints will result in a satisfactory fence, but each has particular qualities that you should consider. For instance, the butt joint is not as strong as the others and should not be used if the fence needs to withstand any force. In that case, the mortise-and-tenon joint might be your best bet.

Other factors to affect your decision will be your skill in joinery and the tools you have.

1 **Housing joint.** Cut away part of the post so that the rail will be flush, or very nearly flush, with the post. Set the rail so that it is half-way through the housing (the next rail will fit in the other half) and nail through.

2 **Block joint.** Nail a short piece of 50 x 50 mm timber (the block) to the post to support the bottom of the rail. Rest the rail on the block and skew-nail through the rail and block into the post.

3 **Butt joint.** Set the end of the rail against the post at the required height, supporting the rail to keep it horizontal. Drive

nails at an angle through the rail into the post. (This does not give a strong joint.)

4 **Mortise-and-tenon joint.** Cut a recess (mortise) in the post at the required height. Trim the end of the rail to form a tenon. Place the tenon in the mortise, drill a hole from the side and hammer in a wooden dowel.

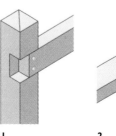

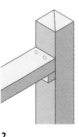

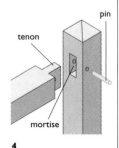

pin

tenon

mortise

1   2   3   4

Using electric saws

- Hold the work with clamps.
- Always keep two hands on the saw and your feet on the ground.
- Unplug the saw when adjusting it.
- Set the saw depth to cut a fraction more than the timber thickness.
- Support the work so that it won't jam the saw blade.
- Never stand behind the saw in case it kicks back at you.
- Keep the work area clean so that there is nothing to trip on.
- Make sure the flex is well clear of the blade at all times.
- Never immobilise or remove the blade guard.

Ladder safety

Working from a ladder is potentially dangerous. When using a stepladder, make sure you stand it on a surface that is level and firm, and open the legs fully.

With an extension ladder, the slope should be about one in four; that is, its feet should be one quarter of its height from the wall. Too steep an angle and it may topple backwards; too shallow, and it could slide downwards. The top section of the ladder should not be extended more than three-quarters of its length. Ideally, the top should be tied to whatever it is leaning against to prevent the ladder from toppling. Make sure an extension ladder stands on a firm surface, placing its feet on a board if the ground is soft.

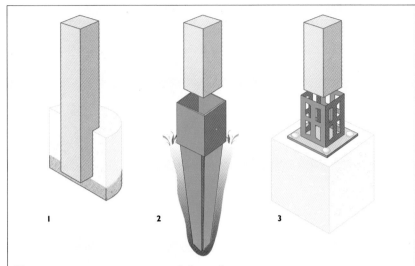

1   2   3

Fixing posts at ground level

There are three main methods of fixing posts:

1 Dig the hole and place a foundation of gravel or brick rubble in the bottom for drainage. Insert the post and add wet or dry concrete mix or tamped earth around it.

2 Drive a steel post spike directly into the ground. Then tap the post down into the socket. It may be necessary to tighten clamping bolts to secure it.

3 Provide a concrete base and drill holes in it to match the baseplate of a post socket. Bolt the socket to the concrete with expansion bolts. Tap the post into the socket. Tighten any clamping bolts.

A concrete base for a post socket should be about double the area of the socket baseplate and at least 300 mm deep. When inserting a post directly into the ground, make the hole 600 mm deep.

With both types of ladder, get someone to hold the ladder while you ascend and descend. Wear shoes with soles that grip and, if you intend climbing on to a roof, make sure it is dry before you attempt to walk on it.

Below: Working with a water level.

Tape one end of a length of clear plastic tubing to the object from which you want to take a level. Tape the other end to a point where you want the same level. Using a funnel, fill the tube with water (perhaps dyed) to within 50 mm of the top. Ensure air bubbles are removed, as these will make your level inaccurate. Mark the height of the water at each end of the tube to get your two exact levels. Plug each end of the tubing ready for use again. Attach a string line between the two points (if you are excavating, for instance) to give a level guide as you work.

adhesive tape

PVC tubing

water level line

remove soil

fill

proposed paving

Glossary

aggregate Crushed stone screened to a size suitable for concrete. The maximum size of stone suitable for general use is 20 mm. Combined aggregate is pre-mixed with sand for concreting.

anchor bracket connector A device securing one part of a structure to another to make the parts stable.

angle iron An iron or steel bar with an L-shaped cross-section.

arris rail A horizontal, triangular-section rail used to reinforce the centre of a boarded fence panel.

ballast Pre-combined aggregate and sand used for making concrete.

baluster A single upright in the handrail of a flight of steps.

balustrade A railing, usually around a deck or balcony. It may be built from timber, steel or cast iron.

bat A cut piece of brick, usually more than half the length (e.g. half-bat, three-quarter bat).

batten A narrow length of wood.

batter boards Support boards, attached to pegs, usually erected in an L-shape to fix the position of a corner post.

bearer In floor construction, the structural member that carries the load of the joists to the structure. Bearers are usually fixed to posts, stumps or to brick piers.

bevel A sloping surface cut at an angle other than 90°.

bird's mouth notch A cut in a rafter so that it fits over a wall plate or beam.

bleeding A feature of unseasoned green timber that will cause staining of concrete until all the sap leaches out of the new timber.

blind To cover a layer of hardcore with a layer of sand to provide a base for paving.

block splitter A hydraulically-operated mechanical device similar to a car jack, used to cut bricks and pavers.

bolster A short-handled chisel with a wide blade (100 mm approx.) used for cutting bricks, etc.

bond (brick pattern) The way bricks are laid in a wall or in paving so that they interlock. The simplest is called 'stretcher bond'. This is laid by placing each successive course, or layer, so that each joint is staggered by one half-brick length.

bond The strength of adhesion between two surfaces.

bracket A prefabricated metal connection device for joining lengths of timber.

bricklaying mortar A general-purpose bricklaying mortar comprises one part hydrated lime, one part Portland cement and six parts sand. Alternatively, a measure of plasticiser can be added in place of the lime. Where a stronger mix is required, use one part cement, half a part lime (or one measure of plasticiser) and four parts sand. Although both are weaker than 1:3 cement mortar, they are more economical and simpler to work.

builders' sand A clean beach sand that has been washed to remove all salt and organic matter. Available in bulk or bagged. Also called soft sand and bricklayers' sand. It has smooth particles, making it suitable for masonry work.

building board Any of the sheet materials used in building.

bullnose A paver or brick having one edge rounded off. Used along the tops of walls and around swimming pools.

butt hinges The flaps of the hinge are of equal size and are screwed to the edge of the movable part and the frame so that only the knuckle of the hinge projects.

calcium-silicate bricks Bricks made of sand and lime and not of clay. Usually white or ivory coloured, they are not recommended for exposed areas.

cantilever A beam or slab with a projecting, unsupported end.

caulk To fill a joint to make it watertight or airtight.

CCA treatment (see also 'pressure treated') Pressure-applied preservative treatment for timber using copper, cadmium and arsenic. Gives timber a characteristic greenish-grey colour and provides long-term protection from moisture and insect attack.

cement Portland cement is used as a basis for all bricklaying mortars and in concrete. One bag weighs 50 kg, which means there are 20 bags to one tonne.

cement mortar A general-purpose mortar for tile laying. It comprises one part Portland cement and three parts sand. This mortar has a grey to off-white colour when set.

chamfer A small bevel or slope on the edge of a board or timber. Also the process of removing the edges of lengths of timber or paving materials.

chuck The part of a drill or other tool that holds a removable cutting implement. In the case of a drill, the bit; similarly, a router has a chuck for the cutters. Chucks are usually operated with a chuck key, although some are locked by tightening one ring against another.

cleat A piece of wood fastened on to something to give support.

clout A nail with a flat, circular head, usually galvanised.

coach screw A screw with a square or hexagonal head that can be turned with a spanner.

compressed cement A thick, dense version of fibre-cement sheeting, used in places susceptible to damp.

concrete Cement, sand and aggregate mixed in varying proportions according to the strength and purpose required. For footings and sundry paving work, a mix of three parts aggregate, two parts sand and one part Portland cement (or 4 parts combined aggregate to one part cement) is satisfactory.

concrete cover The thickness of concrete covering the reinforcement mesh. Adequate concrete cover is essential to prevent concrete cancer which is, simply, the reinforcement steel rusting.

cored bricks An alternative to a frog in a brick (see 'frog'). Usually found in extruded bricks, the cored-out holes reduce the weight of the brick and perform the same function as the frog.

counterboring A method of carpentry that conceals the heads of bolts and nuts in posts and other timber constructions.

countersunk A special drill bit is used to enlarge a screw hole so that the screw head will sit below or flush with the surface.

course In all masonry work, a course is a rise in level of one unit.

cupping (of boards) The bending across the width of a board as the result of shrinkage.

curing The process of finishing a concrete surface that avoids rapid drying so that it will remain strong and not crack.

damp-proof course (DPC) A waterproof layer running around the base of the walls of a house to prevent moisture from the ground rising up through the brickwork.

damp-proof membrane (DPM) A waterproof layer (usually polythene) laid beneath a concrete slab to prevent moisture from the ground from rising through the concrete.

darby float A wooden float or trowel about one metre long.

decking The actual walking surface of a timber deck, usually made from planed and treated boards.

dry-pressed brick The process of making a brick with the use of a dry clay mix, which is put in a mould and pressed in a mechanical press.

efflorescence Salt deposits on the surface of bricks, tiles and other paving materials which often appear after laying.

expansion bolt A bolt with a metal or plastic sleeve that expands to grip the masonry of a pre-drilled hole.

expansion joint A soft material used to fill the joint between two surfaces to allow for expansion and contraction.

extruded brick A wet clay mix is extruded out of a tube to make bricks. The mixture comes out as a long, rectangular block and the bricks are then cut to size.

fall A slope, usually incorporated into paving to ensure efficient drainage of surface water.

fibre-cement sheet A lightweight cladding sheeting made of compressed cellulose fibre and cement.

finial A decorative capping for a post.

footing The lowest part of a building or structure that rests on the ground. Usually constructed from concrete or, in small structures, of bricks.

formwork A timber frame, made out of stakes driven into the ground and perimeter boards, which sets out the level of the top surface of a concrete slab.

foundation The ground on which the footing is built. Sometimes used interchangeably, but incorrectly, with footings. This term relates to the ground, not the building.

frog A recess pressed into a clay brick before firing. The frog assists the levelling of the brick courses and strengthens the wall (see also 'cored bricks').

g (for gauge) A method for measuring thickness of sheet metal, and for the diameters of some fittings like screws and nails.

galvanising An electrolytic process that coats raw steel with a protective layer of zinc, recommended for all exposed external steelwork.

going The width of the tread of a step, from one riser to the next.

gravel board A horizontal board fitted on edge between the posts of a boarded fence and below the vertical boards to protect the end grain of the latter from splashes and, therefore, rotting.

grout Fine cement paste for filling gaps, particularly in ceramic tiling.

halving joint A timber joint made by cutting recesses into both components to a depth of half the thickness of the timber, and overlapping the timbers.

hardcore Building rubble used to form a firm base below concrete or paving.

header brick A brick that is laid across the line of the wall of brickwork so that the narrow end appears in the face of the wall.

header course A course of header bricks, usually flat. Alternatively, a header course laid with bricks on edge is a useful means of providing coping for a wall.

housing joint, housing A method of joining two sections of timber. In carpentry, a joint where components are fitted together, with a portion of each piece being removed to allow them to marry. A housing joint is often used to connect joists or bearers to posts.

in-situ concrete Any concrete poured and left to set where it is intended to remain (e.g. a slab on the ground).

jig A device to hold a component during machining.

jointer A specially-shaped tool for producing a V-shaped or concave mortar joint in brickwork.

joist A horizontal structural member, supporting a floor, deck or ceiling. The joists are fixed to plates in the case of ceiling joists or to bearers in the case of a floor. In pergolas, joists are often called rafters.

joist hanger A U-shaped metal anchor that is attached to the bearer; the end of the joist fits into it.

knee brace A short, diagonal bracing member normally used to reinforce a pergola-to-post connection. Bracing is essential to stop a pergola swaying.

land drains Perforated drainage pipes designed to collect seepage and other subsurface water and carry it away from the site to a soakaway or gully.

lath A thin, narrow strip of wood.

level (see 'spirit level') A measuring tool for determining correct vertical and horizontal alignment.

lime Hydrated builders' lime is supplied in 50-kg bags and is a useful additive for all bricklaying mortars as an aid to workability.

lost-head nail A general-purpose nail with a short, cylindrical head that can be driven down into the wood so that it 'disappears'.

mastic A plastic waterproofing compound that hardens on the outside (so it can be painted), but remains soft (and flexible) underneath.

mortise and tenon A mortise is a rectangular hole cut into one piece of timber. A tenon is a tongue-shaped section designed to fit into a mortise; thus, a mortise-and-tenon joint.

nogging A short, horizontal section of timber between wall studs.

pergola An unroofed or partially-roofed frame, occasionally freestanding, but usually attached to the house, designed to provide a transition space from the inside of the house to the outside, provide a base for climbing plants and to give a degree of shade.

perpends The vertical joints between bricks in a wall.

pilot hole A small-diameter hole drilled in wood to provide a guide for the thread of a screw.

planed all round (PAR) Timber that has been planed smooth on all faces.

planed timber Timber that has been planed smooth on one or all faces.

planning application Many building works must be approved by your local council prior to commencement. The planning application is a formal request for permission to build, and will require specially prepared plans and specifications. Check first with your local council to see if the work you plan will require planning approval.

plate When applied to timber framing, this term means a horizontal load-bearing member. A bottom plate may be found at the base of a stud wall, and a top plate will be at the top of the wall, supporting the ceiling joists and roof structure. A wall plate is fixed to a wall to pick up the rafters of a pergola or similar structure.

plumb A builders' term meaning perfectly vertical or perpendicular.

Portland cement (see also 'cement') The ordinary, grey or grey-blue cement used in building. The name comes from its similarity in colour to Portland stone.

post cap A shaped wooden or plastic cap designed for fitting to the tops of posts to shed water so that it does not soak into the end grain.

post socket A metal socket into which the base of a post fits, with a baseplate that is bolted down to a concrete footing. The post may be simply wedged in place or secured by tightening a pair of clamping bolts.

pressure-treated (see also 'CCA treatment') This is a pressure-applied preservative treatment for timber using copper, cadmium and arsenic. It gives timber a characteristic greenish-grey colour and provides long-term protection from moisture and insect attack.

quadrant moulding A wooden moulding with a profile in the shape of a quadrant of a circle.

rafter An angled supporting member, usually in a roof. In a pergola, where the angle or slope of the rafters is small, the rafter may be confused with a joist.

rebate A recess or step, usually of rectangular section, cut into a surface or along the edge of a piece of timber to receive a mating piece. Sometimes pronounced 'rabbet'. A router is particularly useful for cutting rebates.

reinforcement Steel bar stock and prefabricated mesh used to strengthen concrete work.

ridge The highest part of a roof where the upper ends of the rafters meet.

riser The vertical spacer between steps (treads), or around the edge of a balcony, etc.

router A very useful power tool, which has a vertical spindle and chuck with a high-speed cutter designed to cut recesses with a wide range of profiles.

run (steps) The going or width of a step. The total run is the horizontal distance between the top and bottom of a flight of stairs.

sacrificial joint In concrete paths, this is a false joint only about 25 mm deep in a 100 mm slab. The intention is to cause the slab to break along the joint line as expansion and contraction takes place.

scarf joint A method of joining two lengths of timber by cutting the ends at matching angles so that they overlap and fit together.

screed A layer, usually of mortar or sand, used as a bed for tiles, or as a smooth surface for rough concrete.

screed board A length of board that is used to level the 'screed'; used in conjunction with the screed rails.

screed rails Two lengths of timber used at each side of an area to be paved, which act as the level for the resultant bed.

screeding The task of ruling back mortar or sand to a true and even finish.

shadecloth Woven fabric usually made from synthetic fibres and available in several grades, which are specified by their light transmittance. For pergola and shadehouse use, grades of 80 to 90 per cent are suggested (which will block out 80 to 90 per cent of the light).

sharp sand An alternative to builders' sand, but only suitable for mixing with aggregates when producing concrete and floor screeds. A finer-grade version is known as plasterers' sand and is used for rendering work.

sill The horizontal member at the bottom of a window frame or door frame (also the threshold).

skew-nail To fasten with a nail driven in at an angle. Rafters are connected to plates with a skew-nail driven through the bottom section of both faces of the rafter into the plate below.

slump In concrete, the approximate measure of the amount of water in the mix.

slurry A wet mixture of cement or a semi-fluid mixture of clay or a similar material and water. Used in paving.

soakaway A rubble-filled pit into which surface water is drained.

soft sand A fine grade of sand suitable for use in bricklaying mortars (see also 'builders' sand').

soldier course A course of bricks, often used as coping for a wall or a border to paving, laid with the bricks vertical.

span The horizontal distance between the supports of a roof, floor or beam, etc.

spirit level A device for checking vertical and horizontal alignment, consisting of glass tubes containing an oil or spirit in a metal or plastic frame with accurately formed, flat edges.

spreader A device for keeping apart and spacing parallel objects.

stirrup (metal) A U-shaped support (see also 'bracket').

stop chamfering The chamfering or planing of the edge of a piece of timber, which stops short of the ends. It is often used in traditional timberwork.

straightedge A bar, or strip of wood or metal, of various sizes, having at least one edge of sufficiently reliable straightness to test straight lines.

strap clamp A device for securing objects together by means of a strap.

stretcher bond Common brickwork where the vertical joints (see 'perpends') are staggered by one half brick on each successive course.

stringer (steps) A beam running diagonally up each side of a flight of steps, supporting the treads.

stud, stud framing The vertical timber of a wall frame. Usually the frame is from 75 x 50 mm or 100 x 50 mm timber, and the studs are housed into the plates.

sub-base A layer of crushed rock, gravel or rubble compacted as a strengthening layer beneath the bedding sand of paving.

tamp To consolidate sand, concrete or similar by applying repeated blows.

tenon saw A short, rigid-bladed saw, stiffened with a steel top edge, used for cutting accurate joints.

tolerance An allowance for reasonable accuracy.

tongued-and-grooved joint Two boards joined by the tongue along the edge of one board fitting into the groove along the edge of the other board.

tread The horizontal part of a step that is trodden on.

wall anchors Fittings designed for pre-drilled holes in masonry. Wall anchors hold by expanding within the hole (see also 'expansion bolt'). A wide range of bolts, inserts and studs is available.

wall plate A horizontal length of timber fastened to a wall to support the rafters of a pergola, or joists of a deck or similar construction.

weep hole A small hole left in a retaining wall so that water from the ground behind is free to drain through. This may be provided by leaving a vertical joint between bricks free of mortar, or by building in a length of pipe.

Index

This edition published for Merehurst, 2000
First published in 1998 by Murdoch Books®, a division of Murdoch Magazines Pty Ltd,
GPO Box 203, Sydney NSW 1045, Australia

CEO & Publisher: Anne Wilson
Associate Publisher: Catie Ziller
General Manager: Mark Smith

A catalogue record of this book is available from the British Library

The Complete Garden Makeover Book has been compiled from the resources of Murdoch Books ® and Better Homes and Gardens ®.

Project Manager: Sally Bird/Calidris Publishing Services
Text/Cover Design and Layout: Trevor Hood/*Anaconda Graphic Design*
Editor: Katie Millar
UK Consultant Editors Ian Penberthy and Graham Strong
Diagrams: Di Zign, Sydney
Printed by Toppan, Singapore

© Text, design, commissioned photography and illustrations Murdoch Books® 1998

ISBN 1 85391 832 6

Acknowledgements:
Additional photography by: David Kjaer/Natural History Unit pp. 260 (bottom left); Paul N. Johnson/Natural History Unit pp. 261 (top left);
William S. Paton pp. 260 (bottom right); Graham Strong pp. 234, 235, 236, 237, 238 (bottom), 242, 243 (left), 246 (top), 247, 248 (top), 251, 253,
254, 254, 255, 257, 259, 264 (top), 265, 266 (top), 267 (top), 269 (top), 270 (right), 271, 272, 273; Elizabeth Whiting Associations pp.185 (bottom),
186 (bottom left), 188 (bottom), 189; Mike Wilkes/Natural History Unit pp. 261.